Deradicalizing
Islamist Extremists

Property of Quilliam

Angel Rabasa, Stacie L. Pettyjohn,
Jeremy J. Ghez, Christopher Boucek

RAND NATIONAL SECURITY RESEARCH DIVISION

The research described in this report was sponsored by the Smith Richardson Foundation.

Library of Congress Cataloging-in-Publication Data

Deradicalizing Islamist extremists / Angel Rabasa ... [et al.].
   p. cm.
Includes bibliographical references.
ISBN 978-0-8330-5090-8 (pbk. : alk. paper)
      1. Terrorism—Prevention—Case studies. 2. Extremists. 3. Radicalism—Religious aspects—Islam. I. Rabasa, Angel.

   HV6431.D466 2011
   363.325'17—dc22

                                                                        2010039094

Published 2010 by the RAND Corporation
1776 Main Street, P.O. Box 2138, Santa Monica, CA 90407-2138
1200 South Hayes Street, Arlington, VA 22202-5050
4570 Fifth Avenue, Suite 600, Pittsburgh, PA 15213-2665
RAND URL: http://www.rand.org/
To order RAND documents or to obtain additional information, contact
Distribution Services: Telephone: (310) 451-7002;
Fax: (310) 451-6915; Email: order@rand.org

Preface

Although there has been a great deal of research on the radicalization and recruitment of Islamist extremists, until recently, there has been relatively little research on the *deradicalization* of those who have been recruited into Islamist extremist movements and organizations? Just as there are processes through which an individual becomes an extremist, there are also processes through which an extremist comes to renounce violence, leaves a group or movement, or even rejects a radical worldview. Moreover, there is reason to believe that deradicalization is not merely the radicalization process in reverse: Deradicalization appears to have its own distinct features—some of which are quite different from the factors associated with the initial radicalization. This project sought to identify and analyze the processes through which militants leave Islamist extremist groups, assess the effectiveness of deradicalization programs, and derive judgments about policies that could help promote and accelerate processes of deradicalization.

This research was funded by a grant from the Smith Richardson Foundation, with supplementary funding from the RAND Corporation's Rockwell Prize, and was conducted within the International Security and Defense Policy Center of the RAND National Defense Research Institute, a federally funded research and development center sponsored by the Office of the Secretary of Defense, the Joint Staff, the Unified Combatant Commands, the Navy, the Marine Corps, the defense agencies, and the U.S. Intelligence Community.

iv   Deradicalizing Islamist Extremists

For more information on the RAND International Security and Defense Policy Center, see http://www.rand.org/nsrd/about/isdp.html or contact the director (contact information is provided on the web page).

Contents

Figures

Tables

Summary

There is an emergent consensus among counterterrorism analysts and practitioners that to defeat the threat posed by Islamist extremism and terrorism, there is a need to go beyond security and intelligence measures, taking proactive measures to prevent vulnerable individuals from radicalizing and rehabilitating those who have already embraced extremism. This broader conception of counterterrorism is manifested in the counter- and deradicalization programs of a number of Middle Eastern, Southeast Asian, and European countries.

A key question is whether the objective of these programs should be disengagement or deradicalization of militants. Disengagement entails a change in behavior (i.e., refraining from violence and withdrawing from a radical organization) but not necessarily a change in beliefs. A person could exit a radical organization and refrain from violence but nevertheless retain a radical worldview. Deradicalization is the process of changing an individual's belief system, rejecting the extremist ideology, and embracing mainstream values.

There is a view in the scholarly community that deradicalization may not be a realistic objective and that the goal of terrorist rehabilitation programs should be disengagement.[1] Deradicalization, in fact, may be particularly difficult for Islamist extremists because they are motivated by an ideology that is rooted in a major world religion. The tenets of the ideology, therefore, are regarded as religious obligations.

---

[1] See, for instance, John Horgan, "Individual Disengagement: A Psychological Analysis," in Tore Bjørgo and John Horgan, eds., *Leaving Terrorism Behind: Individual and Collective Disengagement*, New York: Rutledge, 2008.

Nevertheless, deradicalization may be necessary to permanently defuse the threat posed by these individuals. If a militant disengages solely for instrumental reasons, when the circumstances change, the militant may once again take up arms. Conversely, when deradicalization accompanies disengagement, it creates further barriers to recidivism.

Moreover, there may be a tipping point. When enough ex-militants renounce radical Islamism, the ideology and the organizations that adhere to it are fatally discredited. Even short of this tipping point, as greater numbers of militants renounce extremism, radical Islamist organizations will experience greater hurdles in attracting adherents and sympathizers within the Muslim community.

Studies of those who leave gangs and criminal organizations, exit from cults and religious sects, and withdraw from terrorist organizations suggest that individuals follow a similar trajectory when leaving a criminal or extremist group. Certain lessons can be derived from this trajectory.

First, it appears that it is important that efforts be made to facilitate the process of disengagement during the crucial early stages. Individual disengagement begins as a result of a trigger, often a traumatic or violent incident. Although these types of events can impel a person to leave a radical organization, if they are not exploited, they could strengthen the militant's commitment to the group. Therefore, whenever possible, an intervention should be attempted after traumatic events—for instance, a militant's arrest—that may precipitate a cognitive opening.

If extremists who are weighing the costs and benefits of staying or leaving could be identified, it may be possible to influence their strategic calculus. Since most of the rehabilitation programs for Islamist extremists are in prisons, it may be possible for the authorities to recognize conflicted inmates and encourage them to participate in the program.

Second, a government can take actions that make disengagement more attractive and continued extremist behavior less appealing by implementing counterterrorism measures that increase the costs of remaining in an extremist organization while strategically offering incentives that increase the benefits of exiting. Governments must be cautious in calibrating their approaches, however. Repression alone often backfires and causes further radicalization; at other times, it can be an important measure that decreases the utility of remaining in a radical organization. It appears that a dual strategy—including both hard- and soft-line measures—is the best policy for inducing individuals to leave a militant group.

Third, while deradicalization programs focus on convincing jailed Islamist extremists to recant their beliefs, it is important that these programs continue to assist freed, rehabilitated individuals. In particular, the program should assist the ex-militant in finding a job and locating a supportive environment. In addition, it is prudent to require that the ex-militant continue counseling and to monitor his or her behavior and associations closely.

The probability that an individual will disengage or deradicalize appears to be inversely related to the degree of commitment to the group or movement. Commitment can be measured in terms of affective, pragmatic, and ideological bonds. Affective commitment is an emotional attachment to other members of the organization and to the group itself. Pragmatic commitment refers to the practical factors that make it difficult to exit a radical organization, such as material rewards and punishments. The ideological component justifies the actions that the militant is asked to take and the hardships that he or she must endure to achieve the group's objectives.

In this regard, leaving an ideologically based radical Islamist group is not the same as leaving a criminal group or a gang, an essentially nonideological entity. Leaving an Islamist group implies the rejection of a radical ideology or of essential parts of that ideology, particularly the individual obligation to participate in armed struggle. It follows that, even if a militant is inclined to leave the group for other reasons, the articulation of theologically grounded imperatives for renouncing violence by credible authorities is an important factor in catalyzing the decision to leave the group.

Most Middle Eastern and Southeast Asian programs employ a form of theological dialogue in which mainstream scholars and, sometimes, former radicals engage extremists in discussions of Islamic theology in an effort to convince the militants that their interpretation of Islam is wrong. However, the content of the theological dialogue in such programs must be treated with caution. Because the priority of these governments is combating the domestic terrorist threat, the programs stress the unacceptability of terrorism domestically (on the basis that the government is Islamic or that the country is not under occupation), but they may condone it abroad in zones of conflict, such as Iraq and Afghanistan. This approach might address the immediate security needs of the country in question, but it does not truly deradicalize the militants.

There are not enough reliable data to reach definitive conclusions about the short-term, let alone the long-term, effectiveness of most existing deradicalization programs. Many governments closely guard information about their programs and about the militants who have graduated from them. Moreover, the ostensibly good track record of some programs can be misleading because these efforts focus on reforming terrorist sympathizers and supporters, not hard-core militants. This has become increasingly apparent in light of the number of Saudi Guantanamo detainees who have returned to terrorism upon their release.

In contrast, there is more information on the content of European efforts to prevent radicalization, but it is difficult to measure the success of these programs because their effects are more diffuse. In some cases, such as the Slotervaart Action Plan in Amsterdam, measurable indicators to assess the success of the programs have not been developed, and it is very difficult, if not impossible, to estimate the effects of such programs on the exposure group.

It follows that our knowledge of deradicalization programs remains limited and that there are reasons to remain skeptical about the programs' claims of success. Nonetheless, our analysis has a number of policy implications. A key finding is that a deradicalization program should work to break the militant's affective, pragmatic, and ideological commitment to the group. Individuals may vary in the level of each type of commitment, but because it is prohibitively costly to tailor a program to each person, rehabilitation efforts should include components to address each type of attachment. None of these components is sufficient on its own, however. Deradicalization programs appear more likely to succeed when all three components are implemented together so as to provide individuals with multiple reasons to abandon their commitment to the radical group and ideology.

Middle Eastern and Southeast Asian Individual Rehabilitation Programs

Middle Eastern and Southeast Asian governments have established prison-based individual rehabilitation programs that usually promote a particular state-sanctioned brand of Islam. The prototype of this approach was Yemen's theological dialogue model, which was based on the assumption that most militant Islamists do not have a proper understanding of Islam and therefore can be reeducated and reformed.[2] Since these nations (with the exception of Singapore) have explicitly Islamic governments or are Muslim-majority countries, the government is willing to become involved in matters of religious interpretation to promote an official version of Islam. Our examination of these programs has four key policy implications.

First, these efforts seem to hinge on the ability of the state to find credible interlocutors who can develop relationships with imprisoned militants and use their legitimacy and personal ties to convince the radicals of the error of their ways. Credibility may stem from the interlocutor's standing as a theologian, history as a former militant, or personal piety. Using interlocutors whom the militants respect and who are able to connect with the prisoners appears to be essential to establishing rapport with the detainees.

Second, deradicalization programs need to be balanced, with affective, pragmatic, and ideological components that continue after the prisoners have been released. It is clear that prison-based rehabilitation programs cannot rely solely on religious debates to reform detainees. Dialogue alone does not break militants' affective and practical ties to a radical movement or equip them with the skills that they need to

---

[2] As discussed later, the exception to the theological dialogue model is Indonesia, which has no organized religious component.

xviii   Deradicalizing Islamist Extremists

become self-reliant, productive members of their community. More-over, it is difficult to assess whether a militant has truly changed his or her beliefs (although, as discussed later, there are potential means of assessing a change in belief).[3] Since prisoners have an incentive to cooperate with the authorities to earn their freedom, it is best to create a situation that provides incentives for disengagement and disincentives to recidivism.

Third, to ensure that militants remain disengaged, deradicalization programs need to continue to monitor former detainees and offer extensive support after their release. In particular, aftercare should include locating the ex-radical in a supportive environment and facilitating his or her reintegration into society. The best-designed rehabilitation programs (for instance, the one in Singapore) continue to offer (and sometimes require) theological and psychological counseling for those who have been released. Continued interaction with a credible interlocutor provides ongoing emotional support, helps to dispel doubts, and ensures that behavioral and ideational changes endure.

Fourth, programs that include the militant's family appear to increase the probability that the individual will remain disengaged. Deradicalization programs may incorporate militants' families by offering practical support or counseling or by making them guarantors of the former radical's behavior. All of these are effective ways of investing the radical's family in his or her rehabilitation and making it likely that family members will urge the former radical to remain disengaged from extremism.

As noted earlier, the state-sanctioned interpretation of Islam being promoted in some rehabilitation programs often contains radical elements; in particular, some programs propagate the idea that violence at home is unacceptable but that violence in zones of conflict, such as Afghanistan and Iraq, is legitimate and necessary. This suggests that the United States should learn more about these programs before it

---

[3] For instance, whether the prisoner shares credible information with the authorities, whether the prisoner attempts to persuade others to radicalize, whether the former extremist consistently and publicly denounces his or her former beliefs, and whether the former extremist remains disengaged.

agrees to repatriate militants currently held in U.S. detention facilities. The United States should also carefully consider all aspects of a deradicalization program before offering support. Finally, it should encourage states with deradicalization programs to provide more information about their efforts so that they can be better evaluated and improved.

Prison-Based Collective Deradicalization

Collective deradicalization has occurred infrequently—only when a state has defeated an extremist organization by killing or imprisoning most of the group's leaders. Collective deradicalization differs from the programs established to rehabilitate individual extremists in that states in which collective deradicalization has occurred have not established extensive, organized programs to rehabilitate imprisoned militants. Instead, governments have responded to overtures from a radical group's leaders who have already begun to reconsider their positions and then engaged these leaders to facilitate their process of disengagement.

Our analysis of collective deradicalization has a number of implications for policymakers.

First, policymakers should encourage group deradicalization where it seems feasible and facilitate the public disclosure of the writings and arguments of militants who renounce extremism. Demonstration effects are one of the least discussed but most important aspects of deradicalization. When an influential ideologue or operational leader renounces an extremist ideology—and, more importantly, explains his or her reasons for so doing—it raises doubts in the minds of radicals who subscribe to a similar worldview. Because of the stature and credibility of some of the authors, these treatises pose the greatest and most serious challenge to the extremist ideology, which must be delegitimized to permanently remove the threat posed by radical Islamism. Extremists who are still at large will predictably argue that these recantations have been made under duress, so governments should avoid embracing the recanting extremists too closely in order to avoid compromising their credibility.

Second, governments must maintain a high level of international cooperation in suppressing terrorist groups. This is particularly important because Islamist extremist organizations are part of a global network that allows them to survive even if they have been defeated at home. Repression or, more accurately, effective containment of extremist groups is an essential antecedent condition to deradicalization. When a critical mass of a group's key leaders and members are imprisoned with little chance of being released, this hopeless situation precipitates a strategic crisis that is often followed by an ideological crisis. Experience has shown that a mixed strategy—one that relies on hard-line counterterrorism measures as well as soft-line measures—is the most effective way to encourage militants to disengage and deradicalize.

Third, most programs focus on reforming less committed radicals. Although it is extremely difficult to induce committed militants to renounced extremism, governments may want to target the more devoted militants—the activists and the "hard-core"—because these individuals have more influence on the rank and file. Collective deradicalization is the most efficient way to change the behavior and beliefs of a large number of militants at once and ultimately discredit the extremist ideology. Of course, some committed militants may be impervious to efforts to induce them to change. These recalcitrant individuals, or "irreconcilables," may have to be segregated from other group members to prevent them from impeding the rehabilitation of other inmates. However, if some leaders or influential militants show some indications of openness to alternative ideas, it would be advisable to include them in deradicalization programs.

European Counter-Radicalization and Voluntary Deradicalization Efforts

European governments have taken a very different approach to combating Islamist extremism compared to that of governments in the Muslim world. In particular, most European states have been very reluctant to become involved in religious matters and therefore do not directly challenge the extremist ideology. Moreover, rather than attempting to rehabilitate imprisoned militants, European governments have emphasized policies aimed at countering radicalization by enhancing social cohesion and the integration of their Muslim populations, as well as small, voluntary deradicalization programs for young people who are at risk of radicalization but have not yet broken the law. Based on our examination of these efforts, we have identified three policy recommendations.

First, governments must carefully select their partners in the Muslim community to ensure that they are working with authentic voices with grassroots support and not those who promote values contrary to liberal democracy. This is a difficult task, and many European governments have been reluctant to pick and choose partners within their Muslim populations. However, it is not clear that simply promoting democratic and national values, which is the approach that some European governments have taken, is sufficient to ward off radicalization. These governments may need to identify moderate Muslim intermediaries and strengthen these groups to enable them to compete with extremists in the war of ideas. Of course, there is a risk that extremists will attempt to discredit moderates as government tools. As we discussed in an earlier RAND publication, the key question is not whether but *how* governments should channel their assistance and engage prospective partners effectively. Assistance must be channeled in ways that are appropriate to local circumstances and, to the extent possible, involve nongovernmental organizations with existing relationships in the community.[4]

Second, although the voluntary deradicalization programs that some European states have created need to protect the privacy of their participants, these efforts must be critically evaluated. Therefore, baselines and benchmarks need to be established and data collected to permit independent assessments of the programs' effectiveness. If it is found that locally directed interventions are successful, the programs should be expanded. But their effectiveness needs to be verified first.

---

[4] Angel Rabasa, Cheryl Benard, Lowell H. Schwartz, and Peter Sickle, *Building Moderate Muslim Networks*, Santa Monica, Calif.: RAND Corporation, MG-574-SRF, 2007.

Third, given the increasing severity of the problem of Islamist radicalization and recruitment in prisons, European governments may want to consider establishing prison deradicalization programs. The secular character and legal systems of European states make it difficult to emulate some of the practices of prison-based rehabilitation programs in the Middle East and Southeast Asia, but there may be experiences in the case of Singapore, a secular, non–Muslim-majority state facing challenges similar to those confronted by European countries, that are relevant to the European context.

Final Observations

Culture matters. As this monograph shows, the deradicalization programs that we studied all reflect the social and cultural characteristics of the countries in which they have been implemented. The best-designed plans leverage local cultural patterns to achieve their objectives. One implication of this observation is that deradicalization programs cannot simply be transplanted from one country to another, even within the same region. They have to develop organically in a specific country and culture.

That is not to say that best practices cannot be identified. When they appear to be successful, deradicalization programs have been comprehensive efforts that break extremists' affective, pragmatic, and ideological commitment to a radical organization and worldview. This is a very difficult and expensive undertaking that does not guarantee success. Some states—Yemen, for instance—may not have the means to implement a comprehensive program. In other cases, there may be legal or political obstacles that prevent a government from developing programs that intrude on the religious sphere.

Disengagement and deradicalization programs will likely remain a necessary part of larger counter-radicalization and counterterrorism strategies. However, governments cannot afford to be naïve or careless when seeking to rehabilitate extremists. To succeed, deradicalization programs must be extensive efforts that include affective, pragmatic, and ideological components and considerable aftercare. Prison-based deradicalization programs, in particular, need to exercise caution, carefully evaluating each individual before release and implementing safeguards, such as monitoring, to protect against the eventuality that former militants could once again take up arms.

Acknowledgments

We wish to thank all those who made this study possible. We are grateful for the RAND Corporation's Rockwell Policy Analysis Prize, established through the generous philanthropic support of Marshall Rockwell, which enabled us to expand the research.

We also acknowledge the invaluable insights that we gained in our discussions with experts, counter-radicalization practitioners, and government officials in Europe and Southeast Asia. In particular, we thank Ronald Sandee, director of analysis and research at The NEFA Foundation; Doron Zimmermann, a senior civil servant in the Swiss Ministry of Defense; Saskia Tempelman at the Ministry of the Interior and Kingdom Relations in the Netherlands; Jorgen Gammelgaard, chief adviser on counterterrorism at the Danish Ministry of Foreign Affairs; Tony Heal, deputy head of Prevent at the UK's Home Office; Peter Neumann, director of the International Centre for the Study of Radicalization and Political Violence at King's College, London; Michael Whine, director of government and international affairs at Community Security Trust, London; Ed Husain, Ghaffar Hussain, and Noman Benotman of the Quilliam Foundation, London; Dean Godson and Shiraz Maher at Policy Exchange, London; Hanif Qadir at the Active Change Foundation, London; and Alan Johnson, founding editor of *Democratiya*, United Kingdom.

In the Middle East, we thank His Royal Highness Prince Mohammed bin Nayef, Saad al-Jabri, Abdurrahman al-Hadlaq, Shaykh Ahmed Jilani, Abdelaziz al-Ghamdi, Turki al-Otayan, Awadh Alyami, Major General Mansour al-Turki, Lieutenant Colonel Omar al-Zalal, Abubaker al-Qirbi, Major General Ali al-Anisi, and Judge Hamoud al-Hitar.

In Southeast Asia, we thank Ambassador Barry Desker, dean of the S. Rajaratnam School of International Studies, Nanyang Technological University, Singapore, and Rohan Gunaratna, head of the International Centre for Political Violence and Terrorism Research at the S. Rajaratnam School of International Studies. The International Conference on Terrorist Rehabilitation organized by the International Centre for Political Violence and Terrorism Research and the Religious Rehabilitation Group in Singapore in February 2009 provided a global perspective on efforts to rehabilitate terrorists and insurgents and was a valuable resource for this study. We also thank Sidney Jones, International Crisis Group; Indonesian National Counterterrorism Agency chief Ansyaad Mbai; Dharmawan Ronodipuro, special assistant to the Indonesian counterterrorism coordinator; Inspector General Gories Mere, executive director of the National Narcotics Board; Brigadier General (ret.) Surya Dharma, Indonesian national police; and Brigadier General Tito Karnavian commander of Detachment 88, the Indonesian police force's elite counterterrorism unit; Nasir Abas, former Jemaah Islamiyah leader; senior consulting psychologist Sarlito Sarwono of the University of Indonesia; K. Candra Negara, Embassy of the Republic of Indonesia, Washington, D.C., and others who contributed to this study.

At RAND, we thank James Dobbins, director of the International Security and Defense Policy Center, under whose guidance this research was conducted; summer associate Diaz Hendropriyono, for his valuable research on Indonesian counterterrorism; the reviewers of this monograph, Lorenzo Vidino and Sara Beth Elson; editor Lauren Skrabala, production editor Matthew Byrd, artist Carol Earnest, and marketing director John Warren in RAND's Publications department; and our assistants Mary Wallace and Rosa Maria Torres, for their assistance with technical aspects of the preparation of this monograph. Naturally, any errors and shortcomings are the responsibility of the authors.

Abbreviations

ACF	Active Change Foundation
ACG	Aftercare Services Group
AMP	Association of Muslim Professionals
AQAP	al-Qaeda in the Arabian Peninsula
EIJ	Egyptian Islamic Jihad
IG	al-Gama'a al-Islamiyya
ISA	Internal Security Act
ISD	Singapore Internal Security Department
JI	Jemaah Islamiyah
KMM	Kumpulan Militan [or Mujahidin] Malaysia
LIFG	Libyan Islamic Fighting Group
NGO	nongovernmental organization
RICU	UK Research, Information and Communications Unit
RRG	Religious Rehabilitation Group

CHAPTER ONE

Disengagement and Deradicalization

Introduction

Considerable effort has been devoted to understanding the process of violent Islamist radicalization, but far less research has explored the equally important process of deradicalization—how individuals or groups abandon extremist groups and ideologies. This is not simply an academic question. Many nations are struggling to determine whether extremists in their custody can be rehabilitated and safely released, or whether they will return to violence and therefore must be held indefinitely.

The literature on radicalization and deradicalization suffers from a lack of agreement on how some important terms should be defined.[1] Therefore, we seek to clearly define key concepts to avoid confusion. Generally, the term *radicalization* is defined as "the process of adopting an extremist belief system, including the willingness to use, support, or facilitate violence, as a method to effect societal change."[2] Deradicalization, therefore, is the process of abandoning an extremist worldview and concluding that it is not acceptable to use violence to effect social

---

[1] See International Crisis Group, *Deradicalisation and Indonesian Prisons*, Jakarta and Brussels, Asia Report No. 142, November 2007, p. 11.

[2] Charles E. Allen, Assistant Secretary for Intelligence and Analysis and Chief Intelligence Officer, U.S. Department of Homeland Security, Threat of Islamic Radicalization to the Homeland, written testimony to the U.S. Senate Committee on Homeland Security and Governmental Affairs, Washington, D.C., March 14, 2007, p. 4.

change.[3] As a part of the deradicalization process, there is a recognition that social, political, and economic transformation will only occur slowly and in a pluralistic environment.[4]

Islamism is another contested term. Islamists can be defined as Muslims with Islam-based political agendas, but this definition is too broad to be useful. For the purposes of this study, we defined Islamists as those who reject the separation of religious authority from the power of the state. Islamists seek to establish some version of an Islamic political and legal structure. It should be noted that this definition encompasses both violent and nonviolent Islamists.[5] Although there are many different types of Islamists, many of whom are not extremists, our study was concerned primarily with the extremist faction that is strongly influenced by the ideas of the Egyptian theorist Sayyid Qutb. The definition includes, but is not limited to, the brand of terrorism associated with or inspired by al-Qaeda, as well as violent groups with more limited aims, and unaffiliated extremists willing to engage in violence.

In this context, Islamist radicalization involves adopting the belief that, to recreate an Islamic state, Muslims must not only adhere to a strict Salafist or ultraconservative interpretation of Islam but also wage jihad, defined as armed struggle against the enemies of Islam, including non-Muslim nations (especially the United States) and the current rulers of Muslim states who have supplanted God's authority with their

---

[3] We distinguish deradicalization from "counter-radicalization." The latter refers broadly to policies and programs that attempt to dissuade individuals at risk of radicalization—usually young people—from becoming radicalized or "crossing the line and becoming terrorists" (United Nations Counter-Terrorism Implementation Task Force, *First Report of the Working Group on Radicalisation and Extremism That Lead to Terrorism*, September 2008, p. 5).

[4] Omar Ashour, *The De-Radicalization of Jihadists: Transforming Armed Islamist Movements*, New York: Routledge, 2009, pp. 5–6.

[5] This definition is given in Sue-Ann Lee, "Managing the Challenges of Radical Islam: Strategies to Win the Hearts and Minds of the Muslim World," paper presented at the John F. Kennedy School of Government, Harvard University, April 1, 2003. We adopted it in Rabasa, Benard, et al., 2007.

own.[6] Islamist deradicalization is therefore defined as the process of rejecting this creed, especially its beliefs in the permissibility of using violence against civilians, the excommunication of Muslims who do not adhere to the radicals' views (*takfir*), and opposition to democracy and concepts of civil liberties as currently understood in democratic societies.[7]

The Obama administration has sought to close the Guantanamo Bay detention facility despite concerns that prisoners who are ultimately released could return to armed struggle. These concerns received support from a U.S. Defense Intelligence Agency report revealing that 20 percent of the detainees who have been freed have subsequently resumed terrorist activities.[8] Moreover, several of these former Guantanamo prisoners had taken part in Saudi Arabia's deradicalization program after their repatriation and were supposedly rehabilitated.[9] Although the administration would like to release some detainees to their home countries, uncertainty about the effectiveness of existing deradicalization programs has prevented it from pursuing this goal.

---

[6] Fawaz A. Gerges, *The Far Enemy: Why Jihad Went Global*, New York: Cambridge University Press, 2005, pp. 3–9; Angel Rabasa, Peter Chalk, Kim Cragin, Sara A. Daly, Heather S. Gregg, Theodore W. Karasik, Kevin A. O'Brien, and William Rosenau, *Beyond al-Qaeda: Part 1, The Jihadist Global Movement*, Santa Monica, Calif.: RAND Corporation, 2006, pp. 7–14. There is disagreement within the jihadist movement over which enemy—the near or the far—should be the primary target. Qutb called for jihad against the near enemy, the apostate rulers, as a prerequisite to success against the far enemy, the United States and Israel.

[7] Ashour (2009, pp. 5–6) distinguishes between deradicalization, which, in his view, primarily concerns attitudes toward the permissibility of using violence, and moderation, which involves an acceptance of democratic norms.

[8] Mike Mount, "Report: 20 Percent of Released Detainees Returning to Terrorism," CNN, January 11, 2010. While the Yemeni deradicalization program was shut down due to its lack of success, Saudi Arabia's deradicalization program is generally viewed positively, despite some prominent failures. The Obama administration has even reportedly been considering sending the remaining Yemeni detainees at Guantanamo to Riyadh for rehabilitation (Marissa L. Porges, "Can We Retrain Terrorists?" *Philadelphia Inquirer*, November 18, 2009).

[9] According to a Saudi official, approximately 20 percent of the Guantanamo detainees who have completed the deradicalization program have relapsed, while only 9 percent of rehabilitated non-Guantanamo Islamists have recidivated ("Ex-Guantanamo Inmates 'Fail Rehab,'" Aljazeera, June 20, 2010).

This chapter seeks to contribute to the burgeoning literature on *individual* deradicalization by examining a number of questions that have thus far received insufficient attention: Does the process of disengagement—that is, leaving the organization but not necessarily altering extremist beliefs—follow a similar pattern across different types of groups? Do Islamist extremists display unique characteristics that make them different from other types of extremists? If so, what implications do these differences have for their willingness to leave radical organizations, their ability to abandon an extremist ideology, and the likelihood that they will return to violence? Finally, what lessons should be incorporated into deradicalization programs?[10]

In an effort to answer these questions, this chapter surveys the relevant literature, including topics such as leaving gangs and criminal organizations, breaking from cults and religious sects, and withdrawing from terrorist organizations, and considers both Islamist and non-Islamist groups. Based on this survey, we argue that individuals do appear to follow a similar trajectory when leaving a variety of extremist groups.

That said, not all members of radical groups are equally likely to leave. In general, the probability that an individual will disengage or deradicalize appears to be inversely related to the degree of commitment that the person has made to the group or movement. In this regard, there are some important features that distinguish Islamist extremists from members of other groups. On the one hand, it is more difficult for Islamists to renounce their ideology because they consider the precepts of the ideology to be religious obligations. On the other hand, since Islamist radicals are motivated by an ideology that is rooted in a major world religion, there is an opportunity to leverage mainstream Islam to challenge extremist interpretations of the religion. This could facilitate the deradicalization of radical Muslims by making it possible for extremists to renounce extremism without also renouncing their faith.

---

[10] To date, far more attention has been given to the topic of disengagement than deradicalization, due in part to the widespread assumption that the former is more attainable than the latter. Although we discuss the distinction between these two concepts in greater detail later, one goal of this chapter is to examine the extent to which the literature on disengagement can yield insights into the process of deradicalization.

In short, deradicalization may be particularly difficult for Islamists, but the approach may be necessary to permanently defuse the threat posed by radical Islamism.

The following section provides an overview of the key dependent variables—disengagement and deradicalization—and discusses which should be the objective for programs aiming to rehabilitate Islamist extremists. Drawing on the literature on individual disengagement from all types of groups, the subsequent section describes the general trajectory that individual disengagement follows across different types of organizations. It also proposes a method for identifying which radicals are most likely to disengage or deradicalize. The third discusses the features that distinguish radical Islamists and make it more difficult for this type of extremist to deradicalize compared to other extremists. That section outlines the possible implications of these arguments for the development of deradicalization programs and proposes issues that merit further research.

The Dependent Variable: Disengagement or Deradicalization?

While deradicalization is the process of moderating one's beliefs, disengagement is simply the process of changing one's behavior by refraining from violence and withdrawing from a radical organization. John Horgan notes that disengagement can be the product of psychological factors (for example, disillusionment) or physical factors (most notably, imprisonment). He further argues that disengaging from a terrorist organization does not necessarily entail leaving the group; rather, a person disengages from terrorism by not executing violent attacks, even if that person remains affiliated with the radical organization.[11] This is called *role change*. Because role change may involve continued active support for the radical group, which, in turn, enables the group to use violence, we diverge from Horgan and do not consider role change to be an example of disengagement.

----

[11] John Horgan, 2008, pp. 21–27.

Similarly, others have pointed out that disengagement can depend on receiving something in return (conditional disengagement) and that the degree of disengagement can vary (selective engagement).[12] An example of the latter would be an extremist who chooses to distinguish between legitimate targets, such as military personnel, and illegitimate targets, such as civilians. Like the concept of role change, however, neither conditional nor selective disengagement involves abstaining from violence or breaking with a radical group. Therefore, we do not consider these categories as true examples of disengagement.

Another way to think about disengagement and deradicalization is in terms of rational choice theory—specifically, its distinctions between motives, strategies, and structure.[13] From this perspective, deradicalization involves a change in one's fundamental objectives. By contrast, disengagement entails an instrumental change in behavior due to shifting constraints (namely, the costs suffered or benefits gained by pursuing a certain course of action). For instance, a person could exit from a radical organization and forgo violence because a government's counterterrorist measures become increasingly effective or because the government offers financial assistance to those who abandon violence. Although this individual may temporarily leave an extremist organization, he or she could still espouse radical beliefs and return to terrorism in the future when conditions change. In short, a militant will refrain from terrorism only if the expected utility of moderation exceeds the utility of extremism.

A true (and successful) deradicalization program should therefore produce a change in an individual's underlying beliefs, not simply a change in behavior. As noted earlier, behavior can change while objectives remain constant. This suggests several potential problems with deradicalization programs. First, it is extremely difficult to determine whether an individual is truly deradicalized or merely disengaged; the

---

[12] Gordon Clubb, "Re-Evaluating the Disengagement Process: The Case of Fatah," *Perspectives on Terrorism*, Vol. 3, No. 3, September 2009.

[13] Jeffry A. Frieden, "Actors and Preferences in International Relations," in David A. Lake and Robert Powell, eds., *Strategic Choice and International Relations*, Princeton, N.J.: Princeton University Press, 1999, pp. 39–47.

only way to judge an individual's underlying objectives is by observing his or her words and actions, yet words and actions do not always accurately reflect objectives. This problem is particularly acute in the case of Islamist extremists, who often participate in deradicalization programs after being detained and thus have strong incentives to misrepresent their beliefs in an effort to secure their freedom.

Second, even if deradicalization is a viable possibility for some extremists, others are likely to be "irreconcilables"—committed militants who refuse to renounce their beliefs or refrain from the use of violence.[14] Unfortunately, there is no reliable method for identifying these irreconcilables. As a result, some deradicalization programs simply assume that high-ranking members of a terrorist organization or those with blood on their hands are beyond help. There are, however, examples of high-ranking or violent radicals who subsequently disengaged and, in some cases, even publicly renounced their previous extremism.[15]

Third, many deradicalization programs have an ideological component and a material component. In other words, not only do these programs incorporate a theological dialogue in which scholars engage radicals in discussions to try to convince them that Islam does not condone terrorism, they also offer tangible benefits in the form of jobs, training, and subsidies to encourage cooperation. As a result of this dual strategy, it is extremely difficult to determine whether a reformed extremist has experienced a true change in preferences (and is therefore deradicalized) or is merely responding to the inducements that have been offered (and is merely disengaged).

[14] Michael Jacobson, *Terrorist Dropouts: Learning from Those Who Have Left*, Washington, D.C.: Washington Institute for Near East Policy, Policy Focus No. 101, January 2010, p. 25. Some counterterrorism experts maintain that once a radical has used violence, he or she cannot be rehabilitated. See, for example, Richard Barrett and Laila Bokhari, "Deradicalization and Rehabilitation Programmes Targeting Religious Terrorists and Extremists in the Muslim World: An Overview," in Tore Bjørgo and John Horgan, eds., *Leaving Terrorism Behind: Individual and Collective Disengagement*, New York: Routledge, 2008, p. 173.

[15] A few examples of high-ranking militant Islamic leaders who have disengaged or deradicalized include Jemaah Islamiyah (JI) leader Nasir Abas, the historic leaders of the Islamic Group in Egypt, and Egyptian Islamic Jihad leader Sayyid Imam al-Sharif.

Each of these dilemmas is compounded by the fact that deradicalization programs do not have an accurate way to measure success. Instead, they point to recidivism rates, which only measure disengagement.[16] Perhaps more importantly, most deradicalization programs dealing with Islamist extremists boast extremely high success rates, but these claims remain unverified because these programs often lack adequate monitoring.[17]

These issues raise an important question: Should state-sponsored programs aim to deradicalize their detainees, or is disengagement a more reasonable goal? It has been asserted that deradicalization should be the objective because it produces a more enduring change that significantly reduces the likelihood of recidivism.[18] If a militant disengages solely for instrumental reasons, the barriers to recidivism are only as strong as the inducements that are proffered. Conversely, when deradicalization accompanies disengagement, it creates further hurdles against a reversion to extremism.[19] In this view, disengagement is a temporary condition that is costly to realize and often backfires; as a result, more durable attitudinal change must be attempted. Others, like Bjørgo and Horgan, maintain that policymakers should focus on the more attainable goal of disengagement.[20]

After interviewing dozens of former terrorists, Horgan concluded that while they were all disengaged, none was truly deradicalized.[21]

---

[16] Marisa L. Porges, "The Saudi Deradicalization Experiment," Council on Foreign Relations, Expert Brief, January 22, 2010a.

[17] John Horgan and Kurt Braddock, "Rehabilitating the Terrorists? Challenges in Assessing the Effectiveness of De-Radicalization Programs," *Terrorism and Political Violence*, Vol. 22, No. 2, April 2010, p. 276.

[18] Naureen Chowdhury Fink and Ellie B. Hearne, *Beyond Terrorism: Deradicalization and Disengagement from Violent Extremism*, International Peace Institute, October 2008, p. 12.

[19] Omar Ashour, "Islamist De-Radicalization in Algeria: Successes and Failures," *Middle East Institute Policy Brief*, No. 21, November 2008, p. 10.

[20] Tore Bjørgo and John Horgan, "Introduction," in Tore Bjørgo and John Horgan, eds., *Leaving Terrorism Behind: Individual and Collective Disengagement*, New York: Routledge, 2008b, p. 3; John Horgan, *Walking Away from Terrorism: Accounts of Disengagement from Radical and Extremist Movements*, New York: Routledge, 2009, p. 161.

[21] Horgan, 2009a, p. 27.

Political science professor Zachary Abuza concurs and argues that most of Indonesian prisoners who have recanted are not really deradicalized: "At the end of this program, you are probably still going to have someone who is committed to the establishment of sharia, who is probably still going to be less than friendly toward non-Muslims and ethnic minorities."[22] Since it is undoubtedly difficult, if not impossible, to alter a person's fundamental preferences, these scholars argue that disengagement should be the focus of existing programs. Moreover, while an individual's personal beliefs may be abhorrent to mainstream society, it is only the person's actions that truly cause harm. Consequently, efforts to rehabilitate terrorists should focus on changing their behavior.

Consistent with the views of these deradicalization skeptics, some programs seem to be embracing the more modest goal of disengagement. For example, the Saudi government has recently sought to compensate for past failures and increase the effectiveness of its deradicalization program by emphasizing behavior modification over ideological change.[23] While the Saudi program still includes a religious dialogue, it has offered the detainees more financial incentives and increased contact with their families.

Nevertheless, even if deradicalization skeptics are correct and disengagement is a more feasible goal for government-sponsored programs, that does not necessarily mean that deradicalization is impossible. In some cases, disengagement may actually be the first step on a longer-term path to deradicalization. A large body of applied social psychology theory has argued that an extended period of instrumental compliance can lead to identity change through three mechanisms.[24]

---

[22] Quoted in Drake Bennett, "How to Defuse a Human Bomb," *Boston Globe*, April 13, 2008.

[23] Porges, 2010a. In addition, the program has attempted to more carefully assess each prisoner's sincerity and compliance, which includes improved surveillance of those released.

[24] Thomas Risse, "Let's Argue! Communicative Action in World Politics," *International Organization*, Vol. 54, No. 1, Winter 2000, p. 4. Risse explains that "rule-guided behavior [logic of appropriateness] differs from instrumentally rational behavior [logic of consequences] in that actors try to 'do the right thing' rather than maximizing or optimizing their given preferences."

First, an individual may eventually abide by a set of rules or norms due to habit or routinization. In this case, the person has not been persuaded to change his or her mindset; nevertheless, in the absence of incentives or sanctions the person remains disengaged.[25] Second, to avoid psychological dissonance, an individual may adjust his or her preferences to align with imposed behavior, a process referred to as *rationalization*.[26] Third, efforts to justify one's behavior can lead an individual to inadvertently begin an internal dialogue, resulting in the conscious acceptance of new beliefs.[27] In short, there are a number of ways that disengagement could, over time, evolve into deradicalization.

Perhaps more importantly, although many scholars and practitioners emphasize the feasibility and potential effectiveness of disengagement, there are reasons to believe that deradicalization is still the more appropriate goal for programs that seek to counter Islamist extremism. For example, Froukje Demant et al. have suggested that ideology plays a more significant role in motivating some types of extremists—particularly Islamist radicals—than others.[28] Because Islamists are so ideologically motivated, they may be less susceptible to material rewards and punishments. If so, then instrumental disengagement may be difficult to achieve and, especially, to sustain over time, which suggests that deradicalization may be a necessary, if challenging, goal.

Moreover, if a radical ideology is left unchallenged, it is more likely to continue attracting recruits. Even if an organization espousing the ideology fades away, another group is likely to adopt this world-

---

[25] Frank Schimmelfennig, "Strategic Calculation and International Socialization: Membership Incentives, Party Constellations, and Sustained Compliance in Central and Eastern Europe," *International Organization*, Vol. 59, No. 4, Fall 2005, p. 831; Jeffrey T. Checkel, "International Institutions and Socialization in Europe: Introduction and Framework," *International Organization*, Vol. 59, No. 4, Fall 2005, p. 804.

[26] Schimmelfennig, 2005, p. 831.

[27] Thomas Risse, "International Norms and Domestic Change: Arguing and Communicative Behavior in the Human Rights Area," *Politics and Society*, Vol. 27, No. 4, December 1999, p. 531.

[28] Froukje Demant, Marieke Slootman, Frank Buijs, and Jean Tillie, *Decline and Disengagement: An Analysis of Processes of Deradicalization*, Amsterdam: IMES Report Series, 2008, p. 129.

view and continue the struggle. Therefore, to truly extinguish the threat from a radical philosophy, it may be necessary for members to renounce their beliefs and explain why they are erroneous. In other words, a wholesale rejection of this worldview may be required.

The Disengagement and Deradicalization Processes

In addition to studies that focus specifically on disengagement from militant Islamist organizations, we have examined related areas of research, including disengagement from street gangs, desistance from crime, withdrawal from right-wing or racist groups, voluntary departure from cults and religious organizations, and exit from non-Islamist terrorist organizations.[29] Despite the differences among these types of organizations, the literature on exiting these groups suggests that there is a common trajectory for members who consider leaving, attempt to leave, and ultimately succeed in disengaging.

The process of disengagement begins as the result of a trigger, which is frequently a traumatic event or emotional crisis; this creates a cognitive opening and doubts about remaining in the group.[30] During this period of questioning, an individual makes a simple calculation

---

[29] An important limitation of this research is that nearly all of it relies on a biased sample. That is, most studies examine only individuals who have left a radical organization and exclude those who remain in the group (exceptions include Tore Bjørgo, "Processes of Disengagement from Violent Groups of the Extreme Right," in Tore Bjørgo and John Horgan, eds., *Leaving Terrorism Behind: Individual and Collective Disengagement*, New York: Routledge, 2008, and Marc Galanter, *Cults: Faith, Healing, and Coercion*, New York: Oxford University Press, 1989).

In large part, this selection bias is due to the fact that radical organizations are suspicious of outsiders, which makes it difficult, if not impossible, to talk with active members. This is especially true of terrorist organizations, which are clandestine groups on the run from the authorities. Nevertheless, as a result of this selection bias, one cannot eliminate the possibility that individuals who remain in radical groups experience many of the same push and pull factors as those who exit. In a study of members of the Unification Church, Galanter (1989, p. 173) concludes that "little relationship seems to exist between a member's actual dissatisfaction at a random point and the person's eventual departure from the sect."

[30] The trigger is what we generally consider to be a push factor, which is discussed in greater detail later in this chapter.

weighing the pros and cons of exiting. Whether this internal debate ultimately leads a person to exit depends on the strength of "push" and "pull" factors, the benefits of remaining with the group, and the barriers to exit, which together determine whether the expected utility of leaving exceeds the expected utility of remaining. When this condition manifests, the person reaches a turning point and decides to disengage from the radical organization. After exiting, the former radical tries to create a new identity and reintegrate into mainstream society (see Figure 1.1). Four plausible hypotheses—the presence of a moderate social network, whether the individual has a job, whether the individual is accepted or ostracized by society, and whether the individual deradicalizes—can be postulated to influence the likelihood that the former extremist will reengage in radical behavior.

Figure 1.1
Disengagement Trajectory of an Individual Exiting a Radical Organization

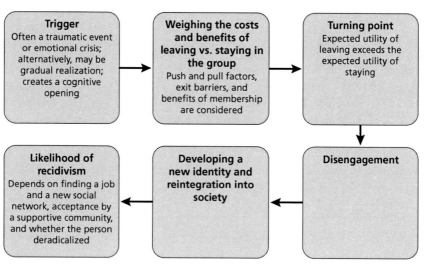

The Trigger

The disengagement process typically begins with a trigger that calls into question a person's commitment to a radical organization.[31] This trigger is frequently a traumatic event that precipitates an emotional crisis.[32] For example, gang members often begin to contemplate leaving a gang after they or someone close to them has been the victim of a violent attack.[33] Violence also plays a role in the decision to leave Islamist radical organizations. The deaths of hundreds of civilians in the October 2002 Bali bombing, for instance, prompted former JI leader Nasir Abas to reconsider his involvement in this militant group.[34] Less dramatic events that cast the group in a negative light can also serve as a trigger. In one example, a couple that eventually left the Church of Scientology began to have doubts about the sect after witnessing a church official striking a subordinate.[35] Similarly, members often leave extreme right-wing or racist organizations due to intragroup conflicts that belie the organization's professed commitment to brotherhood.[36]

Alternatively, the trigger does not have to be a particular event. Instead, it can be an accumulation of events, the dawning conclusion

[31] Fink and Hearne, 2008, p. 3; Stuart A. Wright, "Leaving New Religious Movements: Issues Theory, and Research," in David G. Bromley, ed., *Falling from the Faith: Causes and Consequences of Religious Apostasy*, London: Sage Publications, 1988, p. 152.

[32] Galanter, 1989, p. 173; Renee Garfinkle, *Personal Transformations: Moving from Violence to Peace*, Washington, D.C.: United States Institute of Peace, Special Report 186, April 2007, pp. 11–12.

[33] Scott H. Decker and Barrik van Winkle, *Life in the Gang: Family, Friends, and Violence,* Cambridge, UK: Cambridge University Press, 1996, p. 260; Scott H. Decker and Janet L. Lauritsen, "Leaving the Gang," in C. Ronald Huff, ed., *Gangs in America III*, Thousand Oaks, Calif.: Sage Publications, 2001, p. 58; Liz Carey, "Anderson Teens Share Gang Experiences, Difficulty of Getting Out," *Independent Mail* (Anderson, S.C.), October 26, 2009.

[34] Zachary Abuza, "The Rehabilitation of Jemaah Islamiyah Detainees in South East Asia: A Preliminary Assessment," in Tore Bjørgo and John Horgan, eds., *Leaving Terrorism Behind: Individual and Collective Disengagement*, New York: Routledge, 2008, p. 198.

[35] Laurie Goodstein, "Defectors Say Church of Scientology Hides Abuse," *New York Times*, March 6, 2010.

[36] Tore Bjørgo and Yngve Carlsson, "Early Intervention with Violent and Racist Youth Groups," Norwegian Institute of International Affairs, Working Paper No. 677, 2005, p. 38; Bjørgo, 2008, p. 38.

that the group's ideology does not accurately explain the world, or the realization that it has failed to bring about social or political change.[37] Many Italian Red Brigade activists began to have doubts about their role in the group only after it became apparent that the organization had failed to achieve its objectives and most of its members were in prison.[38] Compassion by an outsider—someone who does not belong to the radical organization—has, at times, led religious radicals to question ideologies that vilify those with different beliefs.[39]

In all of these examples, the trigger brings to light an inconsistency in the radical's worldview. At this moment, when evidence emerges that contradicts an individual's beliefs, there is a cognitive opening, meaning that the individual is now receptive to different ideas.[40] After the militant worldview has proved to be inadequate, the individual may begin a period of reflection and question his or her radical orientation. Furthermore, once doubts arise, they often quickly spread; most radical organizations are total institutions, meaning that every aspect of the group's worldview is interdependent. Thus, if one aspect is called into question, the entire belief structure tends to unravel.[41] If the trauma is minor or further inconsistencies are not readily apparent,

---

[37] Demant, et al., 2008, p. 113.

[38] Donatella Della Porta, "Leaving Underground Organizations: A Sociological Analysis of the Italian Case," in Tore Bjørgo and John Horgan, eds., *Leaving Terrorism Behind: Individual and Collective Disengagement*, New York: Routledge, 2008, p. 69; Alison Jamieson, "Identity and Morality in the Italian Red Brigades," *Terrorism and Political Violence*, Vol. 2, No. 4, Winter 1990, pp. 519–520.

[39] Demant et. al., 2008, p. 117; Garfinkle, 2007, p. 12.

[40] Tufyal Choudhury, *The Role of Muslim Identity Politics in Radicalisation (A Study in Progress)*, London: UK Department for Communities and Local Government, 2007, p. 6. Choudhury explains that radicalization usually begins with a moment of crisis that precipitates the search for a new identity. Deradicalization and disengagement also involve forging a new identity, and the evidence suggests that they begin with a trigger that also creates a cognitive opening.

[41] Helen Rose Fuchs Ebaugh, "Leaving Catholic Convents: Toward a Theory of Disengagement," in Bromley, ed., *Falling from the Faith: Causes and Consequences of Religious Apostasy*, Newbury Park, Calif.: Sage Publications, 1988, p. 106.

however, the radical may simply ignore the discrepancy or rationalize the event to achieve cognitive consistency.[42]

Weighing the Costs and Benefits of Staying or Leaving

A radical enters the second stage in disengagement when he or she begins to seriously consider the pros and cons of exiting the extremist organization.[43] The literature on disengagement and deradicalization has focused on identifying negative factors that encourage disengagement (push factors), positive factors that draw a person away from a radical group (pull factors), and the considerations that make it difficult for a person to leave an extremist organization (exit barriers).[44] In his work on right-wing groups in the Netherlands, Tore Bjørgo popularized these terms, and although he did not explicitly say so, he asserted that members of radical organizations make a crude instrumental calculation about leaving or remaining in a group.[45] Empirical work confirms that these considerations have played a significant role in individual deliberations to exit a radical organization. However, discussions of push and pull factors and exit barriers have suffered from imprecision and, as a result, have overlooked a critical part of an individual's decision calculus.

Push factors—which can run the gamut from perceived ideological failure to intragroup disputes over ideology and strategy to idiosyncratic personal matters—create negative feelings about a radical organization and therefore raise the costs of continued membership. For instance, gang members sometimes leave a gang because its commit-

---

[42] S. Wright, 1988, p. 151; Robert Jervis, *Perception and Misperception in International Politics*, Princeton, N.J.: Princeton University Press, 1976, p. 143; Stuart A. Wright, "Reconceptualizing Cult Coercion and Withdrawal: A Comparative Analysis of Divorce and Apostasy," *Social Forces*, Vol. 70, No. 1, September 1991, p. 131.

[43] Fuch Ebuagh, 1988, p. 109; S. Wright, 1988, p. 152.

[44] Bjørgo, 2008, pp. 36–42.

[45] For example, Bjørgo (2008, p. 47) states that "those who quit the group usually do so because continued membership in the group appears unattractive and is no longer fulfilling their social and psychological needs (push factors), whereas life outside the group appears more attractive (pull factors)."

ment to brotherhood is undermined by infighting.[46] In this instance, the gang's lack of cohesion reduces its attractiveness to its members.[47] Conversely, members of right-wing organizations are often impelled to leave a group when they realize the stigma associated with membership in such an organization.[48] At times, the impetus to leave cults has come from insignificant matters, such as personal disagreements with superiors.[49] On the other hand, a government's counterterrorist measures often place considerable pressure on members of an extremist organization, which, in turn, leads to burnout.[50] A significant number of defectors from militant Islamist organizations have abandoned these groups due to the belief that the groups incorrectly interpret Islam.[51]

In contrast, pull factors are the potential benefits that a person would realize if he or she were to leave the group. Members of gangs and right-wing organizations often express a desire to have a "normal life."[52] Similarly, the establishment of a relationship with someone outside of a cult often persuades members to leave the organization.[53] On the other hand, terrorists are often induced to disengage from violence if a government offers them amnesty or reduced prison sentences.[54]

---

[46] Tore Bjørgo, "How Gangs Fall Apart: Process of Transformation and Disintegration of Gangs," paper presented at the annual meeting of the American Society of Criminology, November 17–20, 1999, p. 1.

[47] Malcolm Klein argues that gang cohesiveness is mainly a function of the presence of external enemies and that more unified gangs engage in more violent behavior. Similarly, Decker and Lauritsen explain that, at times, violence may strengthen a gang's cohesion by rallying its members in the face of a threat, but violent experiences are also the most often-cited reason that former gang members claim for leaving the group (Malcolm W. Klein, *The American Street Gang: Its Nature, Prevalence, and Control*, Oxford, UK: Oxford University Press, 1995, pp. 30, 43; Decker and Lauritsen, 2001, p. 58).

[48] Bjørgo, 2008, pp. 39–40.

[49] Galanter, 1989, pp. 161–165.

[50] Della Porta, 2008, p. 80.

[51] Jacobson, 2010, p. 8.

[52] Decker and Lauritsen, 2001, p. 53; Bjørgo, 2008, p. 39.

[53] S. Wright, 1988, p. 151.

[54] Della Porta, 2008, pp. 69–72; Conciliation Resources and Quaker Peace and Social Witness, *Coming Home: Understanding Why Commanders of the Lord's Resistance Army Choose*

Militant Islamists have left a radical organization in an effort to gain government promises of employment and financial support.[55]

Even if an extremist grows disillusioned with a radical organization and is offered enticements to leave, doing so is often difficult due to a range of obstacles, referred to as exit barriers, which are the costs that one expects to incur by leaving the group. For example, even after gang members leave a group, others often continue to treat them as if they were still members. The police may continue to harass former gang members, and rival gangs often continue to try to harm them.[56] A key barrier to leaving right-wing organizations is the member's fear of having nowhere else to go.[57] The same is often true for cult members, who are ostracized by the group if they choose to leave, often being cut off from friends and family who are still members.[58] Because they are wanted by the authorities, terrorists often feel that they have little choice but to remain with the organization.[59] Islamists face a particularly difficult exit barrier because they will have to disobey or renounce their religious beliefs to leave the organization.[60]

Although exit barriers are important, they are not the only factors that can prevent an individual from leaving a radical group during this stage of the disengagement trajectory. The positive aspects of membership—which are analytically distinct from, but often conflated with, exit barriers—can also be an important influence.[61] Benefits

to Return to a Civilian Life, May 2006, p. 10; Carlos Quita, "The Philippines' Counter-Terrorism Approach," *Asian Conflicts Reports*, No. 5, May 2009.

[55] Christopher Boucek, *Saudi Arabia's "Soft" Counterterrorism Strategy: Prevention, Rehabilitation, and Aftercare*, Carnegie Papers, No. 97, September 2008d, pp. 19–20.

[56] Decker and van Winkle, 1996, pp. 263–264; Decker and Lauritsen, 2001, p. 54.

[57] Bjørgo, 2008, p. 41.

[58] Goodstein, 2010.

[59] Karl Wasmund, "The Political Socialization of West German Terrorists," in Peter H. Merkl, ed., *Political Violence and Terror: Motifs and Motivations*, Berkeley, Calif.: University of California Press, 1986, p. 221.

[60] Dennis A. Pluchinsky, "Global Jihadist Recidivism: A Red Flag," *Studies in Conflict and Terrorism*, Vol. 31, No. 3, March 2008, p. 187.

[61] Bjørgo, 2008, pp. 40–41.

from membership in a gang typically include protection, for example.[62] Members of right-wing groups often gain status and prestige within their circle by belonging to a racist organization.[63] Members of cults often enjoy having all of their needs—religion, employment, friends, and structure—met by the group.[64] Terrorist organizations may provide their members with a sense of excitement or give them greater purpose.[65] Similarly, Islamist organizations give their members a role in implementing God's will, which will earn them an eternal reward in the afterlife.[66]

Ultimately, an individual is likely to leave a radical organization when the expected utility of leaving is greater than the expected utility of staying. Utility is calculated by considering the costs and benefits of a particular course of action, as well as the probability that those costs and benefits will materialize.[67] In making this argument, it is not necessary to assume that individuals are perfectly rational, merely that they engage in a basic means-end calculation when deciding whether to leave a radical group. Since most of the literature on disengagement and deradicalization implicitly assumes that such individuals do indeed make these types of assessments, we have introduced rational choice terminology in an effort to make the discussion more precise.

The Turning Point: The Decision to Exit

If an individual concludes that the expected utility of leaving a radical organization is greater than the expected utility of staying, he or she reaches a turning point. Once the decision to disengage has been

---

[62] Decker and van Winkle, 1996, p. 272.

[63] Bjørgo, 2008, pp. 32–33.

[64] Susan Rothbaum, "Between Two Worlds: Issues of Separation and Identity After Leaving a Religious Community," in David G. Bromley, ed., *Falling from the Faith: Causes and Consequences of Religious Apostasy*, Newbury Park, Calif.: Sage Publications, 1988, p. 205.

[65] Jamieson, 1990, pp. 510–513.

[66] Gabriel A. Almond, R. Scott Appleby, and Emmanuel Sivan, *Strong Religion: The Rise of Fundamentalism Around the World*, Chicago, Ill.: University of Chicago Press, 2003, p. 15.

[67] Jon Elster, "Introduction," in John Elster, ed., *Rational Choice*, New York: New York University Press, 1986, p. 5.

made, the individual must then determine whether to leave covertly, overtly, or publicly. In an effort to avoid a stressful confrontation with other group members, the militant may secretly leave the group. Conversely, after deciding to leave, the militant may discuss the matter openly within the organization but not otherwise publicize the choice. In a public departure, a militant openly broadcasts his or her decision to leave and while doing so often denounces the extremist organization.[68]

Stuart Wright finds that length of membership has an influence on the exit strategy chosen; relatively new members often flee a cult secretly, while more experienced members opt to confront the group or to publicize their decision.[69] Similarly, Bjørgo and Carlsson claim that a radical's position in a right-wing organization often influences the type of departure: High-ranking or prominent members—those who are openly known to be part of the extremist group—often announce their exit, while lesser known members usually quietly and gradually dissociate themselves. At least in part, the high-profile strategy is chosen because well-known extremists cannot discreetly leave a group without their absence being noticed. Each of these strategies has its advantages and drawbacks. A public break is more likely to convince observers that the former radical has sincerely changed; at the same time, it often eliminates the option of returning to the group. Foreclosing return may be viewed as a benefit for a disengaged individual who fears that he or she may be tempted to rejoin the organization. On the other hand, either a covert or overt departure may leave the door open for the individual to return to the organization in the future if circumstances change.

To date, there has been insufficient research on the impact of different types of exit strategies to reach any firm conclusions, but it seems reasonable that there may be a relationship between the exit strategy employed and the likelihood of recidivism. Choosing a public departure means cutting ties to the radical organization in a way that is not easily reparable. For example, Omar bin Laden, Osama bin Laden's

---

[68] S. Wright, 1988, p. 152, and 1991, pp. 136–138; Bjørgo and Carlsson, 2005, pp. 32–35; Bjørgo, 2008, pp. 42–44.

[69] S. Wright, 1988, p. 152.

son, not only left al-Qaeda's camp in Afghanistan but also publicly denounced the September 11, 2001, attacks as "craziness."[70] Although Omar claims to reject al-Qaeda's violence, his comments about his father suggest a deep ambivalence and often make him sound like an apologist for the elder bin Laden. Nevertheless, Omar bin Laden's decisions to open up to the media and to publish an autobiography about his life make it unlikely that he would be welcomed back into al-Qaeda.[71]

On the other hand, some radical organizations permit their members to leave and allow them to return to the fold as long as they do not inform on their comrades. The Irish Republican Army, for instance, reportedly allowed its members to become inactive, provided that the member on leave did not betray the organization by giving information to the authorities. Because it was engaged in a self-proclaimed long war against the British, the group recognized that, at times, a member may become exhausted or burned out, and, consequently, it allowed trusted members to leave on the assumption that they would probably return.[72]

Developing a New Identity and Reintegrating into Society

After exiting, the individual is physically disengaged from the extremist group but still needs to create a new identity and reintegrate into mainstream society. Although there are not enough data to conclusively identify the factors that influence the probability of recidivism, we put forward some plausible hypotheses about the probability of successful reintegration into society or recidivism. If the former militant is able to develop a new social network that encourages moderate behavior, secure steady employment, and be accepted by the community, he or she will be less likely to reengage in radical behavior. Conversely, if the former radical cannot locate a supportive social network, find a job, or is ostracized by the community, the probability of recidivism will correspondingly increase.

---

[70] Quoted in Jacobson, 2010, p. 13.

[71] Guy Lawson, "Osama's Prodigal Son," *Rolling Stone*, January 20, 2010.

[72] Horgan, 2009b, p. 93.

Although many scholars argue that social and affective bonds often explain why individuals join and leave radical organizations, a supportive social network may play an even larger role in influencing whether a former radical remains disengaged. A disengaged radical not only needs friends and family, but the views of these people can shape his or her subsequent behavior.[73] If a former militant leaves a radical organization and returns to a community with radical sympathies, that individual is unlikely to remain disengaged. This may be a particularly difficult problem for members of groups, such as JI, that recruit entire families and extended kinship networks. At times, therefore, deradicalization programs may need to relocate individuals out of communities that encourage radicalism to an environment that is more conducive to disengagement and moderation.

Alternatively, deradicalization programs may be able to sway the attitudes of an ex-radical's family members by providing them with financial and emotional support. If a deradicalization program offers material support and counseling to the family of a former extremist, it may be able to develop the moderate support network needed for disengagement to become permanent.[74] Saudi Arabia's Advisory Council offers social support to the family and tribe of a released extremist, but it also warns that those benefits would be revoked if the former radical commits new offenses.[75]

Since belonging to a radical group is often a full-time activity, it is important that a disengaged extremist find employment and feel productive, independent, and capable of providing for his or her family. Stable employment helps boost the self-esteem of former extremists and wean them off the practical support that the radical organization had offered. This, in turn, suggests that deradicalization programs should directly assist rehabilitated extremists in obtaining a job, which may

---

[73] Giordano, Cernkovich, and Holland make this point when discussing crime (see Peggy C. Giordano, Steven A. Cernkovich, and Donna D. Holland, "Changes in Friendship Relations over the Life Course: Implications for Desistance from Crime," *Criminology*, Vol. 41, No. 2, May 2003, p. 306.

[74] Abuza, 2008, pp. 210–211.

[75] Boucek, 2008d, p. 20.

include supplying additional training or education. The Singapore program's social rehabilitation component, for instance, offers detainees and their families an opportunity to gain additional education and professional training.

Finally, the attitude of the community toward the former extremist can be a critical factor.[76] When a community welcomes a former radical and helps him or her find work and develop new associations, the former extremist is less likely to regret the decision to disengage. By contrast, if a community ostracizes a former radical, that individual is likely to find it difficult to begin a career or find an alternative support network and, as a result, may gravitate back to the extremist group. For instance, the Unionist community in Northern Ireland largely shuns former loyalist militants. Unable to find employment or make new friends, many loyalists have returned to radical or, even more frequently, criminal organizations.[77] This suggests that deradicalization programs should also aim to shape the views of society toward ex-militants.

This trajectory outlines the general path that extremists follow to disengage from a radical organization, but it has little to say specifically about deradicalization. This is because deradicalization occurs independently of disengagement. As discussed previously, there are number of ways in which disengagement could turn into deradicalization, but this does not always occur. The literature on cults has documented cases of ex-members who continue to follow the group's ideology even after leaving.[78] Similarly, former leftist terrorists have often abandoned violence only to join political parties that espoused similar ideologies.[79] It appears that an individual could adopt new preferences at any point

---

[76] Abuza, 2008, p. 194.

[77] James W. McAuley, Jonathan Tonge, and Peter Shirlow, "Conflict, Transformation, and Former Loyalist Paramilitary Prisoners in Northern Ireland," *Terrorism and Political Violence*, Vol. 22, No. 1, 2010, pp. 31–33; Claire Mitchell, "The Limits of Legitimacy: Former Loyalist Combatants and Peace-Building in Northern Ireland," *Irish Political Studies*, Vol. 23, No. 1, February 2008, pp. 14–15.

[78] Galanter, 1989, p. 174.

[79] Della Porta, 2008, pp. 79–80.

along the disengagement trajectory. The current literature is indeterminate as to when and even whether deradicalization will occur.

The preceding discussion suggests that the processes of disengagement and deradicalization appear to be more than merely radicalization in reverse. The reasons that an individual leaves a radical group are not necessarily tied to the reasons for joining the group.[80] An individual may become a member of an extremist organization because of a strong belief in the group's ideology; because friends and acquaintances belong to the group; for practical reasons, such as financial and other incentives provided by the group; or for a combination of these factors. Regardless of the reasons for joining, once an individual is in a radical organization, he or she is socialized to accept the group's ideology, develops deep emotional ties to other members, and relies on the group to provide for many basic needs. Independent of the reasons for the original decision to join, there are other factors that now tie the person to the group.[81]

Level of Commitment

Although there is a general decision process that leads individuals to disengage from all types of radical organizations, clearly, some radicals are more likely to exit than others. To summarize briefly, there is an inverse relationship between the degree of commitment and the likelihood of disengagement or deradicalization. This observation has important implications for the prospects of disengagement and deradi-

---

[80] Horgan and Bjørgo initially agreed with this, but Horgan's recent book supports the theory that the reasons for joining and leaving an organization are related. Fink and Hearne, 2008, p. 9; Horgan, 2009b, p. 151.

[81] In a study of Colombian insurgent movements, Florez-Morris found that members who remained in the group until it collectively demobilized did so as a result of social and practical needs, shared beliefs, and the group's role in boosting their self-identity by making them feel important. In addition to these benefits, insurgents were also deterred from leaving by the lack of other options, a result of the clandestine nature of the organization (Mauricio Florez-Morris, "Why Some Colombian Guerrilla Members Stayed in the Movement Until Demobilization: A Micro-Sociological Case Study of Factors That Influenced Members' Commitment to Three Former Rebel Organizations: M-19, EPL, and CRS," *Terrorism and Political Violence*, Vol. 22, No. 2 March 2010, p. 218.

calization from Islamist organizations and for policymakers designing programs to encourage extremists to change their behavior and beliefs.

It is often pointed out that the longer an individual belongs to a group and the greater his or her involvement in the group's activities, the less likely it is that the individual will leave the group.[82] However, commitment entails more than just length of membership and level of participation. Demant et al. differentiate among normative, affective, and pragmatic commitment.[83] Individuals who believe in a group's ideology often feel a moral imperative to remain in a radical organization (normative commitment). Affective commitment is an emotional attachment to the other members of the organization and to the group itself. Pragmatic commitment refers to the practical factors that make it difficult to exit a group.

It is logical to assume that all three types of commitment increase the longer a member remains in a radical group. Donatella Della Porta argues that commitment is determined by the degree of connection between the three main spheres of life—family, professional, and political—and the radical organization.[84] While this framework is a significant contribution to the analysis of the concept of commitment, it excludes an important part of life: religion. Considering whether the various aspects of one's life are incorporated into the extremist organization provides an objective value that can be measured and can serve as a measure for normative (politics and religion), affective (family and friends), and pragmatic (work and compensation) commitment. The more politics, family and friends, work, and religion intersect, the greater the degree of commitment. Conversely, if these spheres of life are farther apart, there is less commitment and a greater likelihood of defection.

---

[82] Bjørgo, 2008, p. 33; S. Wright, 1991, p. 133; Eileen Barker, "Defection from the Unification Church: Some Statistics and Distinctions," in David G. Bromley, ed., *Falling from the Faith: Causes and Consequences of Religious Apostasy*, Newbury Park, Calif.: Sage Publications, 1988, p. 167; Della Porta, 2008, p. 68.

[83] Demant et al., 2008, pp. 115–116.

[84] Della Porta, 2008, p. 81.

Therefore, commitment depends on the duration of membership in a radical group as well as the degree to which a militant's family, profession, politics, and religion are incorporated into the organization. The two variables may be related because the longer a member is involved, the greater the chances that more aspects of his or her life will be woven into the organization. Taken together, these factors provide a more fine-grained way of assessing the probability that an individual will disengage from a group.

Using these variables, we can create a typology of extremists that helps identify individuals who are more inclined to disengage and deradicalize. Extremist organizations include hard-core members, activists, newcomers, supporters, and sympathizers (see Figure 1.2). The hard core is composed of the most deeply committed members. They have been in the organization for a long period and are usually involved in planning or executing violent activities.[85] Activists are also often involved in violent activities, but they may not have been members as long, and not every aspect of their life is tied into the group. Newcomers are recent recruits who have belonged to the group for a short period and therefore are less likely to have as much overlap between the different spheres of their life and the organization. Supporters have even fewer areas of their life tied to the organization. They are not full-time members but sporadically assist the radical group, for example, by harboring members or supplying them with funds. Sympathizers are not actively involved with the radical organization, but they identify with its goals and ideology and therefore may passively assist the group, for instance by not providing information to the authorities.

The longer a militant is in a radical organization and the more spheres of his or her life that are connected to the group, the less likely it is that the militant will leave the group because the costs of leav-

---

[85] Most individuals who leave radical organizations do so within the first two years of joining (S. Wright, 1991, p. 133; David G. Bromley, "Deprogramming as a Mode of Exit from New Religious Movements: The Case of the Unification Movement," in David G. Bromley, ed., *Falling from the Faith: Causes and Consequences of Religious Apostasy*, Newbury Park, Calif.: Sage Publications, 1988, p. 201.

Figure 1.2
Typology of Radicals Based on Level of Commitment

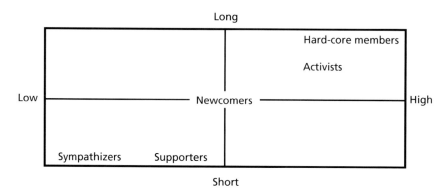

X-axis: Degree to which spheres of life are incorporated into the radical group
Y-axis: Duration of membership in the radical organization
RAND *MG1053-1.2*

ing will be too great.[86] Nevertheless, there are a number of prominent examples of deeply committed individuals disengaging from extremist organizations.[87] In subsequent chapters, we discuss, among others, the cases of JI branch leader Nasir Abas and of the former Hizb ut-Tahrir members in Britain who established the Quilliam Foundation to combat extremism.

Radical Islamists

One of the most glaring gaps in the literature is the failure to examine the similarities and differences between Islamist militants and other types of extremists and then to determine the implications of these findings for the processes of disengagement and deradicalization.

---

[86] A related implication of length of membership is that, over time, one's expectations tend to adapt to circumstances and align with reality; hence, some push factors are less likely to be salient for longer-tenured members. For example, these individuals are less likely to become disillusioned having adjusted their initial—and often unrealistic—expectation to the realities of life in the group. This contradicts Horgan (2009a, 2009b) and Jacobson (2010), who view unmet expectations as a key push factor that often leads to disengagement.

[87] Demant, 2008, p. 113.

Many studies simply assume that there are no relevant differences, while others assert that Islamist extremists are uniquely dangerous and irreconcilable.[88] Although it is evident that religious doctrine distinguishes militant Islamists from other radicals, the effects have not been fully explored. Because they are motivated by faith, Islamist radicals are more committed than nonreligious extremists and therefore are less likely to deradicalize. Nevertheless, precisely because Islamist ideology plays such a central role in these groups, it is necessary to change militant Islamists' beliefs as well as their behavior. Moreover, while it may be difficult to alter the worldview of Islamist radicals, there is an opportunity to use mainstream Islamic theology to undermine radical Islamist ideology.

Most of the existing work on the subject of disengagement presumes that the same factors that impel individuals to exit cults or gangs also spur individuals to leave militant Islamist organizations. One exception to this trend is a study by Demant et al., which classifies the push and pull factors that precipitate a decision to disengage from a radical organization into three broad categories: ideological, organizational or affective, and more mundane, day-to-day factors. All three factors play a role in the decision to leave an extremist group, although to a different degree, depending on the type of organization.[89]

For example, exit from right-wing organizations and gangs is driven primarily by disappointment with the organization and its internal workings or by practical factors, such as the desire for a family or career. Ideology usually plays little to no role in the departure from these groups.[90] Conversely, ideology and, in particular, the perceived failure of an ideology to explain the world or effect social change, often plays a central role in members' decisions to leave cults, terrorist orga-

---

[88] Examples of the former include Bjørgo and Horgan, 2008b; Horgan, 2008, 2009; and Horgan and Braddock, 2010. Examples of the latter are Bruce Hoffman, *Inside Terrorism*, New York: Columbia University Press, 2006, and Jacobson, 2010. Demant et al., 2008, is the exception to this trend.

[89] Demant et al, 2008, p. 115. They call these three factors: ideological, organizational, and continuance.

[90] Demant et al, 2008, p. 126; Bjørgo, 2008, p. 47.

nizations, and militant Islamist groups.[91] (They may also become disillusioned by the behavior of the group or with its leaders, however, especially if they do not seem to be acting according to the group's ideals.) In addition, defectors from these groups often complain about commonplace factors, such as compensation and harsh living conditions.[92] Stuart Wright argues that, for cult members, these practical matters are often ancillary factors that encourage a person to leave, but they are not the principal reason for departure.[93] It is unclear how much importance to assign to each of these factors for Islamist militants, but what is obvious is that ideology (of the consequences of putting the ideology into practice) frequently plays an important role in the process of disengaging from these groups.

This, in turn, raises another question: Is radical Islamism different from other radical ideologies? Ideology plays a central role in all types of terrorist organizations: It helps to attract recruits, legitimizes the group's use of violence, and helps maintain group solidarity. It does so by providing an explanation for the current world order, a picture of a preferred future, and a guide for how to realize the desired state.[94] A study of the German Red Army Faction found that the group's ideology justified its use of violence internally and to an external audience, suppressed the inhibition to kill, and eventually acquired "a quasi-religious character, with a sacrosanct quality."[95]

Although all kinds of militants may be fervent adherents to secular ideologies, religion provides a different type of motivation due to its promise that the devoted will receive an everlasting reward in the afterlife.[96] This has a number of implications for a radical's behavior: Since religious radicals believe that they are fulfilling a divine duty, they are

---

[91] Demant et al., 2008, p. 129; Ebaugh, 1988, p. 104; Jacobson, 2010, p. 8.

[92] Sharon Curcio, "The Dark Side of Jihad: How Young Men Detained at Guantanamo Assess Their Experience," in Cheryl Benard, ed., *A Future for the Young*, Santa Monica, Calif.: RAND Corporation, 2005, pp. 56–57; Jacobson, 2010, p. 12.

[93] S. Wright, 1988, p. 152.

[94] Demant et al., 2008, p. 113.

[95] Wasmund, 1986, p. 220.

[96] Almond, Appleby, and Sivan, 2003, p. 15.

more willing to put aside moral qualms about killing;[97] violence may not be instrumental but merely demonstrative;[98] and they have longer time horizons, which means that they are less likely to admit defeat because they believe that God will reward their steadfastness and suffering by eventually assuring their victory.[99]

Because ideology is such an important driver of violent Islamism, most of the existing deradicalization programs in Muslim countries include an ideological component in the form of a theological dialogue. These prison-based programs enlist imams, Islamic scholars, and sometimes even former radicals to discuss Islamic theology in an effort to convince militants that their interpretation of Islam is wrong. Since the discussions "are based on a common reference to Islam and Islamic law as the ultimate source of truth and legitimacy," they are more compelling than other approaches and, at times, effective in moderating the prisoner's beliefs.[100]

Some have compared the ideological component of these rehabilitation programs to deprogramming—the practice of forcibly detaining cult members in an attempt to reverse brainwashing. However, the similarity between deradicalization and deprogramming does not extend beyond the use of dialogue to convince a member of a radical organization to exit.[101] Although the participants in Islamic deradical-

---

[97] Even James Piazza, who argues that the more salient feature that influences a group's propensity to kill is whether it adheres to a universal/abstract or strategic ideology, finds that "Islamist groups are indeed more lethal and launch attacks that result in higher casualties than non-Islamist terrorist groups" (James Piazza, "Is Islamist Terrorism More Lethal? An Empirical Study of Group Ideology, Organization and Goal Structure," *Terrorism and Political Violence*, Vol. 21, No. 1, January 2009, p. 66).

[98] Mark Juergensmeyer, *Terror in the Mind of God: The Global Rise of Religious Violence*, Berkeley, Calif.: University of California Press, 2003, p. 220; Almond, Appleby, and Sivan, 2003, p. 235.

[99] Juergensmeyer, 2003, p. 165; Almond, Appleby, and Sivan, 2003, p. 96.

[100] Ane Skov Birk, *Incredible Dialogues: Religious Dialogue as a Means of Counter-Terrorism in Yemen*, London: King's College International Centre for the Study of Radicalisation and Political Violence, April 2009, p. 1.

[101] Bromley, 1988, pp. 186–187.

ization programs are imprisoned and therefore do not voluntarily seek out the program, they are not forced to participate.

Moreover, the theological dialogues are usually based on the assumption that the participant is trying to be a good Muslim but has been misled into adhering to an incorrect interpretation of Islam.[102] Studies of participants have confirmed that many of the radicals had little to no formal religious training and therefore were particularly susceptible to extremist propaganda.[103] In contrast, deprogramming rests on the notion that cult members have no free will due to mind control techniques employed by the cult's leader.[104]

Challenging radical Islamist ideology with an alternative interpretation of Islam, if accepted, is likely to not only effect a more permanent change in the militant's worldview but also help weaken the radical Islamist movement by discrediting its ideology. The recantation of prominent radicals poses a credible challenge to the movement. For example, the recantation written by former Egyptian Islamic Jihad (EIJ) ideologue Sayyid Imam al-Sharif (also known as Dr. Fadl) resonates with radicals because "nobody can challenge the legitimacy of this person [al-Sharif]."[105]

In addition to well-known militant ideologues such as Dr. Fadl, lesser-known ex-radicals can also have a dramatic impact. A former British Islamist militant, Usama Hasan explains,

> I think I'm listened to by the young because I have street cred from having spent time in a [jihadist] training camp. . . . Jihadist experience is especially important for young kids because otherwise they tend to think he is just a sell-out who is a lot of talk.[106]

---

[102] Boucek, 2008d, p. 11; Horgan and Braddock, 2010, p. 275.

[103] Boucek, 2008d, pp. 14–15.

[104] Bromley, 1988, p. 191.

[105] Gamal Sultan, Islamist writer and publisher, quoted in Lawrence Wright, "The Rebellion Within: An Al Qaeda Mastermind Questions Terrorism," *New Yorker*, June 2, 2008.

[106] Quoted in Bergen and Cruckshank, "The Unraveling: Al Qaeda's Revolt Against Bin Laden," *New Republic*, June 11, 2008.

These critiques by former radicals can lead extremists to question their beliefs in addition to deterring those who may be at risk of radicalization. Moreover, there may be a tipping point: When enough ex-militants denounce radical Islamism, that ideology and the organizations that adhere to it are fatally discredited. Even short of this tipping point, as greater numbers of militants renounce extremism, radical Islamist organizations will experience greater hurdles in attracting adherents and sympathizers within the Muslim community.

Conclusions

The arguments put forth here have a number of important implications for policymakers seeking to encourage Islamic radicals to renounce violence and the Islamist ideology. From the trajectory, one can derive a number of recommendations: The effectiveness of deradicalization programs may depend on their timing, government actions can significantly influence the expected utility of disengagement and continued violence, and the assistance offered by deradicalization programs should continue after the extremist is released.

The next chapter provides an overview of existing deradicalization programs and their philosophies. In addition, it discusses how these rehabilitation efforts should be evaluated and identifies the features that influence the probability that the programs will succeed in reforming Islamist extremists.

CHAPTER TWO

Survey of Deradicalization Programs

In the past decade, a number of states have established programs to counter radical Islamism and encourage imprisoned militant Islamists to disengage and deradicalize. Nearly all of these programs claim to have been successful and boast startlingly low rates of recidivism among the ex-militants who have been released back into society. According to the government of Saudi Arabia, its deradicalization program has succeeded in rehabilitating 80 percent of the militants targeted. Moreover, only 5 percent of the freed Saudi detainees have been rearrested.[1] Similarly, as of June 2008, the U.S.-run Iraqi deradicalization program claims that, of the 10,000 prisoners released, only 33 committed further offenses.[2] Although Singapore's deradicalization program is much smaller than the Saudi or Iraqi program, Singapore's government maintains that only one of the 40 former radical Islamists who have been freed has been detained again.[3]

Taken at face value, these data suggest that prison-based programs aiming to reform militant Islamists are extremely successful and that other states should employ similar methods to combat radicals. However, these assertions need to be further scrutinized before it is possible to reach any conclusions about the efficacy of deradicaliza-

---

[1] The 20 percent who have failed include prisoners who refuse to participate in the deradicalization program, those who failed to complete the program, and those who have been rearrested (Boucek, 2008d, p. 21).

[2] Major General Douglas M. Stone, Commander Detainee Operations, Multi-National Force–Iraq, transcript of press conference, June 1, 2008.

[3] See Chapter Four for more discussion of Singapore's rehabilitation programs.

tion programs. For instance, militants have been released from jail only to return to armed struggle. In particular, the Yemeni Committee for Dialogue has been singled out as particularly weak and ineffective, especially when compared to the more comprehensive Saudi program.[4] This, in turn, highlights the fact that there is great heterogeneity among deradicalization programs and that not all of these efforts are equally effective. Although some programs are noticeably less demanding than others, it remains unclear which aspects of these efforts lead a radical Islamist to disengage from terrorism and deradicalize. Some critics argue that the theological dialogue, the ideological component of a program, is useless and that most militant Islamists make an instrumental calculation to reform their behavior while maintaining their extremist beliefs.[5] Others allege that the "moderate" version of Islam promoted by many deradicalization programs is not moderate enough and continues to spread extremist views.[6]

Despite the reservations of the many skeptics, deradicalization and counter-radicalization programs seem to be gaining popularity, which is probably due to the dawning realization that security measures alone will not defeat violent Islamist extremism. Instead, many states have determined that, to undermine extremist organizations, it is necessary to prevent young people from radicalizing and to rehabilitate those who are not irreconcilable. As a result, many nations have developed programs that address both counter-radicalization and deradicalization, although there is considerable variation in which objective is given priority. Most European countries emphasize counter-radicalization, and their efforts to rehabilitate radical Islamists are a by-product of preventive initiatives. By contrast, most Middle Eastern and Southeast

---

[4]   Marisa L. Porges, "Deradicalisation, the Yemeni Way," *Survival*, Vol. 52, No. 2, March 2010b, p. 28.

[5]   John Horgan and Kurt Braddock, 2010, p. 268; Marisa L. Porges, "Getting Deradicalization Right," *Foreign Affairs*, May–June 2010c.

[6]   Shiraz Maher, "Saudi Care for Jihadis," *Wall Street Journal*, January 11, 2010; Task Force on Confronting the Ideology of Radical Extremism, *Rewriting the Narrative: An Integrated Strategy for Counterradicalization*, Washington, D.C.: Washington Institute for Near East Policy, March 2009, p. 13.

Asian governments pursue both counter-radicalization and deradicalization initiatives.

Prevention and rehabilitation are complementary goals; because of the interaction between these objectives, even European governments are attempting to deradicalize extremists. Denmark recently implemented a pilot deradicalization programs in two municipalities, and the United Kingdom is expanding its intervention program and developing a national deradicalization initiative.[7]

Since a number of crucial questions about deradicalization programs remain unanswered, the rush to emulate these alleged successes may be premature. For instance, how does one measure the efficacy of a deradicalization program? Should a program be judged by the proportion of participants who refrain from reengaging with violent groups upon their release, or by some other criteria? Are there specific features that a program needs to reform Islamist militants? Finally, based on these standards, what are the strengths and weakness of the existing deradicalization programs?

In an effort to answer these questions, the following chapters provide an overview of recent deradicalization programs for militant Islamists and make four principal arguments. First, although we recognize that there are a number of obstacles to accurately evaluating deradicalization programs, we argue that a minimal definition of success is that a majority of the reformed extremists remain completely disengaged—in other words, that the former militants do not participate in any violent activities or join an organization that perpetrates or supports violence. Although any effort to moderate extremists will inevitably experience some failures, the majority of the ex-militants should remain disengaged for a program to be considered a success.

Ideally, truly successful programs would convince ex-radicals to both refrain from violence and moderate their beliefs. This is important not only because a change in beliefs is likely to produce a more enduring change in behavior, but also because it directly challenges the extremist

---

[7]   Danish Ministry of Refugee, Immigration and Integration Affairs, "Denmark's Deradicalisation Efforts," fact sheet, May 2010; HM Government, *The Prevent Strategy: A Guide for Local Partners in England*, London, June 2008, p. 29.

ideology. Other important signs of success include diminishing radicalism in society at large, reforming hard-core radicals instead of just peripheral members, acquiring intelligence on radical groups, and convincing rehabilitated militants to speak out against radical Islamism.

Second, rehabilitation efforts that have affective, pragmatic, and ideological components that continue after the completion of the program are more likely to succeed in moderating radical Islamists because these programs counter all types of commitment to a radical organization and provide continued support as the former militant reenters mainstream society. The most successful programs attend to a radical's emotional well-being by offering counseling and helping the ex-militant locate a supportive social network; address practical factors by, for example, providing training and a job; and work to moderate the radical's beliefs by challenging extremist Islamism. Moreover, to facilitate the reintegration of ex-radicals into society, deradicalization programs should continue to support and monitor those who have reformed.

Third, for the ideological component of a deradicalization program to resonate with extremists, the message that the extremist ideology is flawed should come from a credible voice. Frequently, deradicalization programs rely on mainstream clerics to fill this role, but in some cases, ex-militants who played a significant role in their previous organizations or former ideologues may have greater credibility with extremists.

Fourth, the success of many deradicalization programs is due in large part to the fact that these efforts are aimed at peripheral radicals, such as supporters and sympathizers. Although it is certainly important to reform less committed radicals, even hard-core militants have disengaged and deradicalized. Therefore, rehabilitation efforts should not summarily exclude these more committed militants.

The remainder of this chapter is divided into three sections. The first discusses the general logic behind state-sponsored deradicalization programs. The second section outlines the characteristics that appear to increase the probability of success. The third section addresses how to evaluate programs aimed at rehabilitating Islamist radicals. Chapter Three provides an overview of the disengagement and deradicalization programs in the Middle East. Deradicalization programs in Southeast Asia and Europe are discussed in Chapters Four and Five, respectively.

The Logic Behind Deradicalization Programs

Radical Islamism has been an enduring problem for many nations, but it became a prominent international priority only after the 9/11 attacks. Counterterrorism campaigns in many theaters around the world have produced a mounting number of incarcerated Islamist extremists. These detainees present a dual problem for the nations holding them. First, most states do not want to hold the growing numbers of extremists in their prisons indefinitely, and, in many cases, they lack the resources to do so. They have therefore searched for a way to rehabilitate these prisoners so that they can be released without posing a threat to society. Second, many states have recognized that prisons are often incubators of radicalization, and in an effort to stymie this process, they have sought to tackle radicalization in their penitentiaries by reforming extremist detainees.[8]

To resolve the problems of indefinite detention and radicalization, a number of states created programs to reform captured extremists. In the Middle East and Southeast Asia, these programs were typically premised on the notion that the extremists had been misled into following an incorrect interpretation of Islam; therefore, the prison-based programs sought to reeducate detainees. The militants' worldview was discussed and refuted through a religious dialogue, usually conducted by mainstream clerics. In addition to the theological discussions, some of these programs aimed to assist the ex-militants in reintegrating into society.[9]

---

[8] For more on prison radicalization see Greg Hannah, Lindsay Clutterbuck, and Jennifer Rubin, *Radicalization or Rehabilitation: Understanding the Challenge of Extremist and Radicalized Prisoners*, Santa Monica, Calif.: RAND Corporation, TR-571-RC, 2008.

[9] Jessica Stern, "Mind over Martyr," *Foreign Affairs*, Vol. 89, No. 1, January–February 2010.

These rehabilitation programs saw imprisonment as a potential catalyst for disengagement and deradicalization. Detention may have triggered a period of questioning by some of the militant Islamists who could be identified and then engaged in discussions to encourage their doubts. Moreover, since the extremists were in prison, the authorities were better able to influence the radicals' incentive structure by strategically and conditionally offering benefits in return for moderation. If it could not change the militants' beliefs, the state could at least provide a rational reason for the radicals to change their behavior. Although it has been established that deradicalization and disengagement can and often do occur independently, it seems as if all prison-based deradicalization programs require detainees to reform their beliefs as well as their behavior if they are to be considered for release. The deradicalization programs are also usually part of a larger counterterrorism strategy that includes hard-line security measures as well as broader efforts to discredit the extremist ideology.

European states have taken a somewhat different approach to combating radical Islamism. In particular, the United Kingdom, the Netherlands, and Denmark have implemented voluntary, locally based programs to combat extremism and to identify and reform individuals who are in the early stages of radicalization. Although these efforts have received direction from their respective national governments (as well as the European Union), there is considerable variation in the types of programs and approaches that have been implemented.[10] European counter-radicalization and deradicalization strategies are intended to be flexible so that local authorities can tailor their actions to their community's characteristics, vulnerabilities, and needs. The emphasis on municipal initiatives also stems from the realization that it is the local authorities who are best placed to detect radicalization and therefore intervene early in the process when the prospects of success are greater.

---

[10] For more on the EU's counterterrorism policy, see Oldrich Bures, "EU Counterterrorism Policy: A Paper Tiger?" *Terrorism and Political Violence*, Vol. 18, No. 1, 2006, and Doron Zimmermann, "The European Union and Post-9/11 Counterterrorism: A Reappraisal," *Studies in Conflict and Terrorism*, Vol. 29, No. 2, March 2006.

Thus far the main emphasis of the European programs has been counter-radicalization—efforts to prevent at-risk individuals from radicalizing.[11] However, many of these programs also aim to identify radicalized European Muslims and encourage their moderation. These programs are voluntary and target radicals who have not broken the law, meaning that the targets are typically peripheral members of a radical Islamist group or merely sympathizers. In addition, the European efforts seek to further integrate their Muslim minority populations into society to reduce the feelings of alienation and discrimination that seem to fuel Islamist extremism in Europe. Toward this end, some European governments offer to help Muslim citizens acquire public housing, jobs, education, and vocational training. These efforts are also intended to build strong and moderate Muslim communities that are capable of resisting extremism and provide a supportive social environment to young Muslims at risk of radicalization.

Another feature that distinguishes the European programs from their counterparts in other regions is that the European efforts to combat extremism are not exclusively focused on radical Islamism but instead seek to weaken all types of extremism (in particular, right-wing extremism) and rehabilitate all types of radicals. European approaches are shaped by the fact that Muslims are a minority in secular, nominally Christian-majority countries. As a consequence, European governments recognize that they cannot directly challenge an ideology based on Islam. Rather, European authorities increasingly believe that it is more effective to support Muslim organizations that have the credibility to discredit the extremist creed and foster a free marketplace of ideas.

In sum, there are significant differences among the deradicalization programs that have been created to counter radical Islamism; however, all of these approaches seek to rehabilitate individuals or groups that have radicalized and to prevent others from radicalizing. The Middle Eastern and Southeast Asian prison-based programs priori-

---

[11] Lorenzo Vidino, "Europe's New Security Dilemma," *Washington Quarterly*, Vol. 32, No. 4, October 2009, pp. 61–62; Lorenzo Vidino, "Toward a Radical Solution," *Foreign Policy*, January 5, 2010.

tize the former goal, while the European programs prioritize the latter. Nevertheless, it is not clear that these differences will persist.

What Constitutes Success?

Nearly all of the existing efforts to rehabilitate radical Islamists claim to have been successful; however, it is not clear what constitutes success, nor are these claims backed up with robust empirical support.[12] There are also a number of obstacles to accurately evaluating deradicalization programs.

First, because most of these programs were implemented relatively recently, not enough time has passed to allow an evaluation of their long-term effectiveness. Nevertheless, there should be enough information to assess their short-term impact. However, for reasons discussed later, even this is difficult.

Second, some of the governments sponsoring these initiatives have deliberately withheld information about their programs, probably in an effort to avoid criticism. As a consequence, few programs have reliable statistics about their participants.[13]

Third, information is scarce because it is difficult to track reformed extremists for an extended period, and many programs observe them for only a short time, for instance, one year.[14] After the regime's watchful eye is focused elsewhere, there is little way of knowing whether a rehabilitated extremist reengages with a radical organization or commits acts of violence unless he or she happens to be apprehended by the authorities.

Fourth, the most widely used measure of success is the rate of recidivism, which is not completely accurate because it does not take into account those individuals who are disengaged but not deradicalized, those who undertake radical actions but have not been detected

---

[12] Horgan and Braddock, 2010, p. 268.

[13] Horgan and Braddock, 2010, p. 285.

[14] Yemen monitored reformed militants for one year.

by the authorities, or those who may be assisting a radical organization but in a role that does not involve breaking the law.[15]

Finally, statistics referring to recidivism are problematic because not all deradicalization programs define recidivism the same way.[16] In fact, most of the programs do not clearly identify what constitutes recidivism, but the evidence suggests that at least some of the programs count as successes individuals who do not reengage in violence at home, although they may join terrorist groups abroad. By not challenging the broader claims of radical Islamism, this limited deradicalization approach continues to tolerate an extremist ideology and sometimes even violence in other countries.

Since deradicalization initiatives are proliferating, it is necessary to carefully evaluate these efforts and identify the best and worst practices. Toward this end, deradicalization programs should be encouraged to clearly define recidivism or success, carefully monitor ex-radicals, and increase the transparency of their operations. Because of the significant obstacles, there have been no efforts to develop a common framework to systematically evaluate programs that aim to rehabilitate radical Islamists.[17] Analysis may be difficult due to the shortage of data, but an admittedly limited and preliminary effort is still feasible and necessary.

A minimal definition of success would be disengagement, meaning that ex-militants do not join a radical organization or undertake violent acts on their own. Although it is inevitable that some of the allegedly reformed extremists will reradicalize, a program should be considered a success if the majority of its participants remain fully disengaged. A more robust definition of success would be that most of the former radicals deradicalize as well as disengage.[18] The deradicalization

---

[15] Porges, 2010c.

[16] Horgan and Braddock, 2010, p. 285.

[17] Horgan and Braddock, 2010, p. 286.

[18] Most of the prison-based deradicalization programs that release militants from prison require them to pledge that they have moderated their beliefs and their behavior; however, it is doubtful that all of them have actually done so. In practice, it is difficult to determine whether someone has actually deradicalized, and the only measures that can be used are

component is important because it contributes to the larger objective of weakening the extremist movement and ideology so that it does not continue to inspire militants. Subsidiary considerations that may contribute to the degree of success include whether the reformed militants provide intelligence about their former group, whether they encourage other radicals to moderate and discourage others from radicalizing, and whether the program seeks to reform hard-core militants as well as peripheral members.

Key Components of Successful Deradicalization Programs

Based on our analysis of the individual-level processes of disengagement and deradicalization, we argue that efforts to rehabilitate radical Islamists should be rigorous and comprehensive programs that counter a radical's affective, pragmatic, and ideological commitment to an extremist organization. To effectively challenge radical Islamism, a program must employ an interlocutor whom the militants view as credible. In addition, after the program has been completed, graduates must be carefully monitored and offered continued support to reduce the likelihood of recidivism.

The processes of disengagement and deradicalization are not necessarily linked to the particular reason that an individual radicalized. Once an individual joins an extremist organization, he or she usually develops a number of ties that bind him or her to the group and make exit difficult. For example, even if a person joined an extremist organization because of bonds of friendship and kinship, this individual will probably be indoctrinated into accepting the group's ideology and usually also becomes reliant on the organization to provide for basic needs.[19]

---

whether the person consistently and publicly denounces his or her former beliefs and whether he or she remains disengaged.

[19] Marc Sageman, *Leaderless Jihad: Terror Networks in the Twenty-First Century*, Philadelphia, Pa.: University of Pennsylvania Press, 2008, p. 70.

Therefore, a deradicalization program is not likely to succeed unless these ties can be broken and alternative means to meet the militant's psychological and material needs are provided. Simply refuting the ideology is not likely to result in permanent disengagement or deradicalization if the individual continues to associate with radical peers and has little chance of establishing a new life outside the group. Countering the radical Islamist ideology is necessary but not sufficient to produce permanently rehabilitated ex-radicals.

As discussed earlier, many deradicalization programs focus on discrediting the extremist ideology through theological dialogue. These discussions are more likely to be effective if the militants respect their interlocutor's authority. Such respect may stem from the interlocutor's formal theological training, experience as an accomplished militant, or personal religious devotion.[20] Even credible partners must persistently engage militants who are often initially hostile or unreceptive.

The theological dialogue model is not the only way in which a rehabilitation program can challenge extremist beliefs. Other methods include providing information on Islam through classes or access to religious texts so that the militants, who often have a shallow and truncated understanding of Islam, can gain a deeper and more nuanced understanding of the religion. In the same vein, a program may make information on alternative interpretations available to encourage debate among the militants as a way of indirectly undermining extremism.[21]

In addition, a deradicalization program must also break a radical's affective and pragmatic commitment to the group. To undermine affective commitment to a radical organization, a program must provide the individual with emotional support and help him or her locate peers who are opposed to radicalism. Moreover, many radicals organizations not only provide for all their members' basic needs, but they also offer assistance to their members' families. Thus, deradicalization

---

[20] For more on using religious actors in counterterrorism strategies, see Anna Halafoff and David Wright-Neville, "A Missing Peace? The Role of Religious Actors in Countering Terrorism," *Studies in Conflict and Terrorism*, Vol. 32, No. 11, November 2009.

[21] Heather S. Gregg, "Fighting the Jihad of the Pen: Countering Revolutionary Islam's Ideology," *Terrorism and Political Violence*, Vol. 22, No. 2, April 2010.

programs need to help ex-militants and their families find alternative sources of income, housing, health care, and education. Finally, deradicalization programs need to continue to monitor and support rehabilitated extremists after they have completed the program to facilitate their reintegration into mainstream society. In sum, efforts to rehabilitate Islamist extremists should have affective, pragmatic, and ideological elements, as well as a robust aftercare program. Religious discussions should be led by a credible figure, and the practical support offered should be extended to ex-militants and their families.

CHAPTER THREE

Middle Eastern Programs

Introduction

In the aftermath of 9/11, both Saudi Arabia and Yemen launched rehabilitation programs for Islamist militants and terrorism suspects. While both programs sought, in theory, to accomplish the same goal, in reality, they were very different in approach, motivation, and results generated. The Saudi Counseling Program sought to reduce the likelihood that participants would return to active militancy through religious discussion, extensive social support, and implicit family obligation. It also aimed to short-circuit the radicalization process within a detainee's family. The Yemeni Committee for Dialogue—which predated the Saudi program—was designed to release detainees for reasons of political expediency by seeking to obtain their assurances that they would refrain from violence within the country in exchange for their freedom.

This chapter examines these two influential programs and seeks to explain why the Saudi program has come to be viewed as a relative success while the Yemeni program has not. Both programs trace their origins to a summer 2001 meeting in Cairo of Arab interior ministers, yet the two countries ultimately took different approaches to designing and implementing a rehabilitation and disengagement program. U.S. authorities in Iraq sought to emulate the Saudis' success by establishing their own prison-based deradicalization program. This chapter also provides a brief overview of the lesser-known U.S. effort to rehabilitate Iraqi detainees and assesses whether the concept of deradicalization was appropriate for the situation in Iraq. Finally, we briefly discuss the efforts of the Egyptian and Libyan governments to deradicalize entire militant Islamist organizations.

Yemen

Context of the Yemeni Deradicalization Program

In Yemen, Islamist extremism is the result of a long and complicated history. A large number of Yemeni nationals participated in the jihad against the Soviet occupation of Afghanistan during the 1980s.[1] At the end of the Afghan war, the Yemeni government encouraged its citizens to return and also permitted foreign veterans to settle in Yemen. Many of these Arab Afghans were co-opted by the regime and integrated into the state's various security organizations.[2] Such co-optation was also used with individuals detained by the Yemeni government after 9/11. As early as 1993, the U.S. Department of State noted in a now-declassified intelligence report that Yemen was becoming an important stop for many fighters leaving Afghanistan.[3] The report also claimed that—as is the case today—the Yemeni government was either unwilling or unable to curb these militants' activities. Islamism was used by the regime throughout the 1980s and 1990s against domestic opponents, and during the 1994 civil war, Islamists fought against southern forces. More recently, similar allegations were made that Islamists have fought on behalf of the government in the northwest and against southern separatists.

After several serious terrorist attacks in the early 2000s, such as the attacks on the USS *Cole* and the French oil tanker Limburg, Yemen experienced a brief period of calm. Analysts now believe that this was the result of a short-lived "nonaggression pact" between the govern-

---

[1] Eric Watkins, "Landscape of Shifting Alliances," *Terrorism Monitor*, Vol. 2, No. 7, April 8, 2004.

[2] See Michael Knights, "Internal Politics Complicate Counterterrorism in Yemen," *Jane's Intelligence Review*, February 2006; "Arab Veterans of Afghanistan War Lead New Islamic Holy War," *Compass*, October 28, 1994; and Watkins, 2004.

[3] U.S. Department of State, Bureau of Intelligence and Research, "The Wandering Mujahidin: Armed and Dangerous," *Weekend Edition*, August 21–22, 1993, p. 3.

ment and extremists, as well as enhanced U.S.-Yemeni counterterrorism cooperation.[4] Several years later, however, a generational split saw the emergence of a group of younger extremists not interested in negotiating with what they regarded as an illegitimate and apostate government.[5] Several prison escapes of experienced and dangerous operatives further energized this younger faction, which launched a new campaign of violent attacks against oil facilities, foreign residents and tourists, and government security targets.

Methodology

Following the 9/11 attacks, the Yemeni government arrested a large number of Yemeni nationals suspected of terrorist associations.[6] Those detained included individuals accused of connections to the bombing of the USS *Cole* and other attacks. Also detained were individuals who had traveled to Afghanistan. Others tangentially linked to extremists were held, as reportedly were family members of other individuals wanted by the authorities. As pressure grew within Yemen to end their detention, President Ali Abdullah Saleh sought to a way to release those individuals, some of whom had not technically broken any Yemeni laws. Thus, the government launched its dialogue program. The program was intended to seek guarantees that detainees would not engage in violence within Yemen in exchange for being released from custody.

At the inauguration of the sixth annual party conference of Yemen's ruling General People's Congress on August 24, 2002, President Saleh announced his intention to form a dialogue committee. Several days later, Saleh convened a private meeting of senior *ulema* (religious leaders) to discuss the establishment of the dialogue pro-

---

[4] Gregory Johnsen, "Al-Qaeda's Generational Split," *Boston Globe*, November 9, 2007b.

[5] Gregory Johnsen, "Yemen Faces Second Generation of Islamist Militants," *Terrorism Focus*, Vol. 4, No. 27, August 14, 2007a.

[6] Adapted, in part, from from Christopher Boucek, Shazadi Beg, and John Horgan, "Opening Up the Jihadi Debate: Yemen's Committee for Dialogue," in Tore Bjørgo and John Horgan, eds., *Leaving Terrorism Behind: Individual and Collective Disengagement*, New York: Routledge, 2008.

gram.[7] Present at this meeting were a number of senior government officials, including the prime minister, the vice president, the speaker of parliament, and the deputy of the Supreme Judicial Council. During this meeting, the Committee for Religious Dialogue was established and its objectives were set.[8]

The Council of Ulema held two subsequent meetings to choose the members of the committee. According to former Supreme Court Justice Hamoud al-Hitar, a number of the *ulema* expressed apprehension at the idea of engaging in dialogue with extremists for several reasons, including concerns about personal safety and fears of being accused of being tools of the regime. Ultimately, the only scholar who agreed to interact with the detainees was al-Hitar; fourteen other sheikhs declined to participate in the dialogue sessions. Although the Committee for Religious Dialogue was established under the auspices of the Yemeni state, it was not truly institutionalized, but rather relied almost entirely on al-Hitar.[9]

In September 2002, the committee, which consisted of Judge al-Hitar and three other sheikhs, met for the first time with detainees.[10] The initial meeting included five detainees. The detainees initially questioned whether there were any legitimate clerics in Yemen, adding that, if there were righteous scholars in the country, then the detainees would not be in prison. The detainees further accused the committee members of being regime flunkies. Al-Hitar acknowledged that the *ulema* in Yemen had not been doing their job properly and added that the committee members were there because President Saleh had instructed them to conduct a dialogue. It was explained to

---

[7] Mahmud Ma'ruf, "Chairman of the Committee for Religious Dialogue with al-Qa'ida Supporters in Yemen Humud al-Hattar Tells Al Quds al-Arabi: Violence Is Due to Restricting Freedom of Islamists and the Positions Toward Arab Issues, Especially Palestine," *Al-Quds al-Arabi* (London), December 18, 2004.

[8] "Head of Yemeni Dialogue Committee Interviewed on Work with Afghanistan Returnees," *Al-Quds al-Arabi* (London), March 4, 2004.

[9] Porges, 2010b, p. 28.

[10] Hamoud Abdulhameed Al-Hitar, *Dialogue and Its Effects on Countering Terrorism: The Yemeni Experience*, undated, p. 16.

the prisoners that the dialogue process was an all-or-nothing endeavor and that the detainees should attempt to convince the committee that their interpretations of Islam were correct in the same way that the scholars would work to persuade the detainees of the opposite. Judge al-Hitar put it simply when he told National Public Radio, "We tell them, if you are right we will follow you, but if what we are saying is right, you have to admit it and follow us."[11]

After their participation was secured, al-Hitar offered the detainees two options for how the dialogue process could be conducted—through either direct or indirect dialogue. Direct engagement would be oral discussion and oral back and forth, while the indirect process would be conducted in writing and would therefore require much more time. The detainees chose direct dialogue. Al-Hitar presented the detainees with an agenda, which included the ground rules for the dialogue and the subjects to be discussed. The dialogue rules and ethical guidelines for the discussion stressed mutual respect.[12]

The first issue discussed in the initial session was brought up by the detainees. They asserted that Yemen was not an Islamic state and that the government was pro-Western, which, the detainees argued, meant that the state was fundamentally against the interests of the country's Muslim population. Al-Hitar responded by producing copies of Yemen's Constitution and penal law for the detainees to inspect. He stated that not only do the laws not contradict the Quran or the Sunna, but if the detainees could effectively demonstrate how Yemen's laws were at odds with Islamic law, then the government would amend its laws. After close examination of the Constitution and penal law, the detainees could find nothing that ran contrary to Islamic law.

The next issue discussed was Yemen's international treaty obligations. The detainees objected to some of the country's international treaties, but when challenged to find anything in them that was un-

---

[11] Eric Westervelt, "Growing Repression in Yemen May Feed al-Qaeda," *All Things Considered*, National Public Radio, November 10, 2005.

[12] Based on Al-Hitar, undated. See also Michael Taarnby, "Yemen's Committee for Dialogue: The Relativity of a Counter Terrorism Success," in Cheryl Benard, ed., *A Future for the Young: Options for Helping Middle Eastern Youth Escape the Trap of Radicalization*, Santa Monica, Calif.: RAND Corporation, WR-354, September 2005, and Birk, 2009.

Islamic they were unable to do so. Al-Hitar related to the detainees that even the Prophet Muhammed had engaged in treaties with Christians and Jews.

The legitimacy of the regime and the legality of President Saleh's rule were also discussed at length. The detainees asserted that the government was an apostate regime. They further argued that the regime lacked legitimacy, since Saleh did not govern as a caliph. When challenged to show where in the Quran it was mandated that the head of state be a caliph, the detainees were unable to respond. Al-Hitar argued that President Saleh was elected by the majority of voters and that the election represented the will of the people. Nothing in the way that Yemen had chosen or empowered its leadership, the judge argued, was against anything in the Quran. From this position, it was accepted that obeying the head of state was an obligation.

Another topic of discussion was the permissibility of killing non-Muslims. The detainees began from the premise that these individuals were infidels, arguing that such actions were allowed. Al-Hitar replied that the Quran clearly states that killing can be justified only with a rightful reason, in circumstances of war or oppression, when people are prevented from practicing their religion and are driven from their homes. This was buttressed with further explanation, such as the observations that Muslim armies historically did not kill women, children, the elderly, or Christian priests. Attention was brought to the fact that only one verse in the Quran authorizes Muslims to fight non-Muslims, and such actions are permitted only in self-defense. Compulsion in religion, al-Hitar related, was not sanctioned in Islam, and any act taken under duress is inadmissible. Al-Hitar argued that foreigners in Yemen have the protection of the head of state through a "covenant of security" in the form of a visa issued by the government, and it is therefore not permissible to attack them.

The program made it clear that those who renounced violence would be eligible to participate in an amnesty program.[13] Al-Hitar indicated that it was the government's intention at the outset that indi-

---

[13] Abd al-Mun'im al-Jabri, "Yemeni Interior Minister Discusses Terrorism Issues, Cooperation with US," 26 September News (Sana'a, Yemen), October 17, 2003.

viduals who had engaged in serious acts of violence would be barred from the amnesty program.[14] The judge acknowledged, however, that once the program started, some of the participants were, in fact, individuals who had killed people in various terrorist attacks. These individuals were recognized as having a more acute need for rehabilitation to prevent them from returning to violence. Thus, it was decided that those convicted of murder would be required to complete their sentence prior to release. According to al-Hitar, Yemeni returnees from Guantanamo Bay, subsequently imprisoned in Yemen, have not participated in the dialogue process.[15]

Release

A total of 364 detainees were released through the program after completing the dialogue process, drawn from a variety of backgrounds and representing numerous organizations. Participants ranged in age from 18 to 40 years old.[16] According to the Yemeni government, approximately 90 percent of those who took part in the program were born outside of Yemen to Yemeni parents. It has been alleged that many of these individuals were also radicalized abroad, primarily in Saudi Arabia but in other countries as well, and many of the detainees had spent time in Afghanistan or Pakistan. Detainees were required to sign a document testifying to their renunciation of their previous beliefs in order to be released through the dialogue program. Interior Minister Rashad Muhammad al-Ulaymi explained that an individual's signature or verbal renunciation of violence was only one of several factors taken into consideration.[17] In addition, it was also required that a detainee's

---

[14] Brian Whitaker, "Yemen Overview 2003–4," British-Yemeni Society, August 2005.

[15] Amel al-Ariqi, "Gitmo Returnees Need Rehabilitation Program, Lawyers Speculate," *Yemen Times*, December 5, 2007. As of December 2007, only 13 Yemenis have been repatriated from Guantanamo Bay, with most going straight to prison or put on trial (see Farah Stockman, "Nationality Plays Role in Detainee Release," *Boston Globe*, November 22, 2007).

[16] Two detainees have been reported to be over the age of 40.

[17] Al-Jabri, 2003.

"family and tribal members" vouch for the released individual, and in a sense, be responsible for him.[18]

Upon release from custody, participants in the program were monitored by the authorities, typically for a probationary period of one year. Reportedly, this monotoring was overseen by a special committee within the National Security Bureau. According to Foreign Minister Abubaker al-Qirbi, the Yemeni intelligence and security agencies were charged with supervising released detainees, and a number of those released through the program were given positions with the military and security forces in order to better keep tabs on them.[19]

Al-Hitar stated that some of the released detainees spoke with others after their discharge to convince them to renounce terrorism and violence. It has also been reported by the Yemeni media that one former detainee passed information to the security services that led to the discovery of a large arms cache. Some released detainees have reportedly provided high-value intelligence to the authorities, which, in turn, has resulted in the capture of important targets, such as Mohammed Hamdi al-Ahdal, the alleged mastermind of the USS *Cole* bombing.

Evaluation

There are no good data on the Yemeni Committee for Dialogue. The absence of reliable data about how the program worked complicates assessments and evaluations. Moreover, the Yemeni government has been unwilling to facilitate research into the program or into how Yemeni prisons operate today.

In hindsight, it now appears that Yemen's short-lived rehabilitation program was unsuccessful, if success is defined as changing militants' worldview. It has been charged that the Yemeni government was less interested in actual the disengagement of militants than with political expediency.[20] Several observers have suggested that the dialogue sessions were geared toward securing the detainees' acquiescence on several key points, including recognizing the legitimacy of the Yemeni

---

[18] Westervelt, 2005.

[19] Westervelt, 2005; Peter Willems, "Unusual Tactics," *Middle East*, October 2004, p. 66.

[20] Boucek, Beg, and Horgan, 2008.

government and obtaining assurances from program participants that they would not engage in violence within Yemen. For example, after participating in the rehabilitation program and being released, Nasser al-Bahri, Osama bin Laden's former bodyguard, accused the dialogue of being a charade and claimed that "no long or complex dialogue" or exchange of views took place.[21]

The inability of the Yemeni government to provide adequate postrelease care was central to the program's collapse. The changing nature of the detainee population also played a significant role.[22] Early program participants were older-generation Islamic activists. According to Yemeni officials, these men could be negotiated with and understood hierarchies, based in part on their own experiences in militant organizations. Yemeni officials have suggested that, as the dialogue process went on, younger individuals—radicalized in a different context—were less willing to negotiate with the government. These men did not recognize authority and did not accept that there were rules to follow.

In total, 364 people were released through the dialogue process; there have been repeated reports that some have died in Iraq and in attacks in Yemen. The Yemeni program did not address the issues of participating in violence abroad. It focused solely on activity within Yemen. For instance, al-Hitar told a reporter that "resistance in Iraq is legitimate, but we cannot differentiate between terrorism and resistance in Iraq's situation because things are not clear in this case."[23] This shortcoming has been identified in other evaluations of the program. Despite the reports of Yemeni graduates of the dialogue program returning to extremism, al-Hitar has denied that this is the case. It is unclear what the basis is for his disagreement with these allegations.[24]

---

[21] Quoted in Tim Whewell, "Yemeni Anti-Terror Scheme in Doubt," BBC News, October 11, 2005. See also Boucek, Beg, and Horgan, 2008, p. 189.

[22] Interviews by Christopher Boucek in Sana'a, Yemen, July and August 2007.

[23] Quoted in Johnsen, "Yemen's Passive Role in the War on Terrorism," *Terrorism Monitor*, Vol. 4, No. 4, February 23, 2006.

[24] Hamoud al-Hitar, interview with Christopher Boucek, Sana'a, Yemen, January 2009.

In the end, it appears as if Yemen's program (taken at face value) was based on the flawed premise that a few brief discussions could moderate an individual's beliefs and thereby change his behavior. The Committee for Dialogue reportedly helped place some ex-militants in jobs, but, overall, the program focused on refuting the ideology and did not help break the other types of commitment to extremism.[25] Moreover, little to no care was provided once the militants were released, and they were only monitored for approximately one year; therefore, the ex-militants who had not been reformed simply had to bide their time during their probationary period before they could resume their previous activities. Furthermore, the Yemeni government did not have the resources to provide the comprehensive support necessary to facilitate permanent disengagement and deradicalization and to keep the ex-militants under surveillance long enough to deter recidivism.

Another sign of failure is the reemergence of a significant militant Islamist organization as a serious threat to the Yemeni state—namely, al-Qaeda (most recently as al-Qaeda in the Arabian Peninsula, or AQAP).[26] Since two near-simultaneous car-bombings at oil facilities in September 2006, attacks against energy targets, including bombings of oil pipelines and shootings of oilfield workers, have occurred at a steady pace. Tourists have been killed in bombings and shootings in Marib in 2007 and Hadramout in 2008 and 2009. Starting in March 2008, violence moved to the capital, with a series of attacks on government facilities, a Western housing compound, the offices of a Canadian oil company, and (twice) the U.S. embassy.

Recent counterterrorism measures in Saudi Arabia have forced extremists to seek refuge in Yemen's undergoverned areas. As the kingdom has become a less permissive operational environment, analysts have observed a steady flow of militants following the guidance of local Saudi commanders to relocate to Yemen. By January 2009, the Saudi and Yemeni al-Qaeda affiliates had merged to form AQAP. The video announcing the establishment of AQAP featured two Saudi returnees from Guantanamo who had assumed leadership positions in the newly

---

[25] Horgan and Braddock, 2010, p. 275.

[26] Fawaz A. Gerges, "Al Qaeda Has Bounced Back in Yemen," CNN, January 7, 2010.

formed organization. Following this news, Saudi authorities released a new list of 85 most-wanted terrorism suspects. Of the 85 suspects, 26 were believed to be in Yemen, including a total of 11 former Saudi Guantanamo detainees.[27]

Looking forward, it will be interesting to see how Yemen's plans take shape as it attempts to restart its discontinued rehabilitation program to deal with possible returnees from Guantanamo Bay. It appears that the U.S. government's lack of confidence in Yemen's ability to adequately keep tabs on former detainees has resulted in very few Yemeni nationals being released from custody. While nearly all the Saudis once held at Guantanamo have been repatriated, fewer than 20 Yemeni nationals have been returned to Yemen.[28] Yemenis now account for the largest group at Guantanamo.

The return of Saudi nationals once held at Guantanamo was greatly facilitated by Saudi Arabia's rehabilitation program. Every Saudi returnee went through this program; it was part of the unofficial understanding that made their release possible. To secure the release of its remaining nationals, Yemen has stated that it will restart the Committee for Dialogue. Based on previous experiences and building on doubts about Yemen's capabilities, U.S. officials are skeptical. For much of 2009, Yemeni officials stated that they had delivered to the U.S. government a proposal for restarting the dialogue program. In fact, it appears that the Yemenis have shared their intention or their desire to do so but have not developed a detailed plan showing how it would work in practice.

The Yemeni government has allegedly identified the location of the proposed facility at a Yemeni military base just outside of Sana'a. While a location may have been found, there has been no substantive work on the nuts and bolts of the program. Furthermore, there has been no work to determine the curriculum of the planned center, to

---

[27] One of the Guantanamo returnees featured in the AQAP video, Muhammed al-Awfi, was repatriated to Saudi Arabia in mid-February 2009. Another two of the 85 Saudi most-wanted suspects are believed to have been apprehended in Yemen. See Christopher Boucek, "Examining Saudi Arabia's 85 Most Wanted List," *CTC Sentinel*, Vol. 2, No. 5, May 2009.

[28] Human Rights Watch, *No Direction Home: Returns from Guantanamo to Yemen*, New York, March 2009.

identify the teachers and workers, or to develop a methodology to measure the success of the plan in rehabilitating militants.

Saudi Arabia

Context of the Saudi Deradicalization Program

From 2003 to 2007, the Kingdom of Saudi Arabia experienced a protracted and violent terrorist campaign waged by AQAP.[29] As the birthplace of Islam and the location of the two holy mosques, Saudi Arabia has always been of central strategic and symbolic importance to al-Qaeda. In a statement released on December 27, 2007, bin Laden identified the Saudi regime as the main enemy.[30] AQAP emerged with a series of attacks against Western targets and Saudi security forces beginning in 2003. The opening attack was on a Riyadh housing compound on May 12, 2003. Between May 2003 and December 2004, more than 30 major terrorism-related incidents occurred in the kingdom. At least 91 foreign nationals and Saudi civilians were killed and 510 were wounded, according to former intelligence chief Prince Turki al-Faisal. In addition, 41 security force members were killed and 218 were wounded in these attacks.[31]

Although the scope of the attacks, some of which clearly involved the complicity of elements of the security forces, shocked the Saudi government, by surfacing with a major terrorist campaign without a secure support base, AQAP made itself vulnerable to Saudi counterattacks. According to Saad al-Faqih, the head of the London-based Saudi opposition group Movement for Islamic Reform in Arabia, AQAP made the

---

[29] For the most authoritative account of the violent Islamism in Saudi Arabia, see Thomas Hegghammer, *Jihad in Saudi Arabia: Violence and Pan-Islamism Since 1979*, Cambridge, UK: Cambridge University Press, 2010, and Thomas Hegghammer, "Islamist Violence and Regime Stability in Saudi Arabia," *International Affairs*, Vol. 84, No. 4, July 2008.

[30] Michael Scheuer, "Bin Laden Identifies Saudi Arabia as the Enemy of Mujahideen Unity," *Terrorism Focus*, Vol. 5, No. 1, January 8, 2008.

[31] Nidaa Abu-Ali, "Saudi Arabia: Between Radicalisation and Terrorism," *RSIS Commentaries*, Singapore: S. Rajaratnam School of International Studies, Nanyang Technological University, April 24, 2008.

strategic mistake of targeting security forces and Western civilians. This enabled the government to mobilize the security forces against them.[32] Between 2003 and 2005, the Saudi security forces effectively dismantled the organization. The group's founder and first leader, Yousef al-Ayyiri, a former bodyguard of bin Laden, was killed in June 2003. Al-Ayyiri's successor, Abdul Aziz al-Muqrin, was killed in June 2004. AQAP's third leader, Saud al-Utaybi, was killed in a gun battle at Al-Ras in April 2005, and other senior leaders surrendered or were captured.[33] Al-Utaybi's successor, Saleh al-Aufi, a former police officer and veteran of the Afghan war, was killed in a shootout with police in August 2005.[34]

In addition to intelligence and police measures, Saudi authorities launched a comprehensive counterterrorism strategy designed to eliminate the immediate threat and drive a wedge between the extremists and the general population. The Saudi rehabilitation and disengagement program was and continues to be a central part of this strategy.

Counterterrorism Strategy

Saudi Arabia's "soft" counterterrorism strategy is known as the Prevention, Rehabilitation, and After-Care approach.[35] Rehabilitation and disengagement programs are the middle portion of this three-part approach. Prevention programs are designed to keep an individual from getting into trouble, rehabilitation programs care for the individual while in the state's custody, and aftercare programs are intended to facilitate the individual's return to society after release from custody.

To prevent extremism, the Saudi government has implemented programs to counter radicalization by providing the general public with information about Islam and the threat of extremism. In particular, the program emphasizes that the extremists do not actually care about

---

[32] Mahan Abedin, "Al-Qaeda: In Decline or Preparing for the Next Attack? An Interview with Saad al-Faqih," *Spotlight on Terror*, Vol. 3, No. 5, June 15, 2005.

[33] Abedin, 2005. Al-Faqih states that al-Utaybi, not al-Oufi as was widely believed, replaced al-Muqrin as emir of AQAP.

[34] Roger Harrison and Javid Hassan, "Al-Qaeda Chief in Kingdom Killed," *Arab News*, August 19, 2005.

[35] Christopher Boucek, 2008d.

Muslims, but callously use them to achieve their own objectives. The kingdom has also established a number of social and athletic programs for young Saudis in an effort to keep them away from extremists.[36]

However, it is the Saudi rehabilitation and aftercare programs that have attracted the most attention. There has been extensive research to examine the demographic backgrounds of rehabilitation program participants.[37] For example, two major studies have been completed by the Interior Ministry's Advisory Committee. The first study focused on individuals who had been active in the kingdom until 2004; it included 639 subjects, none of whom were engaged in political violence domestically but may have participated in violence abroad. The second study included 60 subjects who had participated in terrorism in Saudi Arabia until 2006. According to the committee's findings, the vast majority of detainees who have successfully participated in the rehabilitation program did not benefit from a proper religious education during their childhood.

Members of the Advisory Committee argue that, because these individuals did not correctly learn the tenets of their faith originally, they were susceptible to extremist propaganda. Therefore, the program seeks to remove detainees' radical understanding of Islam and to reintroduce and reinforce the official state version of the faith.[38] This is done through a complex process of religious dialogue and instruction, psychological counseling, and extensive social support.

Participants in the first study were typically young (usually in their 20s), from large lower- or middle-class families (ranging from seven to 15 siblings), and their parents typically had limited educations. They came from large urban areas throughout the kingdom. This generally agrees with what is known of the backgrounds of the individuals

---

[36] Boucek, 2008d, pp. 8–11.

[37] This section is based on Christopher Boucek's in-depth field research and interviews in Saudi Arabia in March 2007, October–November 2007, and May–June 2008.

[38] Interview with Advisory Committee members by Christopher Boucek, Riyadh, Saudi Arabia, November 2007.

who participated in the AQAP campaign.[39] Only a small number were determined to have come from more affluent families (3 percent). Most were students, although some were employed in lower- or middle-income jobs; only 6 percent were employed in higher-level white-collar positions. Interestingly, and contrary to assumption, it was found that only a very small minority (5 percent) were employed in so-called religious professions, as prayer leaders or members of the Commission for the Promotion of Virtue and Prevention of Vice, for example.

Roughly one-third of the study participants had gone abroad to participate in jihad, primarily to Afghanistan, Somalia, or Chechnya. It is currently unclear to what extent these individuals actually engaged in combat abroad as opposed to undergoing paramilitary training or simply traveling to or supporting activities in foreign zones of conflict.

Two very interesting trends emerge from the data. First, one-quarter of the 639 program participants had prior criminal histories. Of those, approximately half had been arrested for drug offenses. This tracks with an increasing recognition in Saudi Arabia and throughout the Muslim world of the dangers posed by prison radicalization.[40] The second fact to emerge had to do with the participants' knowledge of religious matters. According to program officials, many of the detainees in the program knew relatively little about Islam, and it was their desire to become more religious that led them to the extremists who propagated, in the Saudi view, a corrupted understanding of Islam. The majority of the offenders were radicalized through a now-well-understood path: extremist books, tapes, videos, and, more recently,

[39] See Thomas Hegghammer, "Terrorist Recruitment and Radicalization in Saudi Arabia," *Middle East Policy*, Vol. 13, No. 4, December 2006, and Abdullah Al-Khalifah, *Suspects' Families and the Relationship with Terrorism and Extremism in Saudi Society*, Riyadh: Imam Mohammed University, 2008.

[40] Saudi officials have recognized the danger of exposure to extremist ideologies among those held in criminal custody. Saudi Ministry of Interior official, interview with Christopher Boucek, Riyadh, Saudi Arabia, November 2007. See also Christopher Boucek, "Jailing Jihadis: Saudi Arabia's Special Terrorist Prisons," *Terrorism Monitor*, Vol. 6, No. 2, January 25, 2008a.

the Internet.[41] According to one report,[42] one of the more popular ideologues among program participants (before rehabilitation) was Abu Muhammed al-Maqdisi, author of *Clear Evidence of the Infidel Nature of the Saudi State*, a publication obviously banned in the kingdom.

The second study—which focused on individuals who had allegedly participated in violence in Saudi Arabia—revealed an equally interesting set of factors. Most significantly, the data show greater domestic problems and troubled homelives for this group. Approximately half came from homes with a father over the age of 50, and one-quarter (26 percent) came from polygamous households. Saudi authorities stress that they believe there is a correlation between less attention received at home and trouble later in life. Similarly, over a third (35 percent) of the second study's subjects came from homes with "family problems," and one-fifth were identified as orphans with no traditional parental oversight.[43]

There was also evidence of previous difficult relationships with authority, including employment termination,[44] arrests for reckless driving offenses, and violent criminal records (e.g., fighting, petty crime). Significantly, at least 10 percent were nonpracticing Muslims, drawing attention to the fact that it is not always the religiously inspired or interested who are driven to political violence in the kingdom.

---

[41] Christopher Boucek, "The Sakinah Campaign and Internet Counter-Radicalization in Saudi Arabia," *CTC Sentinel*, Vol. 1, No. 9, August 2008b.

[42] David Ottaway, "Saud Effort Draws on Radical Clerics to Combat Lure of al-Qaeda," *Washington Post*, May 7, 2006.

[43] Interestingly, there are no data regarding incidents of mental illness or autism. It is known that some Saudi Guantanamo returnees suffer from a range of psychiatric disorders, although accurate numbers are unavailable (Interviews by Christopher Boucek in Saudi Arabia, November 2007). According to U.S. officials, approximately 6–7 percent of current Guantanamo detainees (c. 250) are being treated for mental illnesses (Joint Task Force Guantanamo chief psychiatrist, interview with Christopher Boucek, Guantanamo Bay Naval Base, November 2008). In his sample, Sageman found only a 1 percent incidence of mental disorders, compared to 3 percent in the general population (see Sageman, 2008, p. 64). On autism, see Diego Gambetta and Steffen Hertog, *Engineers of Jihad*, Oxford, UK: University of Oxford, Sociology Working Paper 2007-10, 2007.

[44] Among this group, most worked in the private sector. This is significant because it demonstrates their desire to avoid associating with a government that they view as illegitimate.

There are also very notable differences in the sources of inspiration and motivation between the two groups. This is perhaps best illustrated by the readings popular among study subjects. Among those active in violence abroad but not domestically, the writings of theorists predominate, while those active in terrorist violence within the kingdom were driven by the writings and materials of operational leaders and military commanders. The differences in intellectual motivation can be understood as both a manifestation of differing radicalization processes and a potential indicator of future intent. Perhaps not surprisingly, in both groups, Osama bin Laden was the most popular author.

Among the theorists, influential sources include Hamad al-Uqla al-Shuyabi, who gives his name to an informal collection of influential Wahhabi scholars and is the author of *Meaning and Reality of Terrorism*;[45] Ali al-Khodeir, author of a fatwa defending the killing of civilians; Sulayman bin Nasir al-Alwan, author of the article "Let Us Die as Martyrs,"[46] in which he argues that armed jihad is central to Islam and that a ruler's authorization is not needed for jihad; Abdullah Azzam, godfather of the 1980s Afghan Arabs; Safar al-Hawali, one of the original "Awakening Sheikhs";[47] and Nasir al-Fahd, perhaps best known for a fatwa legitimizing the use of weapons of mass destruction against civilian noncombatants.

In the second group, very different figures emerge as sources of inspiration and motivation, including Abdul Aziz al-Muqrin, Ayman al-Zawahiri, Saleh al-Aufi, Abu Musab al-Zarqawi, and Yousef al-Ayyiri. Ayyiri, Muqrin, and Aufi were all operational leaders of AQAP. These figures are emblematic of military operations against the state,

---

[45] Published online in 2002 in Minbar at-Tawhid wal-Jihad, the article is in the top 20 most-read texts among militants, according to West Point's Militant Ideology Atlas (U.S. Military Academy, *Combating Terrorism Center, Militant Ideology Atlas*, West Point, N.Y., November 2006). See Thomas Hegghammer, *Violent Islamism in Saudi Arabia, 1979–2006: The Power and Perils of Pan-Islamic Nationalism*, dissertation, Paris: Sciences-Po, 2007.

[46] According to the *Militant Ideology Atlas*, this is the 18th most-read text (U.S. Military Academy, 2006).

[47] Mamoun Fandy, *Saudi Arabia and the Politics of Dissent*, New York: Palgrave, 2001; Joshua Teitelbaum, *Holier Than Thou: Saudi Arabia's Islamic Opposition*, Washington, D.C.: Washington Institute for Near East Policy, 2000.

and many of their writings have appeared as independent tracts and in online publications, such as *Sawt Al-Jihad*.

There are also notable differences in the motivation of both groups. For the first group, the motivational factors included audio and video recordings, the militant awakening that took place in the kingdom, and the influence of sheikhs and friends. The second group, however, was found to have been driven much more by immediate paramilitary concerns, including the perceived hegemony of Western forces, a desire for revenge against the security services, aspirations to advance the cause in Iraq, and a wish to develop military and operational skills.

The vast majority of prisoners who participated in the program, according to research conducted by the Advisory Committee, did not have a proper religious education during their childhood.[48] Because these individuals did not correctly learn the tenets of their faith, Saudi officials argue, they were susceptible to extremist propaganda. As a result, the program seeks to remove an incorrect understanding of Islam and replace it with what the Saudi authorities consider to be the correct interpretation.[49]

From an outside perspective, a problem with this approach is that religious extremism in Saudi Arabia is an offshoot of the official doctrine. The "correct" interpretation taught in Saudi Arabia has substantial areas of overlap with the extremists' ideology. Therefore, the Saudi approach is to convince the extremists of the legitimacy and religious rectitude of the Saudi state and not necessarily to change the extremists' worldview. The relevant point is that mainstream Saudi scholars and extremists share common assumptions and methodologies of Quranic interpretation that lead to the justification of violence. Thus, while violence is deemed illegitimate within Saudi Arabia (or against Sunni Muslims in general), it may be considered legitimate in other

---

[48] Abdulrahman Al-Hadlaq, interview with Christopher Boucek, Riyadh, Saudi Arabia, March 2007.

[49] Based on Christopher Boucek's interview with Turki al-Atyan, Riyadh, Saudi Arabia, November 2007, citied in Christopher Boucek, "The Saudi Process of Repatriating and Reintegrating Guantanamo Returnees," *CTC Sentinel*, Vol. 1, No. 1, December 2007, p. 12.

theaters, such as Iraq or Afghanistan, or against Shi'ites or other Muslims considered deviant.

Philosophy

Saudi Arabia's approach to dealing with Islamist extremists is to offer them alternatives. The Saudi approach draws on historical precedents, cultural norms, and the experiences of other countries in counterterrorism and counterinsurgency.[50] It consists of several components, including delivering the message that extremists do not act in the interest of the people. The government therefore strives to go to great lengths to care for detainees and their families. It is also policy to segregate detainees in an attempt to prevent the most ideologically committed individuals from converting more vulnerable ones. Prisoners are also now held at facilities closer to their families to facilitate greater family interaction, incorporate families into the rehabilitation process, and speed a detainee's return to society with the support of a social network that is more conducive to rehabilitation. In large part, it has been observed that the way in which detainees are treated while in custody has an impact on how they will behave after release.

The Saudi program to rehabilitate and disengage militants is part of the self-described "war of ideas" against extremism in the kingdom. The program represents a unique Saudi solution to a Saudi problem, incorporating many traditional Saudi methods of conflict resolution and conflict management. It was developed in secret and not in response to outside pressures, and it began out of the recognition that something had to be done to address extremism, particularly the intellectual and ideological justifications for extremism.

The elimination of immediate terrorist violence provided the government with the opportunity to launch a series of "soft" counterterrorism efforts, including prevention programs, rehabilitation programs, and reintegration strategies. A primary component of these efforts has been the development of a program to rehabilitate violent militants and their sympathizers through an innovative detainee disengagement

---

[50] For example, see Norval Morris, *The Future of Imprisonment*, Chicago, Ill.: University of Chicago, 1977.

program. Known as the "Counseling Program," it is characterized by religious discussion and debate, extensive social support, and implicit family obligation. The Counseling Program is intended to assist individuals who have espoused *takfiri* beliefs as they "repent and abandon terrorist ideologies."[51]

It is important to stress that the only people who have been released through the Counseling Program are terrorist sympathizers and support personnel or, at the most, individuals caught with jihadist propaganda or who have provided logistical assistance.[52] They are not individuals who have been active in terrorist violence in the kingdom; currently, those with "blood on their hands" are barred from release through the Counseling Program. Saudi officials are also very keen to stress that not everyone who participates in the program will be released. Release is contingent upon successfully completing the program and satisfactorily demonstrating to the Advisory Committee's doctors and psychologists that rehabilitation is genuine.

Furthermore, if the Interior Ministry has information that despite having completed the program (or a sentence, for that matter) an individual plans to commit further acts of violence, then the detainee will not be released.

The Counseling Program draws on several Saudi traditions, including a history of prisoner rehabilitation programs and the use of religious figures in the correctional system. The concept of detainee rehabilitation is the latest manifestation of these practices. There are a number of social programs and organizations designed to help released prisoners reintegrate into society, and they are based on established traditions in Islamic legal thought.[53] These entities include government departments, such as the Ministry of Labor and the Ministry

---

[51] Statement by Major General Mansour al-Turki on al-Ikhbariyah Saudi television, April 27, 2007.

[52] This refers to Saudi nationals detained on charges of domestic security offenses. There have been individuals released through this program who have participated in violence outside Saudi Arabia.

[53] Abdulrahman al-Hadlaq, interview with Christopher Boucek, Riyadh, Saudi Arabia, November 2007.

of Health, as well as specialized organizations, such as the Committee for Supporting Prisoners and Their Families;[54] the National Committee for the Protection of Prisoners;[55] the National Committee for the Care of Prisoners, Released Prisoners, and Their Families;[56] the Criminal Investigation Research Center;[57] and the Family Reconciliation Committee.[58] Other organizations, such as the General Directorate of Prisons, the General Administration of Prisons, the Ministry of Social Affairs, and the Ministry of Islamic Affairs, Guidance, and Endowment, also provide essential rehabilitation and reintegration services for prisoners.

The second aspect on which the Counseling Program draws is the use of religious figures in Saudi prisons. There is precedent for a sheikh to visit a prisoner in Saudi Arabia. For instance, asking a religious figure to intercede after the arrest of a loved one is not an uncommon practice. In rural Saudi Arabia, if one's son or nephew were arrested, the village imam was often asked to visit the prison and discuss the situation with the detainee.[59] Muslim clerics have also been used by Saudi security personnel during investigations to "intellectually interrogate" suspected militants by engaging them in theological remonstration.[60] Religious figures have successfully been used to encourage suspected Islamist militants to confess or to urge defendants to cooperate with authorities. Such tactics were used before the May 2003 Riyadh compound bombings and have since increased.[61]

---

[54] Badea Abu al-Naja, "Challenging Task of Integrating Ex-Convicts into Society," *Arab News*, October 28, 2007.

[55] "Saudi Arabia: Official Prison Visit Leads to the Pardoning of 1,000 Detainees," *Asharq Alawsat*, May 4, 2006.

[56] Raid Qusti, "Coupons Instead of Cash for Needy," *Arab News*, September 21, 2007.

[57] Raid Qusti, 2007.

[58] Habib Shaikh, "Makkah Committee Gives 40 Ex-Convicts a Fresh Start in Life," *Khaleej Times* (Dubai), May 8, 2007.

[59] Interviews by Christopher Boucek in Riyadh, Saudi Arabia, March 2007.

[60] Interviews by Christopher Boucek in Riyadh, Saudi Arabia, March 2007.

[61] In fact, one of the first English-language sources to unknowingly allude to the counseling program noted that "Muslim clerics are used to 'verbally beat' the prisoners, telling them

Methodology

Rather than vengeance or retribution, Saudi Arabia's Counseling Program is based on a presumption of benevolence. It presumes that the suspects were abused, lied to, and misled by extremists into straying away from true Islam and communicates that the state wants to help these prisoners return to the correct path. As one senior security official explained, everyone gets a second chance.[62] Additionally, the Saudi government has sought to marshal religious authority in an effort to confer legitimacy on the process. Several former militants have joined the Advisory Committee, adding further legitimacy for some prisoners.

Another critical component of the Saudi Counseling Program is the attention given to a prisoner's social and practical needs. Each participant is evaluated to determine how detention will impact his family and what steps can be taken to assist the the detainee and family members. For example, when a breadwinner is incarcerated, the Committee provides the family with an alternative salary. Other needs, including children's schooling and family health care, are also addressed. This is intended to prevent further radicalization brought on by the detention of family members. Saudi officials recognize that when the government arrests someone, it can have a severe impact on family members, so this social support is intended to partly offset that hardship. The government further recognizes that if it failed to do so, extremist elements could move in to provide this support.[63]

This support continues upon release. Prisoners who complete the rehabilitation process and satisfactorily demonstrated that they will no longer engage in extremism are given assistance in locating jobs and other benefits, including additional government stipends, cars, and housing.

---

that they have misinterpreted Islam and should confess all they know to win favor with God" (in Nicholas Blanford, "Saudis Mount Intense Drive Against Terror," *Christian Science Monitor*, May 29, 2003). See also Megan K. Slack, "Saudis Confront Extremists with Convert's Passion," *Los Angeles Times*, November 17, 2003.

[62] It is important to note that this pertains only to Saudi nationals who have been involved with Sunni militancy (senior Saudi security official, interview with Christopher Boucek, January 2009).

[63] The government's efforts in this regard were driven by the fact that some detainees' families were being financially supported by unidentified militant figures.

Employment assistance includes placement in government and private-sector jobs.[64] Persuading former detainees to accept government jobs is very important, given that many of these individuals would previously not have considered accepting employment with what they regarded as an illegitimate government. The Interior Ministry also helps those who previously had government jobs regain their positions.[65] The Advisory Committee has been working with local chambers of commerce and other certification organizations to develop training courses for program participants,[66] an effort to enable released detainees to start their own businesses when paired with government startup funds.

The relative successes of the overall effort are compounded by the application of these social support programs to a prisoner's larger family network. The Interior Ministry augments this support with the delivery of the message that a prisoner's larger family network is also responsible for his behavior upon release.[67] This makes use of several important Saudi cultural mores, including social responsibility, notions of honor, and the recognition of traditional family and extended-family hierarchies. For instance, when detainees are released for family events, such as weddings or funerals, three family members must guarantee his return; should the detainee not return, then those family members would have to take his place.[68] To date, no prisoner

---

[64] Prince Mohammed bin Nayef, Assistant Minister of Interior for Security Affairs, interview with Christopher Boucek, Riyadh, Saudi Arabia, October 2007.

[65] Alaa Al-Hathloul and Johan Bodin, "Aprés Guantanamo" ["Life After Guantanamo"], France 24, December 7, 2007.

[66] Abdulrahman al-Hadlaq, interview with Christopher Boucek, Riyadh, Saudi Arabia, November 2007.

[67] Interestingly, this also applies to non–family members. There have been occasions when furloughed Guantanamo returnees have been monitored by the family members of those still remaining at Guantanamo Bay. This was done to ensure that the returnees did not do anything that would jeopardize the repatriation program for the loved ones yet to be repatriated. Such collective responsibility is a common factor in Saudi rehabilitation and aftercare programs (Boucek, 2007, p. 11).

[68] So far, it has only been male relatives who have signed for a detainee's release. There is no restriction against female relatives signing for a prisoner's release, and the Advisory Committee would like to see female family members get involved in this way (Prince Mohammed

has used this opportunity to escape. The use of Saudi social networks, familial obligations, and extended responsibilities reinforces program objectives when a detainee leaves the committee's formal oversight.

The Counseling Program is organized under the auspices of the Interior Ministry. Within the ministry, the Counseling Program is administered by the Advisory Committee, which is made up of four subcommittees: the Religious Subcommittee, the Psychological and Social Subcommittee, the Security Subcommittee, and the Media Subcommittee.[69]

The Religious Subcommittee is the largest of the four subgroups, consisting of approximately 160 clerics, scholars, and university professors, and directly engages in the prisoner dialogues and the counseling process. Individual clerics are typically approached on a personal basis and asked whether they would like to participate in the committee's activities and engage in dialogue with detainees. Key in selecting a subcommittee member is communication style. It is essential that, when talking with a detainee, a cleric not lecture; the process is not intended to be one-sided. One of the criteria used to evaluate communication style is whether the scholar speaks with a detainee "like his own brother" and whether he is motivated by love, compassion, and a drive to help the detainee. Several subcommittee members have not been invited back to work with detainees after their style was found to be unconducive to dialogue. Moreover, if a subcommittee member cannot successfully engage a detainee, another cleric will be selected;[70] if a detainee and scholar do not interact well, another sheikh will try.

---

bin Nayef, Assistant Minister of Interior for Security Affairs, interview with Christopher Boucek, Riyadh, Saudi Arabia, October 2007).

[69] This information is based on author interviews and research in Saudi Arabia in March 2007, including interviews with Abdulrahman al-Hadlaq, adviser to the Assistant Minister of Interior for Security Affairs, and Major General Mansour al-Turki, official security spokesman at the Ministry of Interior, Riyadh, Saudi Arabia, March 2007.

[70] The availability of qualified religious personnel has been noted as contributing to the program's success. When asked whether the counseling program could work in other countries, al-Hadlaq noted that some countries do not benefit from having so many experts and therefore will have a much harder time finding qualified personnel to run the program

The Psychological and Social Subcommittee comprises approximately 60 psychologists, psychiatrists, social scientists, and researchers. The staff of this subcommittee focuses primarily on evaluating a detainee's social status, diagnosing any psychological problems, and assessing compliance. During the counseling process, members of this subcommittee participate in some of the sessions, particularly in long study sessions. Social scientists and psychologists interact with detainees to assess his progress in the program. The subcommittee also evaluates detainees' participation in an attempt to determine whether or not the rehabilitation is genuine.

This subcommittee is also responsible for determining the type of support the prisoner and his family may need after his release. The Saudi government emphasizes that the extremists do not care about the individual, that they merely seek to use misled youth to advance their own agenda. The state tries to demonstrate that it does not seek to punish the detainees or their families, that it cares about them and will do whatever it takes to rehabilitate the prisoner and support him and his family. This is an essential aspect of the program, and it is a central argument that the government makes in this and other rehabilitation and reintegration programs.

The government is very careful in how it engages with family members in an effort to preserve the framework of compassion and rehabilitation. According to Prince Mohammed bin Nayef, the family needs to feel that everything is being done for them and their loved one; the more a family is involved in the process, the more likely the family will participate in the prisoner's rehabilitation.[71]

The Security Subcommittee performs several functions, although many details remain unknown. The most important function of the subcommittee is to evaluate prisoners for security risks and then make release recommendations based on input provided by the Religious Subcommittee and the Psychological and Social Subcommittee. According

---

(Abdulrahman al-Hadlaq, interview with Christopher Boucek, Riyadh, Saudi Arabia, November 2007).

[71] Prince Mohammed bin Nayef, Assistant Minister of Interior for Security Affairs, interview with Christopher Boucek, Riyadh, Saudi Arabia, October 2007.

to senior officials, the decision regarding release is based on the advice of program staff. They also advise prisoners on how to behave upon release and make suggestions for avoiding rearrest.[72]

The Media Subcommittee produces materials used in the program as well as educational materials for use in schools and mosques. This subcommittee is focused on outreach and education, primarily targeting young Saudi men. Toward this end, the subcommittee has carried out research to determine the best means of delivering its message. Following an assessment of Internet, radio, television, and print media, the subcommittee determined that the most efficient way to reach the target audience was through lectures and study circles held at mosques.

The Media Subcommittee seeks to reinforce several messages through its materials, including the concept that extremists simply use their followers and that those who fall in with militants have misunderstood the basic tenets of Islam. One example of the type of materials produced by the Media Subcommittee is a television program that featured a young Saudi man who was recruited for a terrorist attack. When the young man learned that it was to be a suicide attack, he refused, but the extremists deceived him and remotely detonated the explosives. The character in the program survived but was left severely disfigured. The message of the program is clear: Involvement with terrorists will result in tragic consequences, not only for you but for your entire family.[73]

The Media Subcommittee also produces pamphlets and other written materials. In coordination with the Ministry of Islamic Affairs and the Ministry of Education, the subcommittee helps coordinate lectures and speakers for mosques and schools. The Advisory Committee

---

[72] Although Saudi officials have never stated as much, it would be extremely unlikely that none of the program participants has been used to collect intelligence about former colleagues. It has been suggested that some detainees have been turned in and are then released and observed so they can lead authorities to as-yet-undiscovered associates and networks.

[73] This story is clearly based, in part, on the life of Ahmed al-Shayea. Nic Robertson, "Failed Suicide Bomber Turns on al-Qaeda," CNN, September 14, 2007.

has thus been able to repeatedly deliver its message to a wide range of audiences, in mosques, schools, and at summer camps and clubs.[74]

When members of the Advisory Committee initially meet with a prisoner, one of the first things that they stress is that they are not employees of the Interior Ministry or associated with the security forces.[75] They explain that they are independent and righteous scholars. According to several committee members, initial meetings between counselors and detainees did not go well. At first, detainees would refuse to meet with clerics.[76] According to Sheikh Ali al-Nafisah, the detainees "would not salute or shake hands with members of the committee, because they believed that these members were aides of infidels."[77] This situation has slowly changed, and subsequent encounters have been described as "warm and respectful."[78]

There was initial backlash from extremists who denounced the committee, however. The rehabilitation program was called a sham, and the militant community accused anyone who had gone through the program of being a government spy.[79] Detainees themselves at first thought that the program was another form of interrogation.[80] However, the head of the Interior Ministry's Guidance and Awareness Department has affirmed that "the counseling process has nothing

---

[74] For more on these activities, see Abdallah al-Ziyadi, "Interior Ministry: Seminars and Lectures in Schools and Universities to Combat Terrorist Ideology," *Asharq Alawsat*, November 29, 2006.

[75] Abdulrahman al-Hadlaq and Major General Mansour al-Turki, interviews with Christopher Boucek, Riyadh, Saudi Arabia, March 2007.

[76] Sultan Al-Obathani, "Saudi Arabia: Over 400 Extremist Released in the Last Six Months," *Asharq Alawsat*, November 22, 2005, citing Saud al Musaybih, Director General for Public Relations and Guidance, Ministry of Interior.

[77] Quoted in Turki al-Saheil, "Saudi Arabia: Decisive Turnaround for Takfiris Through Counseling and Release of Detainees for Security Reasons; al-Washm Blast Has Caused Imbalance Within al-Qa'ida Organization's Ranks," *Ashraq Alawsat*, November 30, 2005b.

[78] Sultan Al-Obathani, 2005.

[79] Prince Mohammed bin Nayef, Assistant Minister of Interior for Security Affairs, interview with Christopher Boucek, Riyadh, Saudi Arabia, October 2007.

[80] Abdulrahman al-Hadlaq, interview with Christopher Boucek, Riyadh, Saudi Arabia, November 2007.

to do with the interrogation of those detained for security reasons."[81] According to officials, the counseling process does not begin until the investigation and interrogation phases have ended.

In their first meeting with a detainee, committee members simply listen. They ask what a detainee did that brought him to prison, why he did it, and about other circumstances that brought him to be in prison. Throughout the process, the scholars seek to draw out information about a detainee's beliefs and then attempt to demonstrate that his religious justification for his actions is wrong and based on a corrupted understanding of Islam. First, the committee demonstrates how the prisoners were tricked into believing falsehoods; then, they set to teach him the proper, state-approved interpretation of Islam. Sheikh Abdel Mohsin al-Obaykan has described the process as follows: "The advice is given through discussion sessions in a suitable place. The prisoner is asked to express all the suspicions he has and the evidence on which he relies, and then these are discussed with him, and he is introduced to the truth and to the meaning of this evidence."[82]

Initial sessions, especially those held in prison, are conducted one on one.[83] They can be formal and informal discussions, and much of the counseling process depends on the two individuals involved. Later on, especially once a detainee has moved to the Care Rehabilitation Center, sessions do not simply take the form of religious lectures; informal discussions and dialogues are encouraged.[84] While some counseling sessions take place in classrooms, others occur in very casual settings and often involve subtle negotiations and dialogue about

---

[81] Turki al-Saheil, 2005b.

[82] Quoted in Turki al-Saheil, "Al-Ubaykan: Al-Qa'ida and Books of Abu Qatadah Al-Maqdisi Have the Most Prominent Influence on the Minds of the Deceived Youths," *Asharq Alawsat*, September 9, 2005a. A member of the Advisory Committee, Sheikh Obaykan, is also the judicial adviser to the Justice Ministry and a member of the Majlis al-Shura. For more on Obaykan, see David Ottaway, 2006.

[83] "Extremists Have No Firm Religious Beliefs," *Khaleej Times* (Dubai), November 27, 2005. According to committee members, some meetings did initially occur with several sheikhs present.

[84] Sheikh Ahmed Hamid Jelani and Care Rehabilitation Center staff, interviews with Christopher Boucek, Riyadh, Saudi Arabia, November 2007.

everyday affairs.[85] However, all the while, committee staff are evaluating program participants.

The Advisory Committee runs two programs. The first consists of short sessions, which typically run about two hours. While some prisoners recant their beliefs after a single session, a prisoner typically goes through several sessions.[86] The other program consists of what are called "long study sessions." These six-week courses for up to 20 students are led by two clerics and a social scientist. The ten focus areas of the program include instruction in such topics as *takfir*, loyalty and allegiance, terrorism, the legal rules for jihad, and psychological courses on self-esteem. Instruction is also given on the concepts of "faith, leadership, and community," and the sessions provide guidance on how to "avoid misleading, delusional books."[87] The important role of scholars in Islamic jurisprudence is stressed, and detainees are also taught about sedition and the sanctity of blood in Islam.[88] In addition, detainees study so-called ideological topics, concepts such as *al wala' wal bara* (loyalty to Muslims and enmity toward nonbelievers), the illicitness of supporting nonbelievers and the need to throw them out of the Arabian Peninsula, among others, in an effort to rectify "incorrect" religious interpretations.[89] At the end of the course, an exam is given. Those who pass the exam move to the next stage of the process; those who do not pass must repeat the course.

Release

There is currently no objective process for determining when a detainee should be released from custody. According to Saudi officials, the

---

[85] Even during regular meetings and discussion about nonreligious or contentious topics, committee workers are evaluating program participants' development and progress. Observations made during site visit to Care Rehabilitation Center, Riyadh, Saudi Arabia, November 2007.

[86] Turki al-Saheil, 2005a.

[87] Turki al-Saheil, "Rehabilitating Reformed Jihadists," Asharq Alawsat, September 6, 2007.

[88] Turki al-Saheil, 2007.

[89] Turki al-Saheil, 2005b.

decision to release an individual from rehabilitation ultimately rests with the sheikhs and psychologists who have been working with the detainee. Senior officials have stated that while the Security Subcommittee is responsible for release decisions, its members base their decisions on input from program staff. As a result, an individual's release is very much based on personal impressions.

For a prisoner to be released through rehabilitation, Saudi authorities demand that his rejection of violence and *takfiri* beliefs be sincere, and program staff must also be convinced that, after release, the detainee will not return to militancy. If there are doubts about the latter, the detainee's release is postponed indefinitely.

Upon release, former detainees are required to check in with authorities and are encouraged to continue meeting with the scholars with whom they spoke while in custody. Released detainees are informed that they will be monitored, that monitoring will be both overt and covert, and that their continued freedom is dependent on their staying away from their old associates and habits. Released detainees are encouraged to settle down, marry, and have children, in part because of the belief that it is much more difficult for young men to get into trouble once they acquire family responsibilities.[90] The government has facilitated this effort by paying for weddings, donating dowries, and covering other essential costs, such as furnishing apartments.[91] Senior officials from the Interior Ministry and the Advisory Committee frequently attend the weddings of former detainees. This is all part of the Saudi government's efforts to replace one social network with another that is more conducive for a detainee to remain disengaged from terrorism.

---

[90] See "Saudis Helping Freed Terror Suspects; Trying to Pull Militants Away from Terrorism," *Vancouver Province*, April 26, 2007.

[91] As of October 2007, the Interior Ministry had helped 31 of 60 Guantanamo returnees get married; it has promised similar assistance to other program participants who have not been married before. For more on this topic, see Turki al-Saheil, "Former Saudi Guantanamo Inmates Get a New Start," *Asharq Alawsat*, October 3, 2007b. For other reports of assistance to former detainees, see "Saudis Helping Freed Terror Suspects," 2007.

Evaluation

The Saudi deradicalization program is nested in a larger counterterrorism strategy that seeks to deter people from radicalizing, to rehabilitate radicals, and to provide assistance to them so that they reintegrate into society. The Saudi program has all of the hallmarks of a strong deradicalization program: rigorous dialogues; affective, pragmatic, and ideological support; credible interlocutors; extensive aftercare; and measures to ensure that ex-militants remain disengaged.[92] Nevertheless, as we discuss, there remain serious concerns about the program, especially about the content of the theological dialogue.

According to official data, 3,033 detainees have participated in Saudi prison-based deradicalization programs.[93] Of these, only 231 have been released. It is not known how may have been rearrested. Fewer than 300 detainees have participated in a separate program based at an external rehabilitation facility, including returnees from Guantanamo.[94] As of summer 2009, 161 domestic security offenders had gone through external rehabilitation, with 104 released.[95] It is not known how many of them have been rearrested. Thus far, Saudi authorities claim an 80-percent success rate. The 20-percent failure rate described by Saudi officials includes detainees who refused to participate in the program, those who failed the rehabilitation program, and those who have subsequently been rearrested. According to Saudi authorities, less than 5 percent of all released detainees have been rearrested.[96] Officials admit, however, that there could be more individuals who have been

---

[92] Nicole Stracke, "Arab Prisons: A Place for Dialogue and Reform," *Perspectives on Terrorism*, Vol. 1, No. 4, 2007.

[93] This is the term used by Saudi officials.

[94] Based on official data from the Ministry of Interior, obtained in Riyadh, Saudi Arabia, March 2009. In total, 123 Saudi nationals have returned from Guantanamo (including three deceased); as of the summer of 2009, two had refused to participate, and a further ten are still in rehabilitation.

[95] Based on Saudi documents provided to Christopher Boucek.

[96] This excludes Guantanamo returnees. Of the 123 Saudi nationals who had been repatriated as of November 2009, 26 either are wanted, have been killed, or are in custody for security violations, a relapse rate of over 20 percent.

released through the program and returned to militancy, but they have not yet been identified.

The low recidivism rate in the Saudi rehabilitation program would seem to be an indicator of the program's success, but these figures have to be taken with caution. Thus far, only individuals at the lower end of the terrorism spectrum have been released—that is, individuals detained for playing a supporting role in the terrorist network. Militants closer to the violence and those who are ideologically more committed have not been released. Moreover, detainees who have participated in violence within Saudi Arabia have not been allowed to take advantage of the program. While some critics have pointed out that the release of such low-level operatives is not significant, it is noteworthy that such individuals do not advance to become more involved in militancy. The rehabilitation program, in some respects, prevents the emergence of a new tier of operational leaders in the kingdom.

Despite its claim of success, some aspects of the Saudi rehabilitation program raise questions about its effectiveness in actually deradicalizing militants. First, it is difficult to obtain accurate data. While some information is available, there is not enough to evaluate the program with confidence.

A second area of concern is the content of the ideological component of the program. Salafis and other conservative Muslims, including the Saudis, place certain conditions on participation in armed jihad, i.e., terrorism. For instance, many scholars argue that the tactic is permissible in Muslim lands under occupation. Therefore, there is no outright condemnation of terrorism, only of the circumstances under which it is perpetrated. Given these nuances, extremists may be disengaged from violence within the kingdom but may continue to hold to their radical beliefs and therefore may not be considered truly deradicalized.

A third area of concern has to do with issues of due process. Many detainees have never participated in the legal process. Saudi officials had planned to try approximately 990 detainees in connection with a series of criminal cases.[97] In 2009, it was announced that the first batch

---

[97] Christopher Boucek, "Courts Open New Chapter in Counter-Terrorism," *Arab Reform Bulletin*, September 2008c.

of just more than 130 defendants had been tried and found guilty on a variety of charges, although no details have been made public regarding the names of the convicted, the charges, or the sentences.

Iraq

Early Insurgent Rehabilitation Efforts

As a result of the insurgency in Iraq, by February 2006, U.S. forces held 14,767 prisoners in U.S.-run detention centers. At the time, Task Force 134—the unit charged with overseeing detainee operations in Iraq—had a poor record. The prisons were teeming with detainees, conditions at the facilities were abysmal, and riots occurred regularly. Despite this, the leader of Task Force 134, Army Major General John D. Gardner, instituted a number of programs to facilitate the rehabilitation of detainees, including a religious reeducation program; however, these religion classes were not effective and may have backfired. The classes so incensed some of the participants that they rioted. There were also allegations that some of the imams employed by Gardner were not moderate, but Salafists who used the classes to radicalize their attendees.[98]

In addition, Gardner tried to work with the U.S. Agency for International Development to help detainees from Al Anbar province locate jobs. Although Gardner attempted to implement programs offering ideological and pragmatic assistance to some detainees, managing the nearly constant crises in the detention facilities took up most of his time and prevented him from expanding these small deradicalization initiatives.[99]

---

[98] Stracke, 2007.

[99] Cheryl Benard, Edward O'Connell, Cathryn Quantic Thurston, Andres Villamizar, Elvira N. Loredo, Thomas Sullivan, and Jeremiah Goulka, *The Battle Inside the Wire: U.S. Prisoner and Detainee Operations from World War II to Iraq*, Santa Monica, Calif.: RAND Corporation, forthcoming.

Iraqi Rehabilitation Program Under General Stone

In May 2007, Major General Douglas Stone assumed control of Task Force 134 and quickly concluded that this volatile situation was unsustainable. Stone believed that improving the conditions in U.S.-run detention facilities should be the cornerstone of the U.S. public relations strategy to counter the insurgents' narrative. Toward this end, Stone overhauled the prison system by dramatically improving the treatment of all prisoners. Moreover, in an effort to reduce the detainee population and counter radicalization in Iraq as a whole, Stone implemented a more robust rehabilitation program for prisoners.[100]

Stone's program was premised on identifying the hard-core insurgents—the irreconcilables—and separating them from the rest of the prisoners who could be rehabilitated. Anyone who was likely to take up arms because they opposed the new situation in their country, including militant Islamists, was considered irreconcilable.[101] Stone compared the radical Islamists to "rotten eggs . . . hiding in the Easter basket." Once the hard-core militants were isolated, the behavior of the rest of the detainees would improve.[102] Psychologists, teachers, and imams ran the sorting process in an effort to identify the irreconcilables.

Although Stone initially assumed that most of the detained insurgents were motivated by religion or economic deprivation, it was later determined that the vast majority of the prisoners engaged in violence because of local or personal motives, nationalism, the opportunity for profit, or a combination of these factors.[103] The U.S. rehabilitation program sought to persuade detainees to abandon violence by offering them the opportunity to learn new skills so that they could obtain good jobs upon their release.[104] Vocational training was offered, but in 2007, Task Force 134 also established a more traditional, accredited

---

[100] Jeffrey Azarva, "Is U.S. Detention Policy in Iraq Working?" *Middle East Quarterly*, Vol. 16, No. 1, Winter 2009.

[101] Benard et al., forthcoming.

[102] Quoted in Andrew K. Woods, "The Business End," *Financial Times*, June 27, 2008.

[103] The insurgents motivated by opportunism were economically secure and often better off than they had been under the previous regime (Benard et al., forthcoming).

[104] Stone, 2008.

school, Dar al-Hikma, to teach the prisoners Arabic, English, math, science, civics, and geography.[105]

In addition, the rehabilitation program included a course on Islam that was run by clerics who engaged the detainees in discussions about their religion and promoted a nonviolent interpretation of Islam. With the help of reportedly "former al-Qaeda guys that now work for me" Stone had the clerics create a database of radical arguments and prepared refutations supported by citations from Islamic texts.[106] Another theme emphasized in these religious discussions was that the United States and the Coalition Provisional Authority were not against Islam. Even though most of the detainees were not radical Islamists, Stone reasoned that the courses inoculated them against the extremist ideology.[107] Eventually, Stone viewed the religious courses as a way of quieting the detainees by providing them with spiritual comfort.[108] Prisoners who cooperated with the authorities were rewarded with family visits or videoconferences (for the detainees who were held too far away from home for their relatives to travel to the prison).[109]

Well-behaved prisoners who completed the class offered on Islam were considered for release. As a result of Task Force 134's efforts, between January and September 2008, nearly half of the detainees— about 10,000—were freed. The task force reported that, during the same period, only a very small number of those freed—approximately 100 people—were again imprisoned. To further reduce the likelihood of recidivism, Stone revived a 1957 Iraqi law that required prisoners scheduled for release to swear that they would abide by the law, and another person, who would be legally liable for upholding this promise, had to affirm this oath. This pledge and the guarantor program allowed local sheikhs and family members to vouch for the freed prisoners.[110]

---

[105] Azarva, 2009.

[106] Quoted in Woods, 2008.

[107] Azarva, 2009.

[108] Benard et al., forthcoming.

[109] Stone, 2008.

[110] Azarva, 2009.

Although Task Force 134's Iraqi deradicalization program focused on rehabilitating imprisoned Iraqis, Stone saw this as a way to extend counter radicalization across Iraqi society. He called the rehabilitated prisoners "moderate missiles," seeing them as the most effective way to challenge radical Islamism among the broader population.[111]

Evaluation

Stone's Iraqi rehabilitation program was a comprehensive and expensive effort that included affective, pragmatic, and ideological components; however, it is unclear whether U.S. authorities monitored released detainees, and the program did not include serious postrelease assistance. Nevertheless, Stone maintained that the program was effective because very few of the freed detainees were rearrested. The dramatic reduction in the number of terrorist attacks in Iraq seems to support this claim, but it is unclear whether the increased security was due to the deradicalization program or other factors, such as the improved ability of the Iraqi forces to provide security. Moreover, and perhaps most important, the Iraqi deradicalization effort excluded those who were considered to be jihadists. Therefore, it focused on the easiest targets, those who did not espouse extremist beliefs but engaged in violence for instrumental reasons.[112] By contrast, Gardner's earlier effort at reeducating even mildly radicalized prisoners not only failed, but increased instability in the detention facilities. Although data are scarce, the rehabilitation program in Iraq did seem to succeed in preventing many detainees from further radicalizing. As Stone explained, "This used to be a jihadi university that was just breeding more terrorists," but "now we are engaging the detainees and using detainee operations to teach the Iraqis here and improve their perception of Americans."[113]

---

[111] Quoted in Woods, 2008; see also Azarva, 2009.

[112] Woods, 2008.

[113] Quoted in Amit R. Paley, "In Iraq, 'A Prison Full of Innocent Men,'" *Washington Post*, December 6, 2008.

Collective Deradicalization: Egypt and Libya

Characteristics of the Egyptian and Libyan Approaches

In contrast to the individually focused programs discussed thus far, the Egyptian and Libyan governments worked to moderate entire militant Islamist organizations. The process of collective deradicalization, particularly how it is similar to and differs from individual deradicalization, is discussed in more detail in Chapter Six. Here, we provide a brief overview of the actions taken by Egypt and Libya to encourage radical Islamist groups to renounce violence and their ideology. The Egyptian and Libyan efforts were not structured rehabilitation programs that included classes and counseling, like many of the prison-based programs to reform individual Islamists. Rather, it is probably more accurate to characterize what occurred between the Hosni Mubarak regime and al-Gama'a al-Islamiyya (IG) and EIJ in Egypt and the Muammar al-Qhadafi regime and the Libyan Islamic Fighting Group (LIFG) in Libya as a series of negotiations between the militant groups' leaders and representatives of the government. In return for publicly disengaging and deradicalizing, the states freed the reformed militants from prison and, at times, offered them other benefits.

Egypt: The Deradicalization of al-Gama'a al-Islamiyya and Egyptian Islamic Jihad

In the 1990s, the Egyptian government did not have an explicit deradicalization strategy in place, but it took a number of steps that laid the groundwork for the monumental shifts in the thinking among IG and EIJ leaders. The regime provided the prisoners with religious books and other texts that enabled them to enhance their understanding of Islamic thought. This was important because most Egyptian extremists, like many other militant Islamists, had no theological training and a limited knowledge of Islamic jurisprudence. In addition, the government also deployed mainstream intermediaries in an effort to persuade the imprisoned radical Islamists to disengage and deradicalize. Often, this group of intermediaries included scholars from the prestigious Al-Azhar University and, at other times, from the Muslim Brotherhood.[114]

However, at the time, these limited efforts failed to change the views of the militants. The formal Egyptian effort to facilitate the deradicalization of IG began as a result of the group's decision to unilaterally declare a halt to its attacks against the regime. IG's imprisoned leadership first announced an end to combat operations in 1997 but did not gain approval from the rest of the organization to formally implement this policy until 1999. Nevertheless, after a serious attack on foreign tourists in Luxor in 1997, the IG's military operations ceased, even in the absence of an official armistice.[115]

The Egyptian government initially responded with suspicion to IG's unilateral cease-fire. Some in the government feared that the radicals were trying to dupe the authorities into releasing militants who still desired to overthrow the Mubarak regime. Over time, however, government officials concluded that IG's leadership was sincere in its desire to renounce violence and to moderate the group's ideology. The Egyptian government cautiously began to facilitate the leadership's efforts to deradicalize its followers by, for instance, improving the treatment of the prisoners. In addition to providing the prisoners with some amenities, in 1999, the Egyptian government repealed its ban on prison visits, which had been in place since 1992. However, it was the 9/11 attacks that spurred the government to wholeheartedly embrace the deradicalization process and to provide significant assistance to the IG leadership as it sought to persuade the rest of the group to renounce violence.[116]

After 9/11, the Egyptian authorities allowed IG's leaders to meet in the prisons with rank-and-file members, and, in 2002, the state even

---

[114] Lisa Blaydes and Lawrence Rubin, "Ideological Reorientation and Counterterrorism: Confronting Militant Islam in Egypt," *Terrorism and Political Violence*, Vol. 20, No. 4, 2008.

[115] Omar Ahsour, "Lions Tamed? An Inquiry into the Causes of De-Radicalization of Armed Islamist Movements: The Case of the Egyptian Islamic Group," *Middle East Journal*, Vol. 61, No. 4, Autumn 2007, pp. 622–623.

[116] Ashour, 2007, p. 623; Diaa Rashwan, "The Renunciation of Violence by Egyptian Jihadi Organizations," in Tore Bjørgo and John Horgan, eds., *Leaving Terrorism Behind: Individual and Collective Disengagement*, New York: Routledge, 2008b, p. 129.

permitted the top leaders to visit all Egyptian prisons where IG members were incarcerated.[117] Moreover, the Egyptian government publicized its deradicalization initiative to demonstrate that it was successfully combating radical Islamism. When IG's leaders wrote a number of books denouncing the group's previous actions and recanting their ideology, the state paid for these treatises to be published and disseminated. Finally, as a result of the group's deradicalization, in 2003, the Egyptian government released thousands of IG prisoners who supported the group's new position.[118]

Encouraged by the successful rehabilitation of IG, the Egyptian government implemented a similar effort to deradicalize the imprisoned leaders of EIJ, but this effort did not come to fruition until Sayyid Imam al-Sharif, also known as Dr. Fadl, EIJ's foremost ideologue, was transferred to Egyptian custody from Yemen, where he had been detained after 9/11.[119] The Egyptian government used IG members as interlocutors to persuade EIJ members to support al-Sharif, who authored a book challenging the extremist ideology, *Rationalizing Jihad in Egypt and the World*.[120] The government also facilitated meetings between EIJ's leaders and their followers in prison and held out the promise that they would be released in return for deradicalizing. Once the entire organization, with the exception of EIJ members who had joined al-Qaeda, accepted these revisions, the government serialized and published al-Sharif's criticism of radical Islamic thought in two prominent newspapers.[121] Ultimately, the Egyptian state agreed that it would free the EIJ members who approved of al-Sharif's recantation and promised to create a fund for the ex-militants to help them

---

[117] Ashour, 2007, p. 623; Blaydes and Rubin, 2008, pp. 470–471.

[118] The evidence is inconclusive, but some have argued that the Egyptian government funds the pension program for discharged members of IG's military wing. If the state does not directly pay these subsidies, it at least allowed the IG to fundraise so that it could compensate former hard-core members. See Ashour, 2007, p. 624.

[119] Omar Ashour, 2009, pp. 102–103.

[120] See Blaydes and Rubin, 2008, p. 471.

[121] Ashour, 2007, p. 105.

obtain jobs, acquire medical care, and provide compensation for past mistreatment.[122]

By all accounts, Egypt's efforts to deradicalize the Islamist organizations that had challenged the regime were a success.[123] The two groups that posed the greatest threat to the state denounced both the use of violence and key tenants of radical Islamism. With the exception of a small number of militants who had already merged with al-Qaeda, both organizations were able to successfully disengage from terrorism without any significant radical splinter groups emerging. Egypt sought to deradicalize IG and EIJ to discredit the extremist ideology and to offer limited pragmatic and affective support to the militants who responded positively to these advances. Nevertheless, the Egyptian government provided the ex-militants with only limited assistance after their release, and it is not known whether the state monitored the former prisoners to ensure that they remained disengaged. Despite these lapses, there are few known cases of recidivism, and outside the Sinai, Egypt has not suffered a major terrorist attack in years.

Libya: The Deradicalization of the Libyan Islamic Fighting Group

The Libyan government's efforts to moderate LIFG, a militant Islamic organization dedicated to overthrowing the government of Muammar al-Qhadafi, bear a striking resemblance to Egypt's approach to the deradicalization of IG and EIJ, but there are some important differences. In both instances, the radical organizations had been essentially defeated by the state. In the case of Egypt, it took the government several years to take IG seriously, and the militants were given no guarantees. In the Libyan case, Qhadafi's son and heir apparent, Saif al-Islam al-Qhadafi, quickly embraced the idea of a deradicalization process and guaranteed the results.[124]

There is some debate over who initiated the deradicalization process in Libya. Jarret Brachman, a counterterrorism expert who interviewed LIFG leaders in Libya, says that the initial impetus emerged

---

[122]Ashour, 2007, p. 106.

[123]Rashwan, 2008b, p. 128.

[124]Noman Benotman, interview with Angel Rabasa, London, September 2010.

from midtier sharia officials within LIFG who wanted to avoid the kind of bloodshed that had occurred in Algeria in the 1990s. According to Brachman, LIFG's decision to deradicalize was also, in part, a "top-down decision to concede in order to get themselves out of prison in order to proceed with their broader agenda of religious reform in Libya." The Libyan government became involved only after a number of secret and indirect discussions "between former LIFG militants and trusted government advisers."[125]

Noman Benotman, an exiled ex-LIFG leader who played a key role in the deradicalization process, maintains that Saif al-Islam al-Qhadafi initiated the deradicalization process because he had concluded that a purely security-oriented response was insufficient to eradicate Islamist extremism in Libya. Benotman says that that Saif had been talking to various sectors of the Libyan opposition outside the country—some were liberal, others Islamist, others nationalists—as part of a reconciliation project known as Libya of the Future. At a meeting in London in December 2006, Saif told Benotman that he wanted to launch an initiative to deradicalize imprisoned LIFG militants and that, if the initiative succeeded, he would guarantee their freedom. Saif asked Benotman to go back to Libya to talk to the militants.

Saif arranged for Benotman to fly back to Libya and meet with the six imprisoned members of the LIFG *shura* council. Benotman said that the council's members had not expected this and were shocked to see him, but they reacted favorably to Saif's proposal. At their second meeting, the members asked to invite some midlevel leaders to the talks, people who had fought in Afghanistan. Some were under death sentences. Benotman said he made clear that this was not a negotiation, but an opportunity that the Libyan government was giving them to recant and ameliorate their situation. The authorities facilitated meetings among group members and created a library for their use.

Benotman said that there was opposition to the process among the security services. A particularly risky decision, from the security services' standpoint, was the government's agreement to reestablish the LIFG leadership (the emir and *shura*) within the prison, but this was

---

[125] Jarret Brachman, interview with Stacie Pettyjohn.

deemed necessary to enable the leaders to bring along the rank and file.[126]

As a result of these discussions and the state's promise to release the militants, in August 2009, LIFG leaders released a 417-page tome explaining why their efforts to overthrow al-Qhadafi in particular and their ideology in general were based on an incorrect understanding of Islam.[127] In return, 214 ex-militants, including 40 former LIFG members and key leaders, as well as hundreds of supporters, were released from prison.[128] The LIFG leaders pledged to work to persuade others that the extremist approach was wrong.[129]

The Libyan effort to deradicalize LIFG appeared to be a resounding success, but Tripoli has made very little information about its purported deradicalization program available to the public beyond the fact that religious discussions took place.[130] However, even this fact has been called into question; Brachman observed that "there seems to be virtually no state-directed deradicalization program in place." Rather than programs to rehabilitate the extremists, "the real bulk of the government's effort seems to be placed on forging a lasting truce between the Libyan government and the former militants."[131] In other words, what occurred in Libya was an understanding by which the militants conceded on the crucial point of renouncing their revolutionary aims

---

[126]Noman Benotman, interview with Angel Rabasa, London, September 2010.

[127]Alison Pargeter, "LIFG Revisions Unlikely to Reduce Jihadist Violence," *CTC Sentinel*, Vol. 2, No. 10, October 2009, p. 7.

[128]Noman Benotman, interview with Angel Rabasa, London, September 2010; Ali Shuaib and Salah Sarrar, "Libya Frees Jailed Leaders of Islamist Group," Reuters, March 23, 2010; Nic Robertson and Paul Cruickshank, "In a Bid to Thwart al Qaeda, Libya Frees Three Leaders of Jihadist Group," CNN, March 23, 2010.

[129]Sudarsan Raghavan, "Former Militants Now Wage Battle Within Libya to Discredit al-Qaeda," *Washington Post*, May 29, 2010.

[130]Charles W. Dunne, "Terrorist Rehabilitation and Succession Politics in Libya: Opportunities for the United States?" Middle East Institute, March 31, 2010.

[131]Jarret Brachman, interview with Stacie Pettyjohn.

and the regime accepted a plan that allowed the Islamists to save face and secure their release from prison.[132]

There is disagreement regarding the level of pragmatic support provided to the ex-radicals to facilitate their reintegration into society. According to Brachman, a major concern among senior LIFG leaders is what appears to be the government's lack of postrelease support for lower-level militants. "If unable to find jobs or meaningful integration back into society, there is a real risk that they would return to the same kinds of activities that got them into prison in the first place."[133] Benotman, on the other hand, says that those released from prison receive a grant of 10,000 Libyan dinars (about US$10,000). Those who had jobs prior to their arrest are reinstated, and the government helps those who were not employed find jobs.[134]

It is also unclear whether the government plans to monitor the freed extremists. This last point is of particular concern because while the ex-militants have abandoned their armed struggle against the Libyan state, they continue to defend the right to engage in defensive jihad.[135]

Although it is far too early to assess whether most members of LIFG will remain disengaged and deradicalized, the lack of a rigorous program and significant aftercare indicates that there may be problems in the future. On the other hand, since LIFG was a very hierarchical organization in which the leaders had significant influence over the rank and file, if the top militants remain committed to disengagement and deradicalization, perhaps the rest of the group will as well. Despite the unconventional nature of its deradicalization effort, at least in the short term, the Libyan government has achieved a significant victory against radical Islamism in general and LIFG in particular. Also, a significant number of LIFG supporters in Europe have deradicalized; for

---

[132] Pargeter, 2009, pp. 7–8.

[133] Jarret Brachman, interview with Stacie Pettyjohn.

[134] Noman Benotman, interview with Angel Rabasa, London, September 2010.

[135] Dunne, 2010.

instance, LIFG in Europe issued a statement in the United Kingdom supporting the decision to deradicalize.

Table 3.1 presents an overview of the countries and programs discussed in this chapter. In Chapter Four, we turn to a discussion of programs that have been undertaken in Southeast Asia. Chapter Five profiles rehabilitation approaches in Europe.

Table 3.1
Overview of Middle Eastern Programs

Characteristic	Yemen	Saudi Arabia	Egypt	Libya	Iraq
Location	Prison	Prison	Prison	Prison	Prison
Size	364 released	3,500 prisoners	~15,000 released	~200 released	~15,000 released
Objective	Individual deradicalization	Individual deradicalization, counter-radicalization	Group deradicalization	Group deradicalization, counter-radicalization	Individual deradicalization, counter-radicalization
Radicals included	All	Sympathizers, supporters	All	All	Those not motivated by religion
Interlocutors used	Ulema	Ulema, ex-militants	Ulema, ex-militants	Ulema, ex-militants	Ulema
Affective component	None	Counseling, family visits, funding for weddings	Intragroup discussions	Intragroup discussions	Family visits, counseling
Pragmatic component	Limited assistance in obtaining a job	Support to families and help in obtaining a job, housing, health care	Some help in obtaining a job, health care	None	Vocational training, education
Ideological component	Religious dialogue	Religious dialogue	Providing access to religious texts, religious dialogue	Unclear	Religious dialogue
Postprogram	1 year of monitoring, family held responsible	Monitoring, family held responsible, follow-up with ulema	None	None	Pledge and guarantor program

CHAPTER FOUR

Southeast Asian Programs

The Regional Context

For the most part, Southeast Asian programs aim to rehabilitate extremists associated with the regional Islamist terrorist organization JI, a secretive network established in 1993 by two Indonesian clerics exiled in Malaysia, Abdullah Sungkar and Abu Bakar Ba'asyir. The group is an exclusive, closely knit community with roots in the Darul Islam insurgency of the late 1940s and 1950s in Indonesia. The group has a radical Salafist ideology and culture and seeks to establish a pan-Islamic state in Southeast Asia through armed struggle. Like other extremist Islamist groups, JI adheres to the concepts of *takfir* (heretification of other Muslims), *hijra* (separation from a sinful world), and leaving one's family behind to wage jihad in the path of God.

Initially, JI was organized hierarchically, with an emir, a *shura*, and a regional structure of four *mantiqis* and *wakalah* (local jurisdictions). The norms of the group emphasized respect for seniority—based on Islamic learning and military experience—and hierarchical relationships, for instance, between recruiter and recruit and between *ustazd* and student. Secrecy and exclusiveness are also characteristics of the group. Members of the group trust only insiders, and are reluctant to speak about their backgrounds. Recruitment occurs largely through social networks, whether of kinship, friendship, or discipleship.[1] A small number of radical *pesantren* (Islamic schools) were JI incubators,

---

[1] Brigadier General Tito Karnavian, Indonesian National Police, presentation at the International Conference on Terrorist Rehabilitation, International Centre for Political Violence

including Pondok al-Mukmin in Ngruki (which some have referred to as "the school of terrorists"), Sukohardjo in Solo (Surakarta), Mutaqin in Jabarah, Dar us-Syahadah in Boyolali—all in Central Java; al-Islam in Lamongan, East Java; and the Hidayatullah network in East Kalimantan and Sulawesi.[2]

The context of the deradicalization programs in Southeast Asia is the attrition and fragmentation of the JI organizations. Much of the senior JI leadership has been killed or arrested or has renounced violence. Effective investigative work (with Australian help) after the first Bali bombing in October 2002 led to the arrest of several of the key planners and perpetrators of the attack, including Abdul Aziz (alias Imam Samudra), the reputed organizer of the attack; Mukhlas, also known as Ali Ghufron, who had reportedly become acting JI operational head when his predecessor, Riduan Issamudin (alias Hambali, the only Southeast Asian member of the al-Qaeda *shura*), went into hiding.

Three of the perpetrators of the first Bali bombing, Imam Samudra, Mukhlas, and Amrozi, were sentenced to death and executed on November 9, 2008. Hambali was captured in Thailand in August 2003 and surrendered to the United States. He is currently being held at the prison facility in Guantanamo Bay. Mas Selamat Kastari, the head of the Singapore branch of JI, was arrested by Indonesian authorities and handed over to Singapore. (He subsequently escaped from prison and was recaptured in Malaysia in April 2009.)

The notorious Malaysian master bombmaker Azahari Husin was killed when police raided his East Java hideout in November 2005. Zarkasih (alias Nuaim and Mbah), the emir or spiritual leader of the organization, and Abu Dujana, the military chief, were captured in separate raids in July 2007 by Detachment 88, the Indonesian police's

and Terrorism Research, S. Rajaratnam School of International Studies, Nanyang Technological University, Singapore, February 24–26, 2009.

[2] Zachary Abuza, *Uncivil Islam: Muslims, Politics, and Violence in Indonesia*, New York: Routledge, 2006, p. 31; Sharif Shuja, "Gauging Jemaah Islamiyah's Threat in Southeast Asia," *Terrorism Monitor*, Vol. 3, No. 8, May 5, 2005.

specialized antiterrorism squad.[3] Azahari's associate, recruiter Mohammed Noordin Top, also a Malaysian, was killed after a 16-hour police
siege in August 2009. Another senior JI leader, Dulmatin, and his two
bodyguards were killed in a shootout with police in March 2010.[4]
Overall, 438 suspected terrorists had been detained in Indonesia as of
February 2009.[5]

The government's pressure on the group, as well as ideological differences within the leadership, fragmented JI. A faction represented by JI's spiritual leader, Abu Bakar Ba'asyir, has ostensibly abandoned the armed struggle and emphasized political work through a
legal organization, the Indonesian Mujahidin Council (although it is
unclear whether Ba'asyir has actually renounced violence or has just
given the appearance of having done so). Noordin's faction, which he
named Al Qaeda in the Malay Archipelago, continued to favor spec-
tacular attacks.[6] More recently, a new terrorist configuration emerged,
Lintas Tanzim, a cross-organizational alliance of jihadist groups that
attempted to establish a training camp in the province of Aceh. (The
camp was discovered in February 2010; 13 militants were killed, and
more than 60 were arrested).[7]

Legal Regimes and Types of Programs

JI prisoners across Southeast Asia are held under different legal regimes.
In Indonesia, terrorism suspects are referred to the ordinary criminal
justice system. In Singapore and Malaysia, they are held under each
country's respective Internal Security Act (ISA), special British-era leg-

---

[3] Very little is known about Zarkasih and Abu Dujana, who goes by several aliases. Both
are believed to have fought against the Soviets in Afghanistan and to have established a relationship with al-Qaeda.

[4] Irwan Firdaus, "Noordin M Top Reportedly Killed in a Bathroom After 16 Hour Siege,"
Associated Press (*Jakarta Post*), August 8, 2009; Dicky Christanto, "Dulmatin Confirmed
Dead in Raids," *Jakarta Post*, March 11, 2010.

[5] Karnavian, 2009.

[6] International Crisis Group, "Terrorism in Indonesia: Noordin's Network," Jakarta and
Brussels, Asia Report No. 114, May 5, 2006.

[7] Sidney Jones, International Crisis Group, presentation to the Center for Strategic and
International Studies, Washington, D.C., May 24, 2010.

islation that provides for preventive detention. The differences in legal regimes have significant implications for the framing of rehabilitation programs. In Singapore and Malaysia, the subjects of rehabilitation are detainees and their families. In Indonesia, the effort is directed largely at prisoners but also seeks to reach militants outside the prison system. As the Indonesian National Counterterrorism Agency chief Ansyaad Mbai noted, many terrorist collaborators are free because the Indonesian legal system permits the prosecution of only those who have been directly involved in acts of terrorism.[8]

Southeast Asian programs fall into two categories. One model, represented by the Singaporean and Malaysian programs, is government-led (in the case of Singapore, with participation from Muslim community organizations), highly structured and focused, and well resourced; these programs have the mechanisms to monitor the behavior of a relatively small number of released detainees. The Indonesian model is very much ad hoc, run by a small number of senior police officers who have intimate contact with detainees, with little or no support from other government agencies. In fact, the programs are funded largely by private donors. Indonesia also has a much larger number of terrorist detainees—about 200, not counting over 260 who have been released since 2002[9]—in contrast to some 60 in Singapore (of whom about 40 have been released) and a similar number in Malaysia. A program that does not neatly fall into either of these categories is the Thai deradicalization effort for Malay Muslims. The program in Thailand differs from the other Southeast Asian programs because its primary target is Malay Muslim separatists. Given the primarily nationalist nature of the conflict there, it is not clear that the Thai government is correctly applying the concept of deradicalization, which, in turn, suggests that its effort is likely to fail.

---

[8]   Indonesian National Counterterrorism Agency chief Ansyaad Mbai, interview with Angel Rabasa, Jakarta, March 2009.

[9]   Correspondence from Sidney Jones, International Crisis Group, October 2010.

Singapore

Singapore is officially a multiethnic state with an ethnic Chinese majority. Muslims—mostly ethnic Malays—constitute about 15 percent of Singapore's population. The authorities in Singapore have consistently sought to blur ethnic and religious distinctions and to encourage the development of a national identity independent of ethnicity and religion. Over the past two decades, Singapore's government has made efforts to remove impediments and disabilities that in the past relegated the local Malays to the bottom rungs of the socioeconomic scale. As a result, over the past two decades, there have been significant improvements in the educational level, income, and standard of living of Singaporean Malays.[10] Nevertheless, Singapore has not been immune to radical Islamist militancy.

The Singapore program is probably the most comprehensive of all disengagement or deradicalization programs. Singapore set up the program after the arrest of 13 alleged members of a cell of the regional terrorist organization JI in December 2001, before they could carry out plans to launch terrorist attacks, and of another 21 terrorist suspects in September 2002. All of the 13 suspected terrorists captured in the first wave of arrests were Singaporean citizens. All had attended national schools in Singapore, and six had completed military service. For the most part, they were businessmen, professionals, and technical personnel. One was an aerospace technician who took photographs of Paya Labar Air Base and the U.S. Air Force aircraft deployed there, targets of a potential attack.[11]

The members of the Singapore cell had been recruited in religious classes run by the cell's leader, Ibrahim Maidin, a religious teacher recruited by a senior Indonesian JI figure, Mohammad Iqbal Rahman (alias Abu Jibril). Of the 13, at least eight had gone to Afghanistan for training in al-Qaeda camps. The training included the use of AK-47s

---

[10] Raj Vasil, *Governing Singapore: A History of National Development and Democracy*, St. Leonards, Australia: Allen and Unwin, 2000, pp. 222–223.

[11] Government of Singapore, Ministry of Home Affairs, "Singapore Government Press Statement on ISA Arrests," January 11, 2002. See also Government of Singapore, *The Jemaah Islamiyah Arrests and the Threat of Terrorism*, white paper, January 2003, Annex C.

and mortars and military tactics. A letter on an encrypted diskette nominated two of the militants for specialized training in one of three areas: ambush and assassination, sniper tactics, and bombmaking.[12]

Several considerations led the Singaporean authorities to establish a rehabilitation program. The authorities did not want to keep detainees under lock and key indefinitely but could not release them if they posed a security threat. The lead Singapore government agency in the rehabilitation program, the Internal Security Department (ISD) of the Ministry of Home Affairs, found that some of the detainees did not have a well-grounded knowledge of Islam and could be rehabilitated if led to a correct interpretation.[13]

Like the Malaysian program, Singapore's rehabilitation program is informed by the experience of dealing with the communist insurgency in the 1950s,[14] and it is structured in accordance with the ISA, which dates from the British colonial era and permits the detention of individuals deemed to be a security threat. The program has several stages, and the detention of the militants is reviewed every two years, in accordance with the provisions of the ISA; detainees who are no longer considered to pose a threat may be released.[15]

Singapore's program consists of several interlocking components: psychological rehabilitation, religious rehabilitation, social rehabilitation, and community involvement and family support.

---

[12] Government of Singapore, 2002, 2003, pp. 10–15 and Annexes A and C.

[13] Closed presentation by the director of ISD at the International Conference on Terrorist Rehabilitation, International Centre for Political Violence and Terrorism Research, S. Rajaratnam School of International Studies, Nanyang Technological University, Singapore, February 24–26, 2009.

[14] Angel Rabasa's discussion with Ambassador Barry Desker, dean of the S. Rajaratnam School of International Studies, Nanyang Technological University, Singapore, March 2009.

[15] Detainees under the ISA are not subject to trial, but detention under the ISA is subject to various checks and balances, including access to the courts through habeas corpus and judicial review (Richard Magnus, senior fellow at the S. Rajaratnam School of International Studies and former Chief Judge in Singapore, presentation at the International Conference on Terrorist Rehabilitation, International Centre for Political Violence and Terrorism Research, S. Rajaratnam School of International Studies, Nanyang Technological University, Singapore, February 24–26, 2009.

Psychological Rehabilitation

The rehabilitation process begins in prison, where detainees are regularly assessed by psychologists. There are about 30 psychologists in the Ministry of Home Affairs, but not all of them work with detainees. According to one psychologist, the detainees experience feelings of loneliness and separation from their families, so visits are allowed once a week. These family visits are therapeutic; the detainees realize that their families are suffering. A psychologist talks to each detainee about his situation and feelings but does not try to change his values. The detainee needs to do that himself, the psychologist said. The detainees go through several emotional stages (e.g., denial, anger, and acceptance) while psychologists help them manage their emotions and develop better cognitive tools. The detainees eventually realize that they had been gradually indoctrinated by JI, were initially unaware of JI's terrorist agenda, became emotionally affected by the suffering of Muslims abroad, failed to question JI teachings, and felt bound by obligation to be obedient. At the end of this process, some detainees undergo a catharsis—their value structure breaks down and is reconstructed. With some, this happens very quickly. With others, it can take a very long time.[16]

A key part of the rehabilitation process—which is also true of the very different Indonesian program—is the development of relationships of trust with case officers. According to an ISD officer, some detainees develop confidence that the advice given to them is well intentioned. One was grateful to his case officer for speaking to his wife and mediating family problems. Some have been released and have continued to maintain good relationships with their case officers.[17]

For Singapore's government, rehabilitation and release are not the ultimate goal, since not all detainees can be rehabilitated. Some detainees deploy defense mechanisms, believe that they are being

---

[16] Angel Rabasa, discussions in Singapore, February 2009.

[17] Closed presentation by an ISD officer, International Conference on Terrorist Rehabilitation, International Centre for Political Violence and Terrorism Research, S. Rajaratnam School of International Studies, Nanyang Technological University, Singapore, February 24–26, 2009.

unjustly persecuted, or refuse to accept the necessity of rehabilitation. One believed that his detention was a violation of Islamic law. Another used meetings with case officers and psychologists to preach his version of Islam. Other detainees refuse to talk.[18] The goal is to neutralize the threat posed by the detainees, and rehabilitation is one means to achieve that goal.[19]

Religious Rehabilitation

Like other rehabilitation programs, Singapore's program includes an element of the theological dialogue model, in which extremists are engaged in theological discussions by mainstream scholars with the intent to convince them that their radical interpretation of Islam is incorrect and to accept an alternative, mainstream interpretation. To this end, the authorities enlisted the help of a group of religious teachers and scholars from the Singapore Muslim community who had the necessary credentials and authority: the Religious Rehabilitation Group (RRG).

The RRG is composed of a panel of senior and respected scholars (including the president of Singapore's Shariah Court) and a secretariat to assist with administrative, research, and logistical matters. There are 38 counselors engaged in religious counseling of the detainees. The counselors are male and female, graduates of local madrassas and Islamic institutions abroad, including Al-Azhar University, Medina University, and the International Islamic University of Malaysia. RRG staff have produced religious counseling manuals and guidelines and conduct training sessions for counselors.[20]

---

[18] Closed presentation by an ISD officer, International Conference on Terrorist Rehabilitation, International Centre for Political Violence and Terrorism Research, S. Rajaratnam School of International Studies, Nanyang Technological University, Singapore, February 24–26, 2009.

[19] Closed presentation by the director of ISD, International Conference on Terrorist Rehabilitation, International Centre for Political Violence and Terrorism Research, S. Rajaratnam School of International Studies, Nanyang Technological University, Singapore, February 24–26, 2009.

[20] Ustaz Mohamed Feisal Mohamed Hassan, Secretary of the Religious Rehabilitation Group, presentation at the International Conference on Terrorist Rehabilitation, Interna-

From their initial meetings with JI detainees, RRG staff observed that the detainees' worldview was characterized by a distorted ideology, the promotion of violence, a simplistic paradigm, hatred and anger, and a sense of exclusiveness.

The religious counseling is meant to open the minds of the detainees to a more inclusive understanding of Islam. Through discussions with the detainees and their families, the RRG works at what it calls "extricating" and "negating" incorrect tenants of JI's ideology, such as the notion that Muslims are involved in a perpetual jihad against infidels, that true Islam can be practiced only in an Islamic state, and that Muslims must hate and avoid non-Muslims.[21] The manuals and guidelines are organized by theme and include references to the Quran and hadith, stories from the life of the Prophet and Islamic tradition. They seek to correct misinterpreted religious concepts such as *al wala' wal bara* (loyalty to God and Muslims and disavowal of infidels), *jama'ah* (community), *bai'ah* (the oath of allegiance to leaders), *ummah* (the Muslim community), jihad, and *daula Islamiyah* (the Islamic state).[22] Detainees learn that hatred and violence are not supported by Islam, that Muslims can live in a secular environment and in a multireligious society, and that there are legitimate means and channels to help those suffering in conflict zones.[23]

Social Rehabilitation, Community Involvement, and Family Support

Social rehabilitation involves improving educational and employment opportunities by providing the detainees with training to develop vocational skills so that they can obtain good jobs upon their release.

---

tional Centre for Political Violence and Terrorism Research, S. Rajaratnam School of International Studies, Nanyang Technological University, Singapore, February 24–26, 2009.

[21] Kumar Ramakrishna, "A Holistic Critique of Singapore's Counter-Ideological Program," *CTC Sentinel*, Vol. 2, No. 2, January 2009, p. 9.

[22] Hassan, 2009.

[23] Closed presentation by an ISD officer, International Conference on Terrorist Rehabilitation, International Centre for Political Violence and Terrorism Research, S. Rajaratnam School of International Studies, Nanyang Technological University, Singapore, February 24–26, 2009.

At times, the government has even arranged for the ex-radicals to have jobs waiting for them when they were discharged.[24]

Community involvement is a critical part of Singapore's counter-radicalization and rehabilitation programs. The government depends on the Muslim community to police itself and ensure the proper interpretation and teaching of the religion. This helps create a domestic environment that is unequivocally against terrorism, so individuals are not under the impression that the broader community tolerates terrorism.[25]

Toward this end, ISD has worked with Pergas, the association of Islamic scholars in Singapore, to counter radicalization within Singapore's Muslim community. In September 2003, Pergas held a conference for *ulema* on challenging radical Islamism. Based on the discussions held at this meeting, Pergas published *Moderation in Islam in the Context of Muslim Community in Singapore*, which used Islamic theology to refute jihadist arguments. Pergas also sought to disseminate the conference's findings with follow-up talks at public forums and mosques. The RRG also has made a significant effort to reach out to Singapore's Muslims by holding public discussions, publishing moderate texts, and establishing a website that provides information about its deradicalization program. By using credible Muslim interlocutors to discredit radical Islamism, Singapore's government has sought to build the resiliency of its Muslim community and make it an inhospitable environment for extremism.

The community-based Aftercare Services Group (ACG), which provides pragmatic and emotional support to the families of detainees, is meant to ease the resentment families may feel toward the detention of family members and to prevent such sentiments from spilling over into the general Muslim population. A related goal is to address the concerns of vulnerable families so that a second generation of extrem-

---

[24] William J. Dobson, "The Best Guide for Gitmo? Look to Singapore," *Washington Post*, May 17, 2009.

[25] Presentation by the director of ISD, International Conference on Terrorist Rehabilitation, International Centre for Political Violence and Terrorism Research, S. Rajaratnam School of International Studies, Nanyang Technological University, Singapore, February 24–26, 2009.

ists does not arise.[26] The family's attitude may have a significant impact on the detainee's willingness to accept rehabilitation. In some cases, the families urge detainees to cooperate with the authorities; other families are fixated on the idea that the husband or father is a victim of a conspiracy and has done nothing wrong. These families usually refuse help and do not cooperate with the aftercare program.[27]

ASG began with three community-based groups, which developed a joint strategy to provide a range of services to the families of the first JI cell members arrested in December 2001. The members of the ACG are Taman Bacaan (the Singapore Malay youth organization), Yayasan Mendaki (a Muslim educational foundation), and the Association of Muslim Professionals (AMP), together with a number of community partners, including the Islamic Religious Council of Singapore, the Community Development Council, the National Council of State Services, the Singapore Malay Journalist Association, the Family Service Center, and others. Aftercare caseworkers provide counseling, financial assistance, and skill training for spouses and children of detainees and free or subsidized tuition fees for children's education. They also mentor detainees' children, facilitate employment, assist families in handling government paperwork (e.g., applications for housing mortgage deferment), and provide postrelease support to ensure that released detainees seamlessly reintegrate into society.[28]

Each ACG agency also runs its own initiatives to provide further assistance to families, in line with its organizational objectives. Taman Bacaan arranges for eligible families to collect free used textbooks, provides school pocket money for students, and conducts other educational and youth-oriented activities.[29] Yayasan Mendaki focuses on

---

[26] Halim Kader, President, Taman Bacaan, presentation at the International Conference on Terrorist Rehabilitation, International Centre for Political Violence and Terrorism Research, S. Rajaratnam School of International Studies, Nanyang Technological University, Singapore, February 24–26, 2009.

[27] Kader, 2009.

[28] Kader, 2009.

[29] Kader, 2009.

disadvantaged groups in the Muslim community to help them improve their condition through education.[30]

AMP handles 20 cases with six counselors. It takes a holistic approach—an "adopt a family and youth" model, in which a family is "adopted" financially. Home visits are conducted so AMP staff can get to know the family and identify its needs. AMP then determines whether families in need of assistance require long-term or short-term support; for instance, short-term support might include one-time assistance or arrangement of an installment plan to pay off rental or utility arrears.

An example given by Zaleha Ahmad of AMP is Mrs. Hani, a 38-year-old with six school-age children and one infant. The sudden removal of her husband, the family's sole breadwinner, created serious problems for the family. AMP discussed Mrs. Hani's needs with her, especially the needs of the children. She was initially placed in the long-term assistance plan. AMP counselors addressed issues of single parenting; provided emotional support and monetary assistance for the purchase of schoolbooks, uniforms, and a personal computer for the children; and referred her to Singapore's Islamic Council for financial assistance, school pocket money, and educational trust-fund support from Yayasan Mendaki. Mrs. Hani was trained in job skills at home. After seven years, she went through further skill training and is currently employed, earning a wage that is double her previous income. She is emotionally stable, and all her children are reportedly doing well in school.[31]

---

[30] Sharifah Sakinah Ali-Alkaff and Yayasan Mendaki, presentation at the International Conference on Terrorist Rehabilitation, International Centre for Political Violence and Terrorism Research, S. Rajaratnam School of International Studies, Nanyang Technological University, Singapore, February 24–26, 2009.

[31] Zaleha Ahmad, presentation at the International Conference on Terrorist Rehabilitation, International Centre for Political Violence and Terrorism Research, S. Rajaratnam School of International Studies, Nanyang Technological University, Singapore, February 24–26, 2009.

Release

Every year, ISD reviews the status of each detainee to determine whether there is a basis for a detainee's release. There is no single criterion for release. ISD seeks to gather all information available about the detainee, including the assessments of religious counselors, prison wardens, psychologists, and case officers. It takes account of the individual's level of involvement in terrorism and makes an overall assessment. The recommendation is then forwarded for approval by the Minister of Home Affairs and the Cabinet. Once the Cabinet approves, the individual can be released.[32]

The second stage is a restriction order, as allowed by the ISA. The person under a restriction order can work but has to observe a curfew (7:00 p.m. to 7:00 a.m.) and must report a change of job or personal condition to the police. ISD also requires that the released militant continue religious counseling. The idea is to provide a continued and constant source of positive religious guidance. In the authorities' view, this also helps address the concern that the released militant may not have been completely rehabilitated.[33]

Evaluation

Singapore's terrorist rehabilitation program comes as close as any program can to the ideal type. It comprises the components that we have identified that increase the likelihood that a deradicalization program will succeed: efforts to break a radical's affective, pragmatic, and ideological commitment to an extremist group; continued support and monitoring after the individual completes the formal program; and the use of credible interlocutors to discredit radical Islamism. Establishing a comprehensive rehabilitation program for radical Islamists is a dif-

---

[32] Closed presentation by the director of ISD, International Conference on Terrorist Rehabilitation, International Centre for Political Violence and Terrorism Research, S. Rajaratnam School of International Studies, Nanyang Technological University, Singapore, February 24–26, 2009.

[33] Closed presentation by the director of ISD, International Conference on Terrorist Rehabilitation, International Centre for Political Violence and Terrorism Research, S. Rajaratnam School of International Studies, Nanyang Technological University, Singapore, February 24–26, 2009.

ficult and expensive undertaking, but it is within the means of Singapore. The recidivism rate is very low. Of some 60 JI detainees, about 40 have been released.[34] Only one has been rearrested.[35]

Having said that, Singapore, a modern, well-ordered, and disciplined city-state with efficient security services, can deploy capabilities in its rehabilitation program that are not available to larger, less well-organized polities. In some ways, the challenge that Singapore, a secular non–Muslim-majority state, confronts in seeking to deradicalize its Islamist extremists resembles the challenge confronting secular Western states. Unlike European countries, however, Singapore includes in its program a strong theological dialogue component designed to dissuade extremists from what the government and Singapore's Islamic religious authorities consider to be a deviant interpretation of Islam.

Malaysia

In Malaysia, Muslim Malays are a politically dominant majority in a multiethnic but officially Islamic state (although its political institutions and laws are based on the British model). Part of a terrorist network linked to JI was uncovered in May and June 2001, when the Malaysian police arrested 25 suspected members of a hitherto unknown group, the Kumpulan Militan Malaysia (also referred to as Kumpulan Mujahidin Malaysia, or KMM). In December 2001, the Malaysian authorities arrested another 13 KMM members, including a U.S.-educated former Malaysian army captain named Yazid Sufaat, who had hosted two of the 9/11 hijackers at his condominium in Kuala Lumpur during their visit to Malaysia in January 2000.

As in Singapore, the Malaysian government has created a deradicalization program that offers one of the few ways that the prisoners

---

[34] Closed presentation by the director of ISD, International Conference on Terrorist Rehabilitation, International Centre for Political Violence and Terrorism Research, S. Rajaratnam School of International Studies, Nanyang Technological University, Singapore, February 24–26, 2009.

[35] Abuza, 2008.

can get out of jail. Unlike Singapore, however, Malaysia has not disclosed much information about its efforts to rehabilitate its extremists. What is known is that deradicalization is a government-run effort built around a religious dialogue led by clerics who instruct the prisoners on Islamic jurisprudence and their responsibilities as Malaysian citizens.[36] All Islamist detainees take part in the Tafaqquh Fiddin program, which consists of a monthly religious meeting, but only those who do well in these sessions are enrolled in a more demanding deradicalization program, which meets for four to seven days.[37] As part of these discussions, government representatives try to convince the detainees that Malaysia is already an Islamic state and that the government shares the radicals' goal of fully implementing sharia law. According to the authorities, the militants are told that they need to be patient because the Malaysian legal system is gradually adopting sharia alongside its secular legal code.[38]

Reportedly, the government has granted some assistance to detainees' families in an effort to wean them off JI's welfare network. There is also a dialogue program for the prisoners' wives so that they can consider Islamic issues related to the detention of their spouses.[39] Recently, the Malaysian authorities also began providing ex-militants with a stipend to ease their transition into mainstream society.[40] It is not clear what criteria are used for determining which radicals are released from prison, but according to then–Deputy Prime Minister Najib Razak, those who are freed are "being watched very, very carefully."[41] The Department of Islamic Development, which runs the deradicaliza-

---

[36] Ustaz Iszam Padil, "Terrorist Rehabilitation: Malaysia's Experience," presentation at the International Conference on Terrorist Rehabilitation, International Centre for Political Violence and Terrorism Research, S. Rajaratnam School of International Studies, Nanyang Technological University, Singapore, February 24–26, 2009.

[37] Padil, 2009; Barrett and Bokhari, 2008, p. 179.

[38] Abuza, 2008, p. 207.

[39] Padil, 2009.

[40] Abuza, 2008, p. 207.

[41] Quoted in Abuza, 2008, p. 208.

tion program, also conducts biannual visits to the houses of freed ex-militants to evaluate their behavior and beliefs.[42]

Evaluation

Because of the paucity of information about Malaysia's deradicalization program, it is difficult to assess its effectiveness, or even its strengths and weaknesses. Some of the rehabilitated extremists have taped personal recantations that have been aired on Malaysian television; however, the government does not permit independent journalists and scholars to speak to any of these individuals. One ex-militant explained that he could not discuss the deradicalization program without violating the terms of his release.[43] Furthermore, it is not clear how much social support the state provides to released militants and their families, nor is it known whether any sort of psychological counseling is offered. Malaysia does employ clerics to work with the radical Islamists, but it does not seem to have tried to locate independent scholars or those who may have more credibility with the extremists. Finally, coercion again surfaces as a potentially important factor in Malaysia's program, since the detainees are reportedly treated quite harshly and deterrence seems to be an important reason that ex-militants refrain from taking up arms.[44]

Indonesia

There is no Indonesian rehabilitation program in the sense of the centrally driven, highly structured, and well-resourced programs implemented in Singapore and Malaysia. It is probably more accurate to speak of an Indonesian *approach* to rehabilitation, which was developed and implemented by the leaders of Detachment 88—Indonesia's special counterterrorism police unit—in the course of its interaction with JI detainees.

---

[42] Padil, 2009.

[43] Padil, 2009.

[44] Abuza, 2008, pp. 207–208.

The Indonesian approach to deradicalization operates at two levels: It seeks to develop intelligence on the terrorist network and to return detainees to society. The key objective is not to change the mindset of the terrorists but to obtain intelligence on the terrorist network in order to disrupt it and prevent terrorist attacks. National Counterterrorism Agency head Ansyaad Mbai attributed the relative success of Indonesian counterterrorism since 2005 to the broad and deep knowledge of the terrorist network that Detachment 88 has acquired through its soft approach to terrorist detainees.[45]

In contrast to the Singapore and Malaysian programs, where the official religious establishment plays an important role in seeking to persuade detainees to recant their extremist views of Islam, in Indonesia, police interrogators and former militants, not mainstream clerics, play the leading role in disengagement efforts. A team of psychologists advises the police on interrogation methods.

The Cultural Interrogation Method

The methodology developed by Indonesia is called "cultural interrogation." It requires the interrogator to be immersed in the culture of the detainee, understand his hopes and fears, and speak his language. (According to police consulting psychologist Sarlito Sarwono, the militants speak a jargon heavily laden with Arabic terms.)[46] According to Ansyaad Mbai, when they are arrested, very few of the terrorists are willing to talk. They will speak only to those they trust, and, in their minds, everyone connected to the government is their enemy. Even the most prestigious religious scholars have little credibility with the extremists because they are seen as having failed to establish Islamic law in Indonesia.[47] In the Indonesian approach to deradicalization, therefore, there is no formal "theological dialogue." The most appro-

---

[45] Indonesian National Counterterrorism Agency chief Ansyaad Mbai, interview with Angel Rabasa, Jakarta, March 2009.

[46] Senior consulting psychologist Sarlito Sarwono, interview with Angel Rabasa, Jakarta, March 2009.

[47] Indonesian National Counterterrorism Agency chief Ansyaad Mbai, interview with Angel Rabasa, Jakarta, March 2009.

priate individuals to interact with the terrorists are considered to be, paradoxically, those who are directly involved in the arrest and inter-rogation or ex-militants who can speak with the authority of experience in the extremist group.

The Indonesian approach to deradicalization requires the police to treat the prisoners in a humane way and to develop bonds of trust. One of the leading practitioners of the soft approach, Police Brigadier General Surya Dharma, former commander of the Indonesian police's Bali Bombing Task Force and a devout Muslim, said that he had a reli-gious obligation to help these men find true Islam.[48]

A critical part of the program is reuniting the inmates with their families, to remind them of their earthly responsibilities as husbands and fathers.[49] As Dharma explained, "JI adherents practice *hijra*—they leave their families and property and join the jihad. Our philosophy is to take them from *hijra* and back to their families."

> We arrest a suspect and stay with him, pray with him, discuss family matters. Not jihad. Not *hijra*. We tell him that he has not seen his family for many years. After we gain his trust, we tell him that we can arrange a meeting with his mother, his wife, his children.[50]

The police pay for the families' travel and accommodation and give them some additional financial assistance. Since there are no gov-ernment or police funds available for these activities, the interrogators are forced to raise funds through private donations from friends and supporters.[51]

Those involved in the program estimate that some 85 percent of the detainees respond positively in some fashion. The responses, as

---

[48] Di Martin, "Bali Bomber Now Campaigns to Stop Terrorism," *Australian Broadcasting Corporation News*, September 20, 2007.

[49] Martin, 2007.

[50] Brigadier General Surya Dharma, former head of Detachment 88, interview with Angel Rabasa, Jakarta, March 2009.

[51] Inspector General Goreis Mere, head of the National Police antinarcotics task force and former head of Detachment 88, interview with Angel Rabasa, Jakarta, March 2009.

shown in Figure 4.1, range from accepting assistance to publicly recanting and becoming actively engaged in deradicalization and counter-radicalization activities.

From a terrorism-prevention perspective, the program has been very successful in eliciting information that has enabled the police to disrupt the terrorist network in Indonesia. A number of individuals are cooperating privately with the police to disengage other militants from the network, but their identities have not been revealed. Two former senior JI members have recanted publicly and written books denouncing violence: former Mantiqi III commander Nasir Abas and Ali Imron, an organizer of the first Bali bombing who is serving a life sentence.

Of course, this approach is not successful with all prisoners. Some show no remorse for their involvement in terrorism and tell the interrogators that one day they will switch places, and the terrorists will interrogate the police, or that their struggle will be continued by their

Figure 4.1
Levels of Cooperation in the Indonesian Program

children and grandchildren.[52] A notoriously unrepentant terrorist was Imam Samudra, executed for his role in the first Bali bombing. He wrote two books, *Aku Melawan Teroris* [*I Fight the Terrorists*], published by a JI-linked publisher in 2004 and a best-seller with more than 12,000 copies sold, and *Satu Jihad Sejuta Vonis: Mengungkap Al Haq Menghalau Al-Batil* [*One Jihad, One Million Verdicts: Revealing the Truth and Banishing the Wrong*] in 2008. For several months before their execution, Samudra, Mukhlas, and Amrozi urged their followers to avenge their deaths by killing the president, vice president, minister of justice, prosecutors, and others.[53] Another unrepentant terrorist, Iwan Darmawan, alias Rois and Abu Syaukat, on death row for his role in the 2004 bombing of the Australian embassy, also wrote a book in which he stated that legitimate targets for jihad include nonbelievers, Muslims who abandon their beliefs, hypocrites, those who disobey Islamic law, and despotic governments.[54]

The Indonesian approach also differs from those in Singapore and Malaysia in that there is no explicit linkage between cooperation in a disengagement program and release from prison (although Ali Imron's public repentance spared him the death penalty for his role in the Bali bombing).

The Role of Ex-Militants

The Indonesian approach is unusual in the high-profile role played by former extremists. Indonesia seeks to turn the militants' respect for seniority and hierarchy into a means of deradicalization. The interrogators seek to gain the trust of JI "insiders" and then rely on the insiders to influence the rank and file.[55]

---

[52] Indonesian National Counterterrorism Agency chief Ansyaad Mbai, interview with Angel Rabasa, Jakarta, March 2009.

[53] V. Arianti, "Legacy of the Bali Trio: A Changing Threat Pattern from Jemaah Islamiyah," Singapore: S. Rajaratnam School of International Studies, Nanyang Technological University, November 14, 2008.

[54] Farouk Arnaz, "Embassy Bomb Planner Remorseless in New Book," *Jakarta Globe*, March 15, 2009.

[55] Karnavian, 2009.

The best known of these ex-militants is Nasir Abas, a Malaysian citizen residing in Indonesia who was recently removed from the United Nations terrorist list. As a young man, Abas was recruited by JI co-founders Abdullah Sungkar and Abu Bakar Ba'asyir, before JI was formally established, to fight the Soviets in Afghanistan. Abas, 18 years old at the time, saw it as an opportunity to travel and see the world, as well as a chance to help beleaguered Muslims. In 1987, he and a group of 14 others traveled to Pakistan (ironically, on an Aeroflot flight from Kuala Lumpur, because it was cheaper) and trained with an Indonesian contingent in a military academy run by Afghan mujahidin commander Abdul Rasul Sayyaf. After the Soviets' withdrawal, Abas remained in Afghanistan as a weapon instructor. In 1992, the mujahidin defeated the forces of the communist Kabul government and began fighting among themselves. Abas did not want to be part of a fight among Muslims ("it was sinful," he said) and returned to Malaysia in 1993.[56]

Back in Malaysia, Abas worked as a welder until mid-1994, when the leaders of the newly established JI ordered him to Mindanao to serve as an instructor at the Moro Islamic Liberation Front's (MILF's) Camp Abubakar.[57] Abas trained MILF leader Salamat Hashim's bodyguards and was given permission to open a training camp for Indonesians and Malaysians in the main MILF camp, Camp Abubakar, that he called Camp Hubaydah. In 1996, he was ordered to return to Malaysia, and in 1997, he was appointed chief of the JI *wakalah* (agency) in Sabah, eastern Malaysia. The *wakalah* was responsible for arranging the border crossings of militants between Indonesia, Malaysia, and the Philippines. In April 2001, he was selected as the Man-

---

[56] Nasir Abas, interview with Angel Rabasa, Jakarta, March 2009.

[57] Abas said that, before leaving Malaysia for Afghanistan in 1987, he had inadvertently sworn loyalty (*bai'a*) to Darul Islam, the group with which Abdullah Sungkar was then associated. Abas said that the night before he left, a group of Indonesians, some with tears in their eyes, shook Sungkar's hand and murmured some words in Bahasa Indonesia. He did the same and was subsequently informed that he had pledged allegiance to Darul Islam. In January 1993, his superior in Afghanistan, Zulkarnaen, explained to him that Sungkar and Ba'asyir had split from Darul Islam and established a new group (JI) and asked him to choose. Abas chose JI and pledged bai'a to Abdullah Sungkar for the second time.

tiqi III chief, responsible for JI activities in the Philippines, Eastern Malaysia, and Sulawesi. Abas eventually returned to Indonesia with his family in January 2002, after the Malaysians began to arrest JI members in Sabah. He was arrested in Bekasi, near Jakarta, in April 2003 during an Indonesian crackdown in the wake of the first Bali bombing.[58]

Abas said that he was surprised by his arrest because he had nothing to do with the Bali bombing—in fact, he says, he did not have previous knowledge of the attack, although his sister was married to Ali Ghufron, one of the organizers.[59] Even before his arrest, Abas had had concerns about JI's involvement in terrorism (which he attributed to the influence of Hambali). He had disagreed with the 2000 Christmas Eve bombing, which he thought was counterproductive, did not advance jihad as he understood it (as defensive military operations, not attacks on unarmed people), and was contrary to Islamic law.[60]

After his arrest, Abas recalled, he refused to answer any questions but was troubled by his own question: Why did God not let him die? He had told the people he had trained that it was better to be killed than to be taken prisoner. He concluded that his arrest was God's will and that there was something that God wanted him to do. After the church bombings, he, Zulkarnaen, and two other militants (Mustapha and Ahmad Roichan, now serving time in the Krobokan prison in Bali for shielding Bali bombing organizer Mukhlas) had warned Hambali not to carry out any more bombings. "Now, they had done it again and everything was ruined," Abas said. Abas expected the worst from the police, but his first interrogator, a Christian policeman, never used abusive language and treated him with respect. Abas then began to talk but "with a heavy heart," because he was not an ordinary JI member; he had trained other people to keep the group's secrets. He asked to

[58] Nasir Abas, interview with Angel Rabasa, Jakarta, March 2009.

[59] Abas said he learned of Ghufron's involvement two weeks after the bombing, when Ghufron told him that he and his brother Mukhlas were responsible.

[60] The Quran, in Abas's view, does not allow destruction of places of worship or the killing of civilians. If offensive operations are to be undertaken, they must be within a defensive framework.

speak with the task force commander one on one, and the commander agreed. His handcuffs were removed and the two were left alone in the cell. This surprised Abas, and he decided to return the commander's trust. He told him that he would cooperate with the police "to stop [JI's] crimes, so that they will sin no more."[61]

After that, Abas began to speak with JI detainees to urge them to cooperate with the police. He described his method as follows: First, he tells the detainees that they have a good spirit and a good intention to defend Islam but that Muslims are not afraid to speak. "Why don't they talk to the police? Are they ashamed of what they have done [their involvement with JI]?" A Muslim, he tells them, has to acknowledge his responsibility, whether others think he is right or wrong. Sometimes, Abas said, they ask whether the police are infidels and whether it is sinful to speak to the police. Abas asks them, "How can a policeman who prays and fasts be an infidel?" He reminds the detainees that the Prophet said that Muslims should not call their brothers infidels or the accusation will fall back upon them. When talking to a policeman, he tells them, talk to him as a policeman, a man doing his job, not as an enemy or an infidel.[62]

Abas's message is about means rather than ends. He does not seek to change the JI members' goal of an Islamic state, but based on the life and sayings of the Prophet Muhammad and his own experience in Afghanistan, he tells them that the Islamic state should not be their priority. He explains that, in 1992, the mujahidin established an Islamic state in Afghanistan, but the following year the Taliban rose up and attacked the government of the mujahidin. This shows that an Islamic state is not the solution to a country's problems.[63]

According to Abas, he has met with between 150 and 200 militants, including some who are not in prison. Some are persuaded and agree to cooperate with the police. Some are ambivalent. Others refuse and call him a traitor, a *murtad* (apostate). A number of ex-militants

---

[61] Nasir Abas, interview with Angel Rabasa, Jakarta, March 2009.

[62] Nasir Abas, interview with Angel Rabasa, Jakarta, March 2009.

[63] Nasir Abas, interview with Angel Rabasa, Jakarta, March 2009.

have joined him in trying to persuade others to renounce violence; most prefer to remain anonymous.[64]

Aside from Abas, other repentant extremists include Ali Imron and Mubarok, both of whom are serving life sentences for their role in the first Bali bombing. Since 2004, Imron has been providing information to the Indonesian police about the terrorist network and speaking out against terrorism. Unlike his brothers, Mukhlas and Amrozi, Imron was spared the death penalty. "I will continue to ask for forgiveness from the victims and their families, from anyone affected by violence in which I was involved," he said. The police have, on occasion, taken Imron out of jail to tell his story. During a radio interview in a Jakarta hotel room in September 2007, Imron explained,

> I help [the] police because I know what the terrorists think. I know how they will try to get their weapons and explosives. I know what kind of place they will target for what kind of action and I know how they would carry that out. I know how to hide from the police on the run, how the terrorists recruit new members and who is most vulnerable to the radical message. I am giving all this information to [the] police so I can stop violence and terrorism.[65]

From prison, Imron preaches a nonviolent interpretation of jihad as a spiritual struggle in God's name on audiocassette recordings that he sends to his family's *pesantren* in east Java. Like Abas, he is working with the police to deradicalize other imprisoned terrorists.

Evaluation

The Indonesian approach to deradicalization is unique because, unlike the top-down approaches found in the Middle East, Singapore, and Malaysia, it has been developed based on experience interacting with detainees and implemented by police interrogators with very little participation by religious authorities or, indeed, other entities of the Indonesian state. This might seem unusual from a non-Indonesian perspec-

---

[64] Nasir Abas, interview with Angel Rabasa, Jakarta, March 2009.

[65] Martin, 2007.

tive, but in fact it is consistent with the culture of Indonesian security agencies, which are often left to their own devices to raise funds from donors or their own business enterprises. More recently, Search for Common Ground, a conflict-transformation organization that receives much of its funding from European governments, has been implementing a program to disengage militants.[66]

Despite the ad hoc nature of the Indonesian effort and the lack of incentives to induce cooperation, the program has achieved some degree of success. According to the current commander of Detachment 88, the Indonesian police's counterterrorism unit, more than half of the terrorist detainees in Indonesia have cooperated with the police by publicly repenting, providing information about networks that has led to arrests, and accepting offers of assistance.[67] On the other hand, according to media reports, of several hundred militants detained since the October 2002 Bali bombing, only 20 are considered reformed and are actively working with police. There have also been cases of recidivism. Bagus Budi Pranoto was in the deradicalization program while serving a four-year sentence for his role in the 2004 Australian embassy bombing in Jakarta. After his release, he helped carry out the 2009 attacks on the J. W. Marriott and Ritz-Carlton hotels in Jakarta. At least 20 recidivists were involved in the terrorist network uncovered in Aceh in March 2010, including some who had previously been arrested for ordinary crimes, such as drugs and, in one case, murder. Seventeen have been rearrested and three are on the most-wanted list.[68] One high-profile terrorist who reportedly cooperated with the rehabilitation program, Abdullah Sonata, was released from prison in 2009 on good behavior, then rearrested in 2010 in connection with a plot to carry out terrorist attacks in Jakarta.[69]

As already noted, one of the most successful aspects of the Indonesian approach has been inducing high-ranking detainees to recant

---

[66] Sara Schonhardt, "Terrorists Go Back to School in Indonesia," *Asia Times*, July 22, 2010.

[67] Karnavian, 2009.

[68] Correspondence from Sidney Jones, International Crisis Group, October 2010.

[69] "Terrorist 'Rehab' a Failure: Minister," *Jakarta Globe*, June 26, 2010.

and denounce violence and to work with the police to persuade other detainees to cooperate. These accomplishments are all the more remarkable considering that, under Indonesian legal procedures, the detainees can be held by the police for only three months before being transferred to the custody of judicial authorities. Nevertheless, some critics of the Indonesian program argue that the ex-militants have not truly deradicalized because they do not promote a truly moderate ideology. Although these ex-militants oppose the killing of civilians, they continue to espouse radical beliefs.[70] Moreover, some argue that the turn against violence on the part of ex-radicals like Abas actually predated the deradicalization program and that many of the militants who have cooperated with the police did so because they were already opposed to the indiscriminate killing of civilians.[71] A conversation with Abas for this study confirms this view. However, Abas made it clear that it was his capture and the unexpectedly decent treatment that he received from the police that crystallized his decision to leave JI.[72]

The weakness of the Indonesian approach is the lack of a coordinated effort by other state agencies. Police officers who have been involved in the rehabilitation of detainees acknowledge that there is insufficient institutional support. For instance, the government has not allocated funds for the program or to implement some form of post-release monitoring. One official frankly acknowledged that the problem comes down to a lack of political will. This, he added, is because the fight against terrorism is linked to Islam and therefore a very sensitive issue in Indonesia.[73] Another concern is the lack of information about the rehabilitated militants who have been released. Although prisoners are not freed in return for deradicalizing, they frequently secure their release due to the short prison sentences common in the Indo-

---

[70] Kristen E. Schulze, "Indonesia's Approach to Jihadist Deradicalization," *CTC Sentinel*, Vol. 1, No. 8, July 2008, p. 9.

[71] Schulze, 2008, p. 9.

[72] Nasir Abas, interview with Angel Rabasa, Jakarta, February 2009.

[73] Indonesian government official, discussion with Angel Rabasa, Jakarta, March 2009.

nesian criminal justice system.[74] Despite these problems, the Indonesian program has successfully rehabilitated some high-profile militants, used these ex-radicals as interlocutors to encourage other prisoners to moderate, and acquired important intelligence from those who have cooperated. The efforts to reform incarcerated JI members appear to have achieved a degree of success because they have a strong emotional component, offer some pragmatic support, and employ credible ex-militants to challenge the extremist ideology.

Thailand

In Thailand, the military has directed a number of efforts to rehabilitate Muslim Malays suspected of involvement in the insurgency in southern Thailand. This conflict differs from most of the others examined in this study because although the militants are Muslim, the insurgency in the south is driven primarily by ethnonationalist grievances. (Some of the militants subscribe to radical Islamist ideologies, however.[75]) What began as sporadic attacks against institutions and symbols of the Thai state slowly spread into a full-blown separatist insurgency in the predominantly ethnic Malay southern provinces of Yala, Narathiwat, and Pattani. The rebels have increasingly adopted jihadist rhetoric, raising concerns that these fighters are becoming a part of the global jihadist movement. Nevertheless, the Malay Muslim rebellion is driven primarily by local and nationalist concerns; so far, there are no indications of al-Qaeda involvement.[76]

The ISA, which came into effect in February 2008, gave extensive authority to the Internal Security Operations Command, a unit of the Thai military tasked with combating internal security threats. In particular, Section 21 of the ISA authorized the command, with the

---

[74] Abuza, 2008, pp. 199–200.

[75] Peter Chalk, *The Malay-Muslim Insurgency in Southern Thailand—Understanding the Conflict's Evolving Dynamic: RAND Counterinsurgency Study—Paper 5*, Santa Monica, Calif.: RAND Corporation, OP-198-OSD, 2008, p. 13.

[76] Chalk, 2008.

permission of a court, to drop charges against a suspected insurgent if the individual confessed and agreed to attend a six-month reeducation program. The rehabilitation effort is based on a short-lived reeducation program that began in 2007; the revised and expanded effort is called the "political school project." The program aims to reintegrate into society the Malay Muslims who "have been imbued with misguided religious teaching and ethno-nationalist ideology."[77] Detainees who "recognize the damage inflicted by their violence and repent from such terrorist acts . . . can be reintegrated into society and their wrongdoing forgiven."[78] To avoid legal problems, the military requires those who enroll in the schools to sign a written consent form. In May 2008, the political school program opened, offering a 20-day course; as of August 2009, approximately 1,550 detainees had completed the class.[79]

Little is known about the content of the courses at the political schools, although they reportedly emphasize the positive qualities of the Thai state as well as a "correct" version of Islam.[80] Both of the Thai reeducation projects seem to be efforts to emulate other rehabilitation and amnesty programs (including a Thai one used against communist insurgents). Applying the rehabilitation concept to Muslims is based on the premise that the state can convince the insurgents that ethnic nationalism is wrong and that the Thai state is benevolent and good.[81] In fact, the Thai government's unwillingness to recognize the distinct Malay Muslim identity is one of the major grievances that fuel the insurgency. Some have suggested that most of the individuals detained

---

[77] Charnchao Chaiyanukit, "Vision for Establishing a Rehabilitation Programme in Thailand," presentation at the International Conference on Terrorist Rehabilitation, International Centre for Political Violence and Terrorism Research, S. Rajaratnam School of International Studies, Nanyang Technological University, Singapore, February 24–26, 2009.

[78] Chaiyanukit, 2009.

[79] International Crisis Group, *Southern Thailand: Moving Towards Political Solutions?* Bangkok and Brussels, Asia Report No. 181, December 8, 2009b, pp. 12–13.

[80] Olivia Rondonuwu, "Changing the Militant Mindset: Few Signs of Success," Reuters, September 24, 2009.

[81] International Crisis Group, 2009b, p. 13.

and forced to attend the political school leave the program even more aggrieved against the state.[82]

Thai efforts to reeducate Malay Muslims detainees are part of a broader counterinsurgency strategy that includes a state-funded economic development plan for the southern provinces.[83] Bangkok has also attempted to implement a counter-radicalization policy, but this effort was not well thought out and, as a result, appears to have had little effect. Although the government sponsored the publication of *Clarifications on the Distortion of Islamic Teaching in Berjihad di Patani*, which argued that ethnic nationalism was in contradiction to the universality of Islam, this volume was published only in Thai and not in the local Jawi language that most Malay Muslims speak.[84]

Evaluation

There is insufficient information to assess the efficacy of the Thai military's political schools. These efforts appear to be focused on challenging the distinct Malay Muslim identity, but it is not clear whether they include pragmatic or emotional assistance. Nor is it known whether the military and the police monitor those who have completed the program. Unlike most of the deradicalization programs targeting radical Islamists, the Thai program seems to challenge the militants' identity, which would be equivalent to trying to get radical Islamists to renounce Islam altogether. This policy seems to be an incorrect application of the deradicalization concept that is likely to fail.

Table 4.1 presents an overview of the countries and programs discussed in this chapter. In Chapter Five, we examine rehabilitation approaches in Europe.

---

[82] Rondonuwu, 2009.

[83] International Crisis Group, 2009b, pp. 8–10.

[84] International Crisis Group, *Recruiting Militants in Southern Thailand*, Bangkok and Brussels, Asia Report No. 170, June 2009a, p. 17.

Table 4.1
Overview of Southeast Asian Programs

Characteristic	Singapore	Malaysia	Indonesia	Thailand
Location	Prison	Prison	Prison	Military camps
Size	40 released	~100	~100 cooperated	1,550 participants
Objective	Deradicalization and counter-radicalization	Deradicalization and counter-radicalization	Intelligence and counter-radicalization	Deradicalization and counter-radicalization
Radicals included	Peripheral members	Unknown	All	Peripheral members and civilians
Interlocutors used	Ulema	Ulema	Prison guards, ex-militants	Military
Affective component	Psychological counseling for detainees and families	Unknown	Cultural integration method, family visits	None
Pragmatic component	Education, training, help in obtaining a job, support for families	Support for families	Support for militants and families	No individual assistance; economic development plan
Ideological component	Religious dialogue	Religious dialogue, counseling for detainees' wives	Discussions with ex-militants	Classes on Islam and nationalism
Postprogram	Close monitoring, religious counseling	Close monitoring, start-up stipend	Start-up assistance	None

CHAPTER FIVE

European Approaches

The Regional Context

Europe has become a main theater of Islamist terrorism, with the dramatic terrorist events in Madrid and London only the tip of the iceberg. With the exceptions of the July 7, 2005, bombings in London and the March 11, 2004, Madrid train bombings, numerous mass-casualty terrorist attacks have been prevented in Europe. There have also been plans to assassinate political leaders and other figures of public life in a number of European countries. One of these succeeded: the public murder of Dutch filmmaker Theo Van Gogh in Amsterdam in November 2004. Europe has also been a launching pad for attacks outside the continent. Known instances include 9/11 itself, the suicide bombings at the Djerba synagogue in Tunisia in April 2002 and at a café in Tel Aviv in April 2003, the 2006 transatlantic plot to detonate liquid explosives on board at least ten airliners traveling from the United Kingdom to the United States and Canada, and Umar Abdulmutallab's plot to detonate a bomb aboard a flight from Amsterdam to Detroit on Christmas Day 2009.

For European authorities, the most worrying aspect of the Islamist terrorist threat in Europe is the rising level of extremism within Europe's large and growing Muslim diaspora and the alienation of Muslim communities from their governments and society at large. The isolation of European Muslims is further enhanced by their concentration in ethnic enclaves, a lack of education and employment opportunities (with unemployment rates three to four times higher than the national average in Denmark, Sweden, Finland, and the Netherlands and double the national average in France and Germany),[1] and the rise of anti-immigration movements.

European governments, no less than governments of Muslim-majority countries, are seeking to develop strategies to counter the radicalization of their Muslim populations. But unlike Muslim-majority countries, where counter-radicalization and deradicalization programs include a significant theological component, European governments, even those that maintain a link with an official church or churches, find it difficult or impossible to promote a particular interpretation of Islam as part of their counter-radicalization programs. Rather, Europeans see radicalization in the context of the broader social problem of integration of the continent's Muslim communities. The integration problem is seen, first and foremost, in terms of inadequate economic, social, and political participation; high unemployment rates; criminality; urban fragmentation; and other social ills. This state of mind is reflected in efforts to move beyond police and security approaches by addressing the factors that encourage and facilitate recruitment into extremist and terrorist groups, as in the "Prevent" component of the British counterterrorism strategy, CONTEST.

Two elements have shaped the European approach to counter-radicalization: the lack of a broad political consensus on how to tackle the Islamist extremist vector and the tools to confront the ideological dimension of the radicalization process. Instead, the path chosen by European governments to counter radicalization has been piecemeal and varies considerably from country to country (although the European Union has sought to create an overarching counter-radicalization structure, the EU Strategy for Combating Radicalization and Recruit-

---

[1]   Robert S. Leiken, "Europe's Angry Muslims," *Foreign Affairs*, Vol. 84, No. 4, July–August 2005; Paul Gallis, Kristin Archick, Francis Miko, and Steven Woehrel, *Muslims in Europe: Integration Policies in Selected Countries*, Washington, D.C.: Congressional Research Service, RL33166, November 18, 2005; S. Mansoob Murshed and Sarah Pavan, *Identity and Islamic Radicalization in Western Europe*, Brighton, UK: MICROCON, Research Working Paper 16, August 2009.

ment to Terrorism, within its Counter-Terrorism Strategy, which is to serve as a strategic template).[2]

Because of the difficulties of secular Western governments in directly addressing the ideological component of radicalization, European governments, to the extent that they have a counter-radicalization strategy, have taken the indirect approach. That is to say, they support Muslim nongovernmental organizations (NGOs) that have, in the view of these governments, sufficient credibility within the Muslim community to mitigate the risk of radicalization. This raises the issue of selecting appropriate interlocutors and, in particular, whether Islamists should be engaged as partners.

Some European governments are willing to recognize and promote Islamists on the grounds that Islamist groups, such as the Muslim Brotherhood, have evolved to support pluralistic democracy and that Islamists are more likely to be successful in dissuading potential terrorists from committing violence than are non-Islamist clerics.[3] In some cases, this seems to stem more from an inability to distinguish Islamists from liberal Muslims than from a conscious policy.

Since about 2005, some governments, such as in the UK, that in the past had worked with Muslim organizations controlled by Islamists have moved to distance themselves from Islamist groups and redirect their support to non-Islamist groups and even organizations that are actively confronting Islamists.

The discussion of European counter-radicalization programs focuses on the most developed programs—those of the United Kingdom and the Netherlands—with additional discussion of other countries as appropriate. By and large, these approaches are focused on counter-radicalization, with deradicalization a by-product rather than a central focus of the programs.

---

[2] Council of the European Union, *The European Union Counter-Terrorism Strategy*, Brussels, November 30, 2005, p. 3.

[3] This argument was made bluntly to one of the authors by a representative of the Dutch Foreign Ministry.

The British Counter-Radicalization Approach

Although the United Kingdom first implemented its broad counterterrorism strategy in 2003, it was not until after the July 7, 2005, bombings in London that this plan, called CONTEST, was fully developed. The CONTEST strategy has four components: Prevent (preventing terrorism by addressing the factors that produce radicalization), Pursue (pursuing terrorists and their sponsors), Protect (protecting the British public and government), and Prepare (preparing for the consequences of a terrorist attack).[4] Initially, the emphasis of CONTEST was on the last three P's. In the most recent iteration of the strategy in March 2009, referred to as CONTEST-2, greater emphasis was placed on a more proactive approach predicated on Prevent. The new coalition government does not believe that Prevent is working as effectively as it could and has undertaken a review to develop a strategy that is effective and properly focused. A clearer boundary between Prevent and the Department of Communities and Local Government's new integration strategy, supported by a new program to tackle extremism more broadly (also led by the department) will form the three elements of the government's policy in this area.[5]

The Prevent strand of CONTEST focused on combating radicalization in the United Kingdom by partnering with the police, local governments, and NGOs to challenge radical Islamism, disrupt those who promote violent extremism, support individuals who are vulnerable to radicalization or who have begun to radicalize, increase the capacity of communities to resist violent extremism, and address grievances that violent extremists exploit.[6]

Initially, CONTEST restricted its efforts to countering violent extremism, and as a result, the British government was willing to partner with Salafi organizations, even though in the long run these radical groups could undermine Britain's social cohesion. British authorities

---

[4]   HM Government, *Countering International Terrorism: The United Kingdom's Strategy*, London, July 2006, pp. 1–2.

[5]   British official, discussion with Angel Rabasa, London, August 2010.

[6]   HM Government, 2008, p. 16.

prioritized the short-term objective of reducing the immediate security threat posed by violent Islamists. More recently, as discussed later in greater detail, British authorities have withdrawn their support from Islamist-dominated organizations, such as the Muslim Council of Britain, and have begun to work with organizations that are combating Islamist ideology.

The first strand of Prevent aims to counter radical Islamism and bolster those who espouse a moderate Islamic ideology. After the 2005 London bombings, the government organized seven working groups of prominent Muslims tasked with recommending how the government could stop the spread of violent extremism in the country. Called Preventing Extremism Together, these committees submitted their list of proposals to the British government in September 2005. Their recommendations included creating a mosque and imam national advisory board, a traveling scholars' road show called the Radical Middle Way, and forums discussing Islamophobia and extremism.[7]

The second component of Prevent seeks to impede the efforts of those trying to radicalize others in places such as mosques, schools, prisons, and community centers and on the Internet. Efforts in this area include criminalizing actions that support terrorism so that individuals who promote and assist terrorists can be prosecuted, obtaining intelligence about imprisoned radicals, and raising the standards in mosques.[8]

The third element of Prevent is supporting vulnerable individuals. It consists of proving mentoring programs and training opportunities for young Muslim leaders so that they have the knowledge and skills to counter radicalism.[9] The government wanted to avoid imprisoning at-risk individuals as part of this effort; instead, the authorities sought

---

[7]   For the working groups' recommendations see *"Preventing Extremism Together" Working Groups, August–October 2005*, London: UK Home Office, October 2005. See also Michael Whine, "The Radicalization of Diasporas and Terrorism: United Kingdom," in Doron Zimmermann and William Rosenau, eds., *The Radicalization of Diasporas and Terrorism*, Zurich: Center for Security Studies, ETH Zurich, 2009, pp. 31–33.

[8]   HM Government, *Pursue Prevent Protect Prepare: The United Kingdom's Strategy for Countering International Terrorism*, London, March 2009, pp. 88–89.

[9]   HM Government, 2008, pp. 27–29; HM Government, 2009, pp. 89–90.

to help those who were moving toward violent extremism but had not yet broken the law by organizing local interventions. Toward this end, the British instituted the Channel Project, a local, community-based program that relies on the police, local authorities, and local communities to identify individuals who are radicalizing and then help them to return to the right path. Community partners refer to the authorities those individuals who are exhibiting alarming behavior, such as visiting terrorist websites, discussing and promoting violence, or other indicators of radicalization.

The Channel Project assesses referred individuals to determine whether they are likely to become involved in violent extremism and whether they have influence over others. The project's focus "is on preventing radical beliefs escalating to violent extremism and not on preventing individuals, groups or places from expressing radical or extreme views or behaviour."[10] If the project determines that an individual is moving toward violent radicalism, local partners and authorities decide how to stage an intervention, which may include the individual's family, the police, and local imams. Guidance provided to local partners recommends that the Channel Project's interventions deal with many of the factors that lead to radicalization, not just ideology.[11]

The fourth strand of Prevent involves increasing local communities' resilience to violent extremism by strengthening moderate Muslim leaders and empowering young Muslim men and women.[12] For instance, Leeds created the Bringing Communities Together project. This seven-month plan aimed to help young Muslims resist and confront extremism and was operated by a local charity, the Hamara Healthy Living Centre, and a number of other local Muslim NGOs.

---

[10] Audit Commission, *Preventing Violent Extremism: Learning and Developing Exercise*, London, October 2008, p. 46.

[11] HM Government, 2008, pp. 28–29. Annex I of *The Prevent Strategy: A Guide for Local Partners in England* identifies factors that make individuals vulnerable to radicalization, including personal crisis, a changed situation or circumstances, underemployment, links to criminality, identity, social exclusion, grievances, and a lack of trust in political structures and civil society. See also HM Government, *Channel: Supporting Individuals Vulnerable to Recruitment by Violent Extremists*, London, March 2010a.

[12] HM Government, 2009, pp. 90–91.

The program included a poster campaign designed by young Muslims from Leeds that challenged common stereotypes. Bringing Communities Together also offered training courses for young Muslims to help them discredit extremism and Islamophobia.[13]

Similarly, the borough of Harrow instituted an online safety awareness course to train Muslim women who have children or work with children. The course was designed to increase awareness about the dangers of online radicalization and to equip the women so that they could identify the signs of radicalization and discuss with youths the material that they may encounter online.[14]

The fifth and final component of Prevent aims to address grievances that extremists use to mobilize support by reducing discrimination and inequality. In addition, the British government promotes discussion about its foreign policy so that it can explain and rebut extremists' criticisms.[15]

Countering the Radical Message

Effective communication with target audiences is a key part of the British counterterrorism approach. The Research, Information and Communications Unit (RICU), composed of personnel from the Home Office, the Foreign and Commonwealth Office, and the Department of Communities and Local Government, is the organization charged with developing a single interdepartmental approach to implementing the strategic communication component of CONTEST-2. To fine-tune the government's message, RICU is trying to understand audiences in more detail, in terms of both demographics and attitudes. To this end, it has carried out studies of attitudes toward violence, the state, extremism, and media consumption and has developed meth-

---

[13] UK Department for Communities and Local Government, *Building Community Resilience: Prevent Case Studies*, London, December 2009, pp. 5–7. Some of the London 7/7 suicide bombers had frequented the center, however. According to a British media report, a concerned worker at the center notified the police of his suspicions that it had been exploited as a front for the radicalization of young Muslims (Russell Jenkins, "Killers May Have Been Recruited at Youth Centre," *Sunday Times*, July 16, 2005).

[14] UK Department for Communities and Local Government, 2009, pp. 14–16.

[15] HM Government, 2009, p. 91.

odologies to identify which channels are most effective to reach audiences with the government's message and to evaluate the effect on the intended audiences.[16]

The goal of the communication strategy is to engage target audiences on issues that are relevant to them and to try to influence attitudes based on a shared starting point. For instance, what should the authorities be saying to reach these audiences most effectively? And what are the most effective channels to deliver these messages? These channels need not be exclusively media; they also include local practitioners and trusted parties in the communities.[17]

Partners: Moderate British Muslim Organizations

Because the British government recognized that it could not directly challenge Islamist extremism, Prevent emphasizes supporting "those who can best explain how to rebut it."[18] In practice, this entails the British authorities partnering with mainstream Muslim organizations and providing them with the funds to disseminate their message. For the first few years of CONTEST, British authorities chose to work with ostensibly nonviolent Islamist-dominated organizations, such as the Muslim Council of Britain.[19] The underlying assumption in this approach was that Salafis and conservative Muslims are more likely to

---

[16] Head of research and knowledge management, RICU, interview with Angel Rabasa, London, November 2009. See the RICU reports British Muslim Media Consumption Report, London, March 2010a; Counter-Terror Message Testing: Qualitative Research Report, London, March 2010b; Credible Voices: Exploring Perceptions of Trust and Credibility in Muslim Communities, London, March 2010c; Understanding Perceptions of the Terms "Britishness" and "Terrorism," London, March 2010d; Young British Muslims Online, London, March 2010e.

[17] See the previously mentioned RICU reports.

[18] HM Government, Pursue Prevent Protect Prepare: The United Kingdom's Strategy for Countering International Terrorism, Annual Report, March 2010b, p. 12.

[19] For more on the decision to work with Salafis, see James Brandon, "The UK's Experience in Counter-Radicalization," CTC Sentinel, Vol. 1, No. 5, April 2008. See also Vidino, 2009, pp. 65–71.

have the credibility to effectively undermine violent Islamists and can also supply better intelligence on extremists.[20]

Critics of this approach, on the other hand, maintain that engagement with Islamists and Salafis would only empower groups that espouse beliefs contrary to British values and that Salafist organizations, even if they do not formally espouse violence, function as conveyor belts to violent extremism.[21] More recently, there has been a noticeable shift in the approach of some British government agencies. The government's lead agency for engaging the Muslim community, the Department of Communities and Local Government, has sought to shift the government's engagement with the Muslim community away from conservative Salafist organizations and toward liberal and Sufi groups. CONTEST-2 seeks to "challenge views which fall short of supporting violence and are within the law, but which reject and undermine our shared values and jeopardise community cohesion."[22] The former Labour Party government's Home Secretary, Jacqui Smith, argued that the government must challenge nonviolent Islamists who "skirt the fringes of the law . . . to promote hate-filled ideologies."[23]

Although Islamists and extremist groups and individuals have long been operating in the United Kingdom, Britain is also home to moderate Muslim organizations as well as notable moderate Muslim intellectuals and community leaders who are well acquainted with and supportive of liberal Western values and institutions. Of the various Muslim organizations in the United Kingdom, the one with the most liberal coloration is Progressive British Muslims. Progressive British Muslims was launched after the July 2005 London bombings to pro-

---

[20] Robert Lambert, "Empowering Salafis and Islamists Against al-Qaeda: A London Counterterrorism Case Study," *PS: Political Science and Politics*, Vol. 41, No. 1, January 2008; Robert Lambert, "Salafi and Islamist Londoners: Stigmatised Minority Faith Communities Countering al-Qaida," *Crime Law and Social Change*, Vol. 50, Nos. 1–2, September 2008.

[21] For more on the conveyer belt and firewall arguments, see Marc Lynch "Islam Divided Between Salafi-Jihad and the Ikhwan," *Studies in Conflict and Terrorism*, Vol. 33, No. 6, June 2010, p. 468.

[22] HM Government, 2009, p. 81.

[23] Quoted in Alan Travis, "Time to Tackle the Non-Violent Extremists, Says Smith," *Guardian*, December 11, 2008.

vide a voice for progressive British Muslims who felt unrepresented by existing Muslim groups. The group's goal is to work with the central government and local authorities to combat violent extremism, promote Muslim integration into British society, and advance liberal values, such as gender equality, freedom of speech, respect for all faiths, human rights, and democracy.[24]

Another moderate organization, the British Muslim Forum, is an umbrella group launched in March 2005 with some 250 affiliated mosques and other organizations.[25] The forum claims to be the voice of traditional Sunni Islam, which incorporates Sufism. It has the largest share of elected seats in the UK's Mosques and Imams National Advisory Board. The group supported the British government's decision to ban the radical groups al-Muhajiroun and Islam4UK in January 2010, but it also urged the government to look for long-term solutions by addressing the structural inequalities and grievances felt by the majority of mainstream Muslims and to consider banning those far-right organizations that promote racism and hatred and incite violence.[26]

The Sufi Muslim Council was launched with British government support in July 2006 to challenge the Islamist-dominated Muslim Council of Britain's claim to represent British Muslims. The Sufi Muslim Council seeks to reconcile traditional Islamic scholarship with contemporary society and provides advice to British Muslims on practical matters based on traditional Islamic teachings. The council condemns terrorism in all forms and declared its intention to educate British policymakers, agencies, academia, and media outlets on the irreconcilable differences between traditional Islam and the radical tenets of extremist groups and to work with all organizations to discourage and disrupt the promulgation of extremist Islamist ideology within the Muslim community at home and abroad.[27]

---

[24] For more on the group, see Progressive British Muslims, homepage, undated.

[25] "British Muslim Forum: Sufis Rise," *MPACUK: Muslim Discussion Forum*, April 28, 2005.

[26] For more on the group, see British Muslim Forum, homepage, undated.

[27] Sufi Muslim Council, "Sufi Muslim Council's Core Principles," web page, undated.

Ruth Kelly, the former Labour Party government's Secretary of State for Communities, Conservative, and Liberal Democrat members of parliament, as well as Anglican clergy and members of the Jewish community, attended the Sufi Muslim Council's launching ceremony. Communities Secretary Kelly welcomed the council's core principles condemning terrorism in all its forms and its partnership approach to taking forward joint initiatives and activities.[28]

Faith Matters is another British NGO fighting radicalization. It is run by Fiyaz Mughal, a councillor of the London Borough of Haringey from 2006 to 2010 who was previously a councillor in Oxford. He is deputy president of the Liberal Democrat Party, the coalition partner of the current British government. Mughal has also campaigned heavily for black and minority ethnic groups' inclusion in political parties and discourse. He was appointed to the Working Group for Communities, which was linked to the Extremism Task Force developed in 2005 after the London bombings, and was the chair of the Ethnic Minority Liberal Democrats from 2002 to 2006.[29]

The Quilliam Foundation, a London-based Muslim counterextremism think tank established by two former members of Hizb ut-Tahrir, Ed Husain and Maajid Nawaz, is one of the most active and certainly the most visible British Muslim group involved in counterradicalization. The Quilliam Foundation carries out research, training, and outreach activities to advance its agenda of providing an alternative to Islamism and encouraging Islamists to return to mainstream Islam.[30] Ed Husain said that Quilliam was established, in part, to explain the distinction between Islam, a religion, and Islamism, a political ideology. Before Quilliam began its work in 2007, he said, Islam was synonymous with Islamism in the United Kingdom. The Islamist-dominated Muslim Council of Britain was the British government's preferred interlocutor in the Muslim community. Husain believes that there has been a change in the British public sphere, much of it due to Quilliam exposing what Islamism is. He said that this change was

---

[28] Dominic Casciani, "Minister Backs New Muslim Group," BBC News, July 19, 2006.

[29] Faith Matters, "Board of Directors," web page, undated.

[30] Quilliam Foundation, "About Us," web page, undated(a).

evident in the language in the CONTEST-2 document and Quilliam's influence would also be reflected in the Prevent review.

The other goal in establishing the Quilliam Foundation was to develop a Muslim identity that is at home in the West. This, Husain believes, is a tougher line of work than drawing distinctions between Islam and Islamism. In addition to contesting Islamists, Quilliam has been at the forefront of the fight against what Husain calls anti-Islam forces. Otherwise, he said, Islam would be defended only by Islamists.

Explaining the Quilliam Foundation's work program, Husain said he disagrees with the assumption that Muslims can only be reached in Muslim venues. He said that he has written for the mainstream media and toured university campuses. Every six months, he added, the foundation organizes gatherings at St. Paul's Cathedral for young Muslim thinkers to discuss such issues as freedom of conscience and the Muslim community's relations with the media, the police, and the Jewish community. He said that Quilliam has also helped facilitate access by Muslim activists to high British government and political circles.[31]

According to Ghaffar Hussain, head of outreach and training for the Quilliam Foundation, the foundation's work consists of the following:[32]

- *Media activities.* It disseminates articles in the mainstream British media and through electronic media.
- *Training.* It trains national and local government personnel and police. Hussain noted that Quilliam even held a two-day workshop in the United States (in West Virginia) to train U.S. Department of Homeland Security and U.S. Immigration and Customs Enforcement personnel on radicalization awareness.
- *Work in academic institutions.* The foundation's work in this area is usually at institutions of higher education. For instance, Hussain mentioned his presentation at the London program of Syracuse University on the promotion of pluralism.

---

[31] Ed Husain, interview with Angel Rabasa, London, September 2010.

[32] Ghaffar Hussain, interview with Angel Rabasa, London, November 2009.

- *Community events.* A community event in the north of England included a morning session with local imams, followed by an afternoon session with stakeholders (teachers, politicians, police, and local government officials). The themes discussed included terrorism, the Islamic state, Muslims in politics, and homosexuality.
- *Debating Islamists.* Quilliam Foundation personnel also engage in public debates with Islamists. Ghaffar Hussain mentioned, for instance, that Ed Husain had debated the prominent Muslim intellectual Tariq Ramadan, grandson of Muslim Brotherhood founder Hassan al-Banna.

Assessing Quilliam's impact on the British Muslim scene, Ed Husain noted that when the Quilliam Foundation was established, it was very much an outsider, under attack by Islamists who accused it of being an agent of the government and Zionists. Currently, there is greater acceptance on the part of the Muslim community, and Quilliam is central to the discussion of Islam in Britain. Now, he added, the foundation is in regular communication with the Muslim Council of Britain (which, Husain said, is seeking to reposition itself to regain its relevance).[33]

The Quilliam Foundation is active in Pakistan. Quilliam co-director Maajid Nawaz leads the foundation's events in Pakistan. In 2009, Nawaz embarked on a lecture tour of universities in that country. His purpose was to try to dispel the idea that the Iraq War was a war on Islam and articulate how this was a very simplistic reading of a very complicated situation. (Years earlier, as a member of Hizb ut-Tahrir in Britain, Nawaz had helped establish Hizb ut-Tahrir in Pakistan.[34])

While these groups are engaged in countering Islamist ideology, none appears to be involved in deradicalization per se, with the possible exception of the Active Change Foundation (ACF), an NGO based in Waltham Forest, a mixed neighborhood in London's North End with a predominantly ethnic Pakistani and African population. ACF works with young people at risk of radicalization and is led by individuals

---

[33] Ed Husain, interview with Angel Rabasa, London, September 2010.

[34] Ghaffar Hussain, interview with Angel Rabasa, London, November 2009.

with personal experience with gang culture and religious extremism: the brothers Hanif and Imtiaz Qadir and Mike Jervis, a Briton of Afro-Caribbean ancestry who was previously the Waltham Forest Council's violent-crime lead officer. Hanif Qadir, who is ACF's Prevent Violent Extremism director, is a former extremist who traveled to Pakistan in 2002 to participate in the fighting in Afghanistan but became disillusioned by his experience and turned against violent extremism.[35]

ACF staff work in direct personal contact with disaffected young people and use an approach they call "chaos management" to deal with disorder in disaffected communities. There are three elements in the approach: (1) recognition of the reality of the problem, (2) adoption of a change strategy tailored to the particular nature of the problem and the needs of those involved, and (3) transformation of the individuals involved through the employment of diversion techniques (e.g., deprogramming, personal intervention).[36]

The ACF methodology is as follows: The social services provided by the foundation—the social center, the gym, the boxing club—are the means used to "filter" (i.e., identify) young people at risk of radicalization. ACF's outreach team (staff members from different walks of life) collects more information on the individual. For instance, who are his friends? What are his beliefs? What drives him? On the basis of that information, the team develops a targeted intervention. It brings together a group of young people, including some of the individual's friends, so that the targeted person does not feel singled out. The program lasts three to four days and involves what Hanif calls "cohesion work"—that is, physical and intellectual activities designed to build group cohesion. During this time, more information is collected about the targeted individual's thoughts and beliefs. Once the main driver of the target's radicalization (what Hanif calls the individual's "Achilles' heel") is identified, the individual is confronted about his (violent) beliefs and the likely consequences of those beliefs.

---

[35] Camilla Cavendish, "From Drug Dealer to Bomber in Weeks," *Times* (London), July 12, 2007. For more on the ACF, see Active Change Foundation, homepage, undated.

[36] Active Change Foundation, undated.

Hanif said that he uses theology in his interventions, as well as cultural, intellectual, and emotional arguments and tools, depending on the driver of radicalization. For instance, he draws on his own experience in Afghanistan. He tells participants that he was supposed to join a holy war, but there wasn't anything holy about the hypocrisy of the commanders who, he says, treated certain favored groups (Arabs) better than others and used the rank and file as cannon fodder. If the subject of the intervention is incensed about the occupation of Muslim lands, he tells him that he is right to be upset about Palestine, Iraq, or Afghanistan but that the response should be through nonviolent means. If the grievance has to do with some perceived insult to Islam, he cites episodes from the life of the Prophet Muhammad showing how Muhammad suffered insults during his lifetime but did not retaliate with violence. (There are times, he said, when retaliation is required, but only for specific reasons. The Prophet always displayed wisdom, he noted.)

Hanif asserts that the most devout young people are not necessarily the most at risk of radicalization. Youths who are not disenfranchised and do not come from dysfunctional families are drawn into a militant mindset because of the belief that there is a crusade against Islam by the West. He said that this is because of the way in which the war on terrorism has been conducted, the number of civilian casualties in Iraq and Afghanistan, and statements by Western leaders. When young people believe that there is a war against Islam, Hanif added, even those who know nothing about their faith sign up for the jihad. Most, he said, join before they discover their faith. Once they join, theology is given to them in small doses, together with videos of violence against Muslims in Palestine and Iraq.

Hanif said that he tries to take the violence out of this perspective but takes a nuanced view of what constitutes extremism. If the government wants to define the goal as preventing extremism in general rather than preventing violent extremism, then he would need to know how extremism is defined and what level of extremism must be addressed. If the government wants to prevent all forms of extremism, he said, then it wants a miracle. If a young man wants to go abroad to wage jihad, in Kashmir or Afghanistan, for example, Hanif would neither endorse nor condemn it. He would ask the young man to consider his decision carefully and not to be hypocritical. (For instance, he should not take advantage of his privileges as a British citizen if his goal is to fight against British troops in Afghanistan.) He would also ask where the authority of the commanders to wage jihad comes from. A legitimate jihad, he suggested, requires an emir or legitimate ruler and proper rules of engagement.[37]

It is important to note how diverse these organizations are. Some are secular and others are religious. Some, like the Quilliam Foundation, seek to influence public attitudes and the policy debate, while others, like ACF, operate at the grassroots level to rehabilitate youths at risk; yet, all are equally committed to fighting violent extremism. Perhaps this is the right approach: partnering with many organizations, as each could do the job from a different angle. If radicalization is a highly individualized path, a variety of approaches should be used to counter radicalization.[38]

Evaluation

The effectiveness of the Prevent programs has been the subject of considerable controversy. Some critics note that the relationship between Prevent Violent Extremism programs and terrorism prevention is weak. Criticism has also been levied at the lack of community involvement in local authorities' decisions about Prevent programs, the opaqueness of the local authorities' decisionmaking processes, a lack of understanding of the Muslim communities on the part of local authorities, and Muslim perceptions of being targeted by counterterrorism measures.[39]

A confidential briefing paper prepared by the Quilliam Foundation for the incoming Cameron government, which was subsequently

---

[37] Hanif Qadir, interview with Angel Rabasa, London, September 2010.

[38] The diversity of these organizations was brought to our attention by this monograph's reviewer, Lorenzo Vidino.

[39] Rachel Briggs, "Community Engagement for Counterterrorism: Lessons from the United Kingdom," *International Affairs*, Vol. 86, No. 4, July 2010, pp. 976–979. Largely the same criticisms are made in Jamie Bartlett and Jonathan Birdwell, *From Suspects to Citizens: Preventing Violent Extremism in a Big Society*, London: Demos, July 2010.

leaked to the press, provided a forthright assessment of Prevent's achievements and shortcomings. The paper noted that CONTEST-2, the update of the UK's counterterrorism strategy, expanded Prevent's mandate from challenging only those who promote violent extremism to targeting nonviolent but extremist ideologies as well. In the Quilliam Foundation's view, however, implementing this strategy turned out to be more difficult than formulating it. The paper also noted that although the top tier of the British government understood that Islamist ideology is at the root of violent extremism, the government has been unable to fully implement a strategy based on this understanding. This is because of interdepartmental rivalries, a lack of knowledge of Islamism among key civil servants, recruitment of Islamists to positions in central and local government, successful Islamist lobbying against Prevent among British Muslims, politically driven opposition to Prevent, and a lack of enthusiasm among some local councils and other governmental bodies engaged in counterextremism work.[40]

Although no doubt some of these criticisms are valid, in comparison with terrorism prevention programs in other countries, Prevent is almost unique in its comprehensiveness and sophistication—a response consistent with the elevated level of Islamist terrorist threats that the United Kingdom confronts. As it has been noted, other governments (and the European Union) have looked to CONTEST-2 as a model for their own counterterrorism approaches.[41] The establishment of RICU was a commendable initiative to coordinate and evaluate the impact of the British government's message.

The argument that Prevent disproportionally targets Muslims appears to reflect a campaign by Islamists to discredit the program. In any event, the view that the broad focus of the current approach should be replaced with "a more precise focus on individuals that have the intent to commit criminal acts" (i.e., violent extremists)[42] may be difficult to operationalize and would be a step backward in developing a comprehensive response to Islamist extremism. As a practical matter,

---

[40] Quilliam Foundation, *Preventing Terrorism: Where Next for Britain?* London, undated(b).

[41] Quilliam Foundation, undated(b), p. 3.

[42] Bartlett and Birdwell, 2010, p. 4.

the authorities may not be able to identify prospective terrorists before they cross the line from extremism to violent radicalization. And to the extent that terrorism is ideologically driven or justified, it is appropriate to target the extremist ideology.

That is not to say that there is no room for improvement in Prevent. The Quilliam Foundation briefing paper, for instance, offers pointed criticism of the performance of the British government agencies involved in the program. It notes that the Home Office's work has occasionally been marred by its choice of partners, including an overreliance on Islamists, that RICU's output has been undermined by politically correct terminology, that the police's understanding of Islamism is low or lacking altogether, that the Department of Communities and Local Government has failed to provide adequate direction to local councils about who should be involved in Prevent work and what they should be doing, that the Mosques and Imams National Advisory Board has failed to deliver meaningful results, and that universities are currently excluded from the risk assessments carried out with Prevent funding, although they are potential hubs of extremism.[43]

Prevent activities also go on in prisons. There are more than 10,000 Muslim prisoners in England and Wales, representing more than 12 percent of the overall prison population. About 100 are convicted terrorists or suspects. A prison environment can increase the risk of radicalization among Muslim inmates, but it can also provide the authorities with the tools to promote deradicalization. These tools include the selection of prison imams. The security services conduct background checks on imams before they are allowed to minister to Muslim inmates, and prison authorities insist that the imams speak English at the prisons and translate all texts from Arabic to English to ensure that they do not contain radical messages.[44]

---

[43] Quilliam Foundation, undated(b), pp. 14–30.

[44] Richard Ford, "Jail Imams Vetted by Security Services and Muslim Books Screened for Code," *Times* (London), February 26, 2007.

The Netherlands

There are approximately 900,000 Muslims in the Netherlands, accounting for 5.8 percent of the country's population. Official statistics and census data in the Netherlands do not include religion, so ethnic background is used as a proxy. The three largest non-Western population groups are "Turks" (including Kurds), "Surinamese," and "Moroccans." The Turkish and Moroccan inhabitants are predominantly Muslim (95 percent and 97 percent, respectively), as is an unknown proportion of the Surinamese.[45] The majority of Muslims in the Netherlands live in the four major cities. In Amsterdam, Muslims account for approximately 13 percent of the city's population of about 750,000.[46] There are also significant Muslim communities in Rotterdam, The Hague, and Utrecht.

Historically, the Dutch evolved a specific model of multiculturalism that they refer to as a "pillar society." The pillar system flourished after World War II until the late 1960s. Every pillar had its own media (newspapers, radio, and TV channels), sports clubs, pension funds, labor unions, political parties, retirement homes, and schools. There was a socialist pillar, a Protestant Christian pillar, a Roman Catholic pillar, and a liberal pillar. The pillar system began to disintegrate in the 1960s and had ceased to exist by the 1990s. The model was picked up again by academics and left-wing politicians as they tried to integrate Muslims as a parallel society in the Netherlands. The expectation was that the Muslim community would form a new pillar alongside the majority culture.[47]

---

[45] Froukje Demant, Marcel Maussen, and Jan Rath, *Muslims in the EU: Cities Report—The Netherlands*, New York: Open Society Institute, EU Monitoring and Advocacy Program, 2007. These ethnic categories apply to people of Turkish or Moroccan nationality, immigrants with Dutch citizenship or dual citizenship, and people who were born and raised in the Netherlands but had at least one parent who was born abroad.

[46] Razia Tajjudin, "Islam in Amsterdam," Euro-Islam.info, undated.

[47] The authors are indebted to Ronald Sandee for this description of the pillar system in the Netherlands. Sandee notes that among the reasons for the failure in applying the pillar model to Muslims is that Dutch Muslims themselves are "pillarized" along ethnic lines (correspondence from Ronald Sandee, director of analysis and research, NEFA Foundation, August 10, 2010).

Over time, it became evident that integration was not taking place and that large, closed communities were emerging, isolated from Dutch society; young populations were alienated not just from the majority society but from their own communities as well. A survey undertaken by the Institute for Migration and Ethnic Studies in the fall of 2006 suggests that up to 2 percent of the country's Muslim population is prone to radicalization or predisposed due to conservative religious views in conjunction with a conviction that Islam is under attack and must be defended.[48]

The assassination of controversial film director Theo Van Gogh by a radicalized second-generation Dutch Muslim of Moroccan ancestry in November 2004 catalyzed a debate over the Dutch model of multiculturalism. (Van Gogh had directed the film *Submission*, from a script by Somali-born Dutch member of parliament and feminist Ayaan Hirsi Ali, which dealt with violence against women in Muslim societies and in which Quranic verses were projected on the body of the female narrator.) Van Gogh's killing generated a backlash against liberal immigration policies and the growing Muslim presence in the Netherlands. Even before the killing, the Dutch security services had warned about the danger of radicalization among young Dutch Muslims and the need to address the manifestations of radicalization that, while not directly violent, fostered violence and were harmful to the democratic legal order.[49]

Key Features of the Dutch Counter-Radicalization Approach

Dutch authorities link the process of radicalization and what they refer to as social polarization.[50] The first is defined as "the willingness to

---

[48] Council of the European Union, 2005, p. 28. The Dutch estimate that 2 percent of the country's Muslims may be prone to radicalization may be too low. Other experts believe that the figure may be closer to 4 or 5 percent (correspondence from Ronald Sandee, director of analysis and research, NEFA Foundation, August 10, 2010).

[49] General Intelligence and Security Service, Communications Department, *Annual Report 2003*, The Hague: Dutch Ministry of the Interior and Kingdom Relations, July 2004.

[50] Anne Frank House, *Racism and Extremism Monitor: Eighth Report, Leiden, the Netherlands*, 2008, Chapter 7; Dutch Ministry of the Interior and Kingdom Relations, *Polarisation and Radicalisation Action Plan: 2007–2011*, 2007.

strive for far-reaching changes in society (possibly in an undemocratic manner), to support such changes or persuade others to accept them." Dutch authorities describe the second as "the sharpening of differences between groups in society which can result in tensions between these groups and an increase in segregation along ethnic and religious lines."[51] Neither is defined in terms of religion or religious ideology. The Dutch government views radicalization mainly as a youth phenomenon that occurs when isolated individuals are searching for an identity and their place in society. When a society is polarized, conflicts and misunderstandings arise that result in radicalization and, subsequently, terrorism.

Since the Dutch attribute radicalization to sociopolitical issues, not religion, their counter-radicalization strategy specifically aims to enhance social cohesion by facilitating the integration of alienated groups into mainstream society.[52] The Dutch Polarization and Radicalization Action Plan for the period 2007–2011 is seen primarily as the responsibility of local government. However, the national government sets the general parameters of the counter-radicalization strategy, is responsible for training individuals working to combat radicalization, and partially funds the initiatives. Moreover, central authorities try to address some of the grievances that make individuals susceptible to radicalization by, for instance, reducing discrimination, facilitating employment, providing fair access to government housing, bolstering safety, providing access to health care, and ensuring that all citizens participate in the democratic process.

The plan outlines a three-track approach, the bulk of which is seen as the responsibility of local governments. The first track involves prevention, signaling, and intervention. These actions are to be implemented by local youth workers, truancy officers, the police, and other authorities and are embedded in the municipal or local government's security policy. The second track refers to specific policies at the national level in support of local counter-radicalization policy. The third concerns the international level, with a twin focus on mitigating radi-

---

[51] Dutch Ministry of the Interior and Kingdom Relations, 2007.

[52] Dutch Ministry of the Interior and Kingdom Relations, 2007, pp. 4–5.

calization and polarization within and outside the European Union's boundaries, as well as ascertaining congruency between the national counter-radicalization policy and Dutch foreign political objectives.[53]

At the local level, the *Polarisation and Radicalisation Action Plan* uses hard-line and soft-line measures to prevent radicalization, to identify signals of extremism so that the government can intervene to help those who are in the process of radicalizing, and to repress extremists that have already broken the law.[54] The soft component may include encouraging open debate about conflicting viewpoints on Muslim television programs and Muslim websites funded by the government, organizing public gatherings to discuss differing opinions, extra support for individuals who end up on the margins of the educational system, and facilitating their entry into the labor market. The soft approach is similar to the traditional British practice of neighborhood policing and may even go a step beyond in that it actively seeks to use multiple actors to engage the target community, not just the police. The hard component includes a range of disciplinary and enforcement measures, up to and including the interdiction of politically violent groups or individuals. As part of the hard approach, there has been a significant expansion of the Dutch General Intelligence and Security Service and harsher laws against those who support terrorism or plan to commit acts of violence.[55]

Special emphasis is given to school dropouts. Within the Moroccan community, many male dropouts end up in the criminal circuit and are involved in drug trafficking, petty crime, and pimping. This is also the group most vulnerable to radicalization.[56] Local authorities seek to reintegrate these vulnerable youths into the educational or

---

[53] Dutch Ministry of the Interior and Kingdom Relations, 2007, p. 11.

[54] Dutch Ministry of the Interior and Kingdom Relations, 2007, p. 6.

[55] Froukje Demant and Beatrice De Graaf, "How to Counter Radical Narratives: Dutch Deradicalization Policy in the Case of Moluccan and Islamic Radicals," *Studies in Conflict and Terrorism*, Vol. 33, No. 5, May 2010, p. 417.

[56] Correspondence from Ronald Sandee, director of analysis and research, NEFA Foundation, August 10, 2010.

vocational track through a series of measures, such as establishing so-called neighborhood boarding schools.

Ultimately, the proponents of the dual hard- and soft-line approach seek to balance prevention with repression and to recognize the drivers of radicalization at an early stage. The principal message is that "citizens accept that the Netherlands is an open, pluralistic society where various relationships and lifestyles exist side by side."[57]

The features of this strategy are indicative of the intellectual framework in which these policies were developed. Religious actors and religion are only involved in the programs as stakeholders, but not because radicalization is considered a religious issue. Dutch society is so secularized that it is difficult for Dutch officials to identify with the religious framework of Muslim communities or to understand the religious motivations of Islamist radicals.[58] Dutch authorities treat the process and the polarization phenomenon as a by-product of a social malfunction that they seek to redress by reinforcing social cohesion and managing a multicultural environment.[59] From this perspective, the government's approach to counter-radicalization is the same for right-wing, left-wing, and religious extremists.[60] A guiding thread of these programs lies in strengthening the links between vulnerable individuals and society, avoiding marginalization and exclusion, and helping these individuals to refine their identity and locate their "place in Dutch society."[61] As one report put it, "The goal is to create a reliable and democratic network of key actors in civil society that young people can trust and go to with questions."[62]

Within the broad parameters set by the national authorities, local governments have considerable discretion to devise their own

---

[57] Council of the European Union, 2005, p. 21.

[58] Correspondence from Ronald Sandee, director of analysis and research, NEFA Foundation, August 10, 2010.

[59] Dutch Ministry of the Interior and Kingdom Relations, 2007.

[60] Anne Frank House, 2008, Chapter 11.

[61] Anne Frank House, 2008, Chapter 7.

[62] Slotervaart Council, *Progress Report: Slotervaart Action Plan—Countering Radicalisaton*, Amsterdam, February 2008, p. 5.

approaches to countering radicalization. The soft-line component of the Dutch action plan relies on municipal governments' intimate knowledge of the areas in which to analyze their particular situation and their ability to craft specific policies that address their constituencies' needs. Local authorities work with community-based organizations to increase social cohesion by empowering individuals and promoting alternative ideas to radicalism.[63] In implementing programs aimed at making at-risk individuals feel a part of Dutch society, each municipality has its own unique methods to counter extremism. Next, we examine the approaches taken by the borough of Slotervaart and the cities of Amsterdam and Rotterdam.

The Slotervaart Action Plan

In reviewing the implementation of the Dutch counter-radicalization approach, we focus on the Slotervaart Action Plan, named for an Amsterdam borough with a significant immigrant population. In 2002, out of a total population of approximately 44,000, the borough had 11,000 residents with a Muslim (Moroccan or Turkish) background.[64] Several members of the radical Islamist Hofstad group grew up there, including Theo Van Gogh's assassin, Mohammed Bouyeri. Crime and unemployment are significantly higher than the national average, and one in three young people is a high-school dropout. Violence erupted in the borough in 2006 as rioters burned cars after an incident in which police killed a young man of Moroccan descent who ran into a police station and stabbed a female officer.[65]

In the aftermath of the incident, local authorities implemented a series of programs to curb tensions and prevent additional violence. The projects were driven by Ahmed Marcouch, who became the first Muslim council chairman of Slotervaart in 2006. A Moroccan immi-

---

[63] Lorenzo Vidino, "A Preliminary Assessment of Counter-Radicalization in the Netherlands," *CTC Sentinel*, Vol. 1, No. 9, August 2008, p. 12.

[64] Edien Bartels and Inge De Jong, "Civil Society on the Move in Amsterdam: Mosque Organizations in the Slotervaart District," *Journal of Muslim Minority Affairs*, Vol. 27, No. 3, December 2007.

[65] The man, Bilal Bajaka, was said to be mentally ill and influenced by thoughts of jihad.

Amsterdam's Deradicalization Program: The Information House

In Amsterdam, the authorities believed that specific actions were needed to fill the gap between the general counter-radicalization policies of Wij Amsterdammers and the hard-line actions taken by the police and security services to apprehend terrorists. The city sought to find a way to deal with individuals who had already begun to radicalize but had not yet engaged in illegal activity. These radicalizing individuals were likely to be immune to the general prevention policies, but since they had not violated the law, repressive actions were not appropriate and would likely be counterproductive. As a result, the authorities decided to create a deradicalization program called the Informatiehuishouding (Information House) in the Department of Public Order, Safety and Security.[72]

Until it was closed in 2009, Information House was a case-level municipal warning system that collected reports of radicalization and then determined the best way to intervene. The process depended on the Information House and its employees maintaining good relationships with members of the community who were likely to notice the early warning signs of radicalization and who trusted the organization enough to report their concerns. Reporters were frequently youth workers, teachers, police officers, parole officers, and local activists, but anyone could make a report. To build up this network, Information House linked existing crime prevention networks, community organizations, local government offices, and hotlines to an informal network that was forged with Muslim communities and the frontline workers in these at-risk areas.

Once it received a report, Information House generated a preliminary assessment of the situation and turned the case over to the case management team. The case management team included Information House staff and local specialists from a number of germane fields. The team met every other week to discuss the cases and formulate an action plan tailored to each individual situation. After the members

---

[72] This section is based on Colin Mellis, "Amsterdam and Radicalisation: The Municipal Approach," in *Radicalisation in Broader Perspective, Hague: National Coordinator for Counterterrorism*, October 2007, pp. 43–47.

completed an assessment, they shared their recommendations with the initial reporter of the case, who then was responsible for implementing these actions in an effort to guide the individual or group in question back into mainstream society; Information House, in turn, provided support to the reporter during the intervention.

The course of action recommended for Islamist radicals was usually two-pronged: There was recognition of the importance of challenging the extremist ideology, but there was also a need to strengthen the individual's ties to society through employment, education, apprenticeship, or social relationships. In cases involving the early stages of radicalization, Information House found that the material or social component of the intervention—essentially, making the individual feel accepted and part of society—was sufficient to rehabilitate him or her. However, if an individual had been socialized into embracing radical Islamism, an ideological intervention was also necessary.

A credible interlocutor who was knowledgeable about both Islamic theology and democratic ideals was used to conduct the ideological intervention, which consisted of challenging the political and social underpinnings of the radical narrative as well as its theological foundation. The material/social and ideological interventions ideally occurred simultaneously. Even in cases in which the radical had not internalized extremist beliefs, Information House employed an ideological intervention in an effort to increase the person's resistance to radical ideas. Due to concerns about privacy, Information House was closed in December 2009, and there is little information about how effective its interventions were in rehabilitating radical Islamists.

Rotterdam: Get Involved or Lag Behind

In Rotterdam, which also has a significant immigrant population, the local authorities are seeking to implement a two-pronged approach to counter radicalization: a "soft" approach, based on prevention, and a "hard" approach, based on repression.[73] The city's strategy is called Get Involved or Lag Behind, and its central rationale is to encourage and

---

[73] Anne Frank House, 2008, Chapter 7.

promote citizen participation in society and to monitor and exclude those who reject integration.

The soft pillar is designed to increase interactions between the municipality and key stakeholders and seeks to accelerate integration and promote dialogue. The municipality organizes events to meet these objectives and uses subsidies to influence the actions of community-based organizations. Rotterdam has financed campaigns against discrimination, for instance, as well as workshops that help vulnerable populations integrate better.[74] This approach is designed to offer vulnerable individuals who are seeking religious and personal assistance a nonradical alternative that supports their participation in society.[75]

The hard pillar is based on a close monitoring of individuals who are susceptible of violence. As discussed previously, the municipality and the local police are on the front line. Two reporting systems allow city authorities to address potential threats: the internal police reporting system and the Information Switch Point Radicalization mechanism, which detects indicators of radicalization.[76] Information Switch Point Radicalization also allows city authorities to determine whether a particular individual poses an immediate threat to society or can still be a target of the city's softer approach to radicalization. Interactions between the two systems are limited, however.

Evaluation

The effectiveness of these policies is difficult to measure. The 2008 Slotervaart Action Plan progress report was an effort at self-evaluation by the authors of the plan. A letter from Marcouch to the borough council on August 26, 2008, stated that measurable indicators to assess the success of the programs have not been used and that it is very difficult, if not impossible, to estimate the effects on the exposure group.[77] At the national level, the Ministry of the Interior and Kingdom Rela-

---

[74] Anne Frank House, 2008, Chapter 7.

[75] Anne Frank House, 2008, Chapter 7, p. 6.

[76] Anne Frank House, 2008, Chapter 7, p. 3.

[77] Correspondence from Ronald Sandee, director of analysis and research, NEFA Foundation, August 10, 2010.

tions is seeking to develop a benchmarking method that would allow a comparison of programs across the country. Another means to measure the effectiveness of the program consists of an evaluation by independent experts.[78]

In evaluating the Dutch counter-radicalization program, it is worth taking account of political controversies relating to some of Marcouch's initiatives. Marcouch has made controversial proposals to teach Islam in public schools (as a way of monitoring and controlling the content of the teaching) and to merge boroughs with Muslim populations in Amsterdam-West. "A blooming Muslim community could arise with sufficient social capital. The Muslim minority would then become a positive point," he wrote. "New West could focus on the integration of immigrants." As the result of these proposals, and his affinity for Muslim Brotherhood ideologue Yusuf Qaradawi, Marcouch has been accused of pursuing an Islamization agenda. One of three Slotervaart borough council members who resigned from the Dutch Labour Party over Marcouch's proposal to introduce the teaching of Islam in public schools articulated this concern as follows: "We thought that we were members of a secular party, . . . but Marcouch sees it primarily as his duty as a good Muslim to propagate Islam."[79]

Marcouch's administration of the Slotervaart plan has been criticized for a lack of transparency and for enabling the Muslim Brotherhood to establish a foothold in the borough. There has been a weekly "Moroccans coordination meeting" in Marcouch's office. These meetings are not open to the public and are attended only by Marcouch, the imam, the antiradicalization expert, and other Moroccan influentials in Slotervaart. There has also been a lack of transparency regarding the funding of foundations set up to implement projects under the plan.[80]

---

[78] Dutch Ministry of the Interior and Kingdom Relations, *Operational Action Plan: Polarisation and Radicalisation*, 2008, pp. 4, 9.

[79] "Netherlands-Labour Icon Aims for 'Blooming Muslim Community' in Amsterdam West," NIS Dutch News, January 13, 2009.

[80] Correspondence from Ronald Sandee, director of analysis and research, NEFA Foundation, August 10, 2010.

There is also a notable expansion of the Muslim Brotherhood's presence. In addition to the existing Moroccan mosque, two new mosques are planned. One is the Poldermosque, an initiative of Mohammed Cheppih, the representative of the Muslim World League, which is part of the international Muslim Brotherhood. The second mosque is the FION Mosque, the first mosque of the Federation of Islamic Organizations in the Netherlands (FION), the Muslim Brotherhood organization in the Netherlands.[81]

Denmark

There are some 200,000 Muslims in Denmark, accounting for 3.7 percent of the total Danish population of 5.4 million. Most are first-generation immigrants. The first wave of immigration occurred in the 1970s and included mostly guest workers from Turkey, Pakistan, Morocco, or Yugoslavia. In the 1980s and 1990s, there were mostly asylum seekers from Iraq, Iran, the Palestinian territories, Bosnia, and Somalia.[82] As in the Netherlands and other European countries, there has been a growing concern in the majority society about the cultural divide between ethnic Danes and Muslims and the radicalization of sectors of the Danish Muslim population. These tensions were brought to a head by the controversy over the publication by the newspaper *Jyllands-Posten* of cartoons depicting the Prophet Muhammad; the incident touched off a violent reaction in Muslim countries, which, in turn, paved the way for the rise of anti-immigration forces.

In 2009, the Danish government published an action plan for counter-radicalization titled *A Common and Safe Future: An Action Plan to Prevent Extremist Views and Radicalization Among Young People*.[83] As in many other European nations, the Danish strategy does

---

[81] Correspondence from Ronald Sandee, director of analysis and research, NEFA Foundation, August 10, 2010.

[82] Iben Helqvist and Elizabeth Sebian, "Islam in Denmark," Euro-Islam.info, undated.

[83] Government of Denmark, *A Common and Safe Future: An Action Plan to Prevent Extremist Views and Radicalisation Among Young People*, January 2009. For the proposal of the plan

not focus exclusively on radical Islamism but instead seeks to combat all forms of extremism, primarily by strengthening the country's social cohesion and its citizens' commitment to liberal democratic values. *Extremism* is defined as "totalitarian and antidemocratic ideologies, intolerance to the views of others, hostile imagery and a division into 'them' and 'us.'"[84] Like the Netherlands, Denmark views radicalism as a by-product of inadequate social integration. Consequently, the Danish government's approach is primarily to take preventive measures at both the national and, especially, the local level. These efforts focus on integrating alienated groups into mainstream Danish society and thereby enhancing social cohesion. As part of this strategy, the Danish action plan explicitly seeks to strengthen liberal democracy by educating and socializing its citizens to accept democratic norms and responsibilities.[85] In contrast to many other countries, Denmark separates its counter-radicalization efforts from its counterterrorism plan by designating beliefs as the exclusive purview of its action plan, while the security services respond only to actions taken by radicals who break the law.[86]

The Danish action plan outlines seven focus areas and 22 specific initiatives that encourage tolerance and the democratic exchange of ideas, rather than teaming up with Muslim organizations to influence religious debates. The seven focus areas are as follows:

- Establish direct contact with young people who are at risk of radicalizing or have already radicalized through mentoring programs and other interventions that aim to guide youth back into the fold of mainstream society.[87]
- Strengthen social cohesion by making citizens aware of their rights and their obligations toward others. In line with these

---

see Government of Denmark, *A Common and Safe Future: Proposal for an Action Plan to Prevent Extremist Views and Radicalisation Among Young People*, June 2008.

[84] Government of Denmark, 2009, p. 8.

[85] Government of Denmark, 2009, p. 11.

[86] Interview with an official from the Danish Foreign Ministry.

[87] Government of Denmark, 2009, pp. 12–13.

goals, the Danish government has made an increased effort to reduce discrimination, inform parents about radicalization, and involve them in their children's lives.[88]

- Facilitate dialogue and provide accurate information to the public about the dangers of extremism and about Danish values and policies. In particular, since many Muslims are critical of Danish foreign policy, the state started an outreach program to inform the public about Denmark's relations with the rest of the world, especially Muslim countries.[89]
- Enhance Denmark's democratic cohesion by bolstering civil society.[90]
- Take actions that increase the resilience of communities that are particularly vulnerable to extremism.[91]
- Counter radicalization in prisons by educating prison staff, training religious figures who work in prisons, and offering information about democracy.
- Acquire more knowledge about radicalization through further research, and establish long-term partnerships between international, national, and local governments and community organizations.[92]

In addition to this action plan, in coordination with the European Union, the Danish Ministry of Refugee Immigration and Integration Affairs has partnered with the municipalities of Aarhus and Copenhagen, the East Jutland Police District, and the Danish Security and Intelligence Service (PET) to create a pilot deradicalization program called "Deradicalisation—Targeted Intervention." This program aims to help radicalizing or radicalized young people who have not broken the law. Like other European intervention programs, the

---

[88] Government of Denmark, 2009, pp. 14–15.

[89] Government of Denmark, 2009, pp. 15–17.

[90] Government of Denmark, 2009, pp. 17–21.

[91] Government of Denmark, 2009, pp. 21–22.

[92] Government of Denmark, 2009, pp. 23–26.

Danish programs are voluntary and apply tactics used in preventing crime to countering radicalization. Since these efforts rely heavily on frontline workers in agencies such as the Schools Social Services and the police, the government has invested in training for these local officials as well as for individuals who serve as mentors to troubled youths.

The Danish deradicalization program has two components. The PET directs the first part, which encourages radicalized youth who belong to extremist organizations to exit these groups. The second component is a mentoring program for young people who have expressed extremist or discriminatory views and is jointly administered by the Ministry of Integration Affairs, the municipalities of Aarhus and Copenhagen, and the East Jutland Police District.

When the authorities are alerted to the fact that an individual seems to be radicalizing, the second part of the deradicalization program intervenes by reaching out and engaging the radicalizing youth in discussions. If the individual responds positively to this contact, the program assigns a mentor to provide emotional support and guidance. The mentor tries to convince the at-risk young person not to join a radical organization, and if he or she is already part of such a group, the mentor offers emotional support. In this case, the mentor encourages the individual to withdraw from the extremist organization and helps find positive alternative activities and organizations. Religious issues are not addressed directly.[93]

Evaluation

An early study of Muslim views of Danish counter-radicalization efforts found that many Muslims did not know about the proposed government programs, which had yet to be implemented. Another group viewed the initiatives positively but believed that they were insufficient to diminish radicalism in the community. The final and largest group viewed the efforts negatively and believed that they stigmatized Muslims through their focus on the Muslim community.[94] Since the

---

[93] Danish Ministry of Refugee, Immigration and Integration Affairs, 2010.

[94] Lene Kühle and Lasse Lindekilde, *Radicalization Among Young Muslims in Aarhus*, Aarhus, Denmark: Center for Studies in Islamism and Radicalisation, January 2010,

action plan was implemented so recently, there is very little information about how effective it has been in countering radical Islamism, but the Danish government has organized an independent, in-depth assessment of the action plan that will continue through 2013. While it is too early to evaluate it, the Danish program seems to be hindered by the fact that it refuses to directly challenge the radical ideology and instead focuses on socioeconomic and affective issues. The government acknowledges that, thus far, it has been difficult to persuade at-risk youths to participate in these deradicalization efforts.[95]

Another problem is the growing anti-immigrant sentiment in Denmark that has resulted in an anti-immigrant party gaining influence over the government.[96] As a result, the issue of religion in general and Islam in particular has become extremely politically charged. Because of this sensitivity, the government does not directly challenge the extremist ideology. Moreover, although the Danish plan focuses on intervening to help at-risk youth, since religion is a taboo topic, the deradicalization efforts do not address the ideological aspects of radical Islamism. In short, Denmark's efforts to counter extremism focus on affective issues related to social integration and only address some pragmatic concerns or socioeconomic grievances. At most, Denmark's program indirectly challenges radical ideas by promoting democratic values, but the government refrains from openly confronting radical Islamism.

Table 5.1 presents an overview of the countries and programs discussed in this chapter. In Chapter Six, we present a more in-depth discussion of collective deradicalization approaches and contrast these efforts with those that place an emphasis on individual extremists.

---

pp. 125–126.

[95] Danish Ministry of Refugee, Immigration and Integration Affairs, 2010.

[96] "Denmark and the Far Right: Fear of Foreigners," *Economist*, November 14, 2007.

Table 5.1
Overview of European Approaches

Characteristic	United Kingdom	Netherlands	Denmark
Location	Local communities	Local communities	Local communities
Size	Unknown	Unknown	Unknown
Objective	Counter-radicalization, deradicalization	Counter-radicalization, deradicalization	Counter-radicalization, deradicalization
Radicals included	Radicals who have not broken the law	Radicals who have not broken the law	Radicals who have not broken the law
Interlocutors used	Police, community leaders, local officials, local religious leaders	Police, community leaders, local officials, local religious leaders	Police, community members
Affective component	Mentors	Attempting to integrate participant into social groups; mentors	Encouraging involvement in civil society; mentors
Pragmatic component	Limited efforts to deal with macro-level grievances, such as deprivation	Help in obtaining education, vocational training, job	Development of vulnerable areas and communities
Ideological component	Backing moderate Muslim voices that discredit Salafi-jihadist ideology	Discussing religion, promoting tolerance	No discussion of religion
Postprogram	Unknown	Unknown	Unknown

CHAPTER SIX

Collective Deradicalization

One of the most important developments in the ongoing ideological competition between violent extremist and mainstream interpretations of Islam is that a number of militant Islamist organizations have renounced violence and the ideology that motivated their armed struggle. In August 2009, LIFG issued its *Corrective Studies in Understanding Jihad, Accountability and the Judgment of People*. The document was a stunning reversal for the LIFG, which was a founding member of the Arab Afghan jihadist movement that emerged during the Afghan war against the Soviets, as well as a long-standing partner of al-Qaeda.[1]

Despite the group's militant pedigree, LIFG's new manifesto concluded that "it is religiously impermissible to use violence for reform or change in Muslim countries" and that Muslims were not obligated to participate in jihad, except when infidels invade an Islamic nation.[2] Moreover, LIFG insisted that "there are ethics and morals to jihad," which include "the proscription of killing women, children, the elderly, monks, wage earners (employees), messengers (ambassadors), merchants and the like."[3] Although LIFG always maintained its independence and its national focus on overthrowing Muammar al-Qhadafi's regime, it had considerable ties to al-Qaeda and to the broader global

---

[1] For more on LIFG, see Evan F. Kohlmann, with John Lefkowitz, *Dossier: Libyan Islamic Fighting Group (LIFG)*, NEFA Foundation, October 2007, and Luis Martinez, The Libyan Paradox, New York: Columbia University Press, 2007, pp. 60–70.

[2] Mohmmed Ali-Musawi, trans., *A Selected Translation of the LIFG Recantation Document*, London: Quilliam Foundation, 2009, p. 19.

[3] Ali-Musawi, 2009, p. 18.

jihadist movement. LIFG's repudiation of its extremist ideology raises a number of questions: What impels a radical Islamic organization to disengage from terrorism and renounce its ideology? How is collective deradicalization related to individual deradicalization? Finally, what impact will LIFG's critiques of jihadist ideology have on the broader Islamist extremist movement?

Despite its potential importance, deradicalization at the organizational level has received relatively little attention in comparison to individual-level deradicalization.[4] There has been a considerable amount of work on the related but distinct topic of how terrorism ends, which overviews a litany of possible reasons that a terrorist organization may forgo violence.[5] Nevertheless, this body of work does not explore what happens when a militant organization goes beyond disengagement from terrorism and also renounces its extremist beliefs. This chapter seeks to fill these gaps by examining the issue of collective deradicalization with a particular focus on radical Islamist groups; it also assesses the relationship between individual and collective deradicalization. Moreover, it attempts to determine whether many of the lessons learned from the study of individual disengagement and deradicalization are applicable to groups. Chapter Three provided background information about the Egyptian and Libyan governments' actions to encourage militant Islamist organizations to deradicalize. This chapter focuses on the perspective of the radical organization, particularly on the internal

---

[4]   The only major work on the subject is Omar Ashour's *The De-Radicalization of Jihadists: Transforming Armed Islamist Movements* (Ashour, 2009).

[5]   Audrey Kurth Cronin, "How Al-Qaida Ends: The Decline and Demise of Terrorist Groups," *International Security*, Vol. 31, No. 1, Summer 2006; Audrey Kurth Cronin, "Historical Patterns in Ending Terrorism," in *Ending Terrorism: Lessons for Defeating al-Qaeda*, Adelphi Papers No. 394, November 2007; United States Institute of Peace, *How Terrorism Ends*, Washington, D.C., Policy Brief, May 25, 1999; Martha Crenshaw, "Why Violence Is Rejected or Renounced: A Case Study of Oppositional Terrorism" in Thomas Gregor, ed., *A Natural History of Peace*, Nashville, Tenn.: Vanderbilt University Press, 1996; Seth G. Jones and Martin C. Libicki, *How Terrorist Groups End: Lessons for Countering al Qa'ida*, Santa Monica, Calif.: RAND Corporation, MG-741-1-RC, 2008; Jeffrey Ian Ross and Ted Robert Gurr, "Why Terrorism Subsides: A Comparative Study of Canada and the United States," *Comparative Politics*, Vol. 21, No. 4, July 1989.

decisionmaking and processes that lead a group to renounce violence and its ideology.

In doing so, this chapter makes four principal arguments. In the initial phases, collective deradicalization begins as an elite-level process among one or several key individuals. In other words, it is a process of individual deradicalization at the outset and therefore follows the same trajectory described in Chapter One. In the preliminary stage, a trigger raises doubts about the radicals' commitment to violence. For militant Islamist organizations, this always took the form of a strategic crisis resulting from successful efforts to repress the group. When counter-terrorism measures lead to the apprehension and detention of a large number of key members, the group's leaders are forced to reconsider their tactics, which in the following (deliberative) stage can turn into an ideological crisis.

During this period of reflection, the leaders consider the antici-pated costs and benefits of continuing versus ending the armed strug-gle. When the expected utility of deradicalization exceeds the expected utility of continued militancy (a condition that is, in part, the result of an ideological crisis and incentives proffered by the state), the lead-ers reach a turning point and decide to try to persuade the rest of the organization to accept significant revisions to its strategy and beliefs about Islam.

Second, because collective deradicalization is, by definition, a collective process, it differs from individual deradicalization in several ways. Once militant leaders abandon their ideology and embrace mod-erate reform, they must begin a process of negotiation within the wider group. In these cases, a strong and respected leader must convince the rank and file that the group's ideology was based on an incorrect inter-pretation of Islam. In effect, these persuasive leaders are the trigger for lower-level group members, who then begin to debate the merits of continuing the armed struggle.

Another important difference between individual and collective deradicalization is the impact of peer pressure and social networks. Specifically, in cases of individual deradicalization, extremists who contemplate leaving the group must withdrawal from their social sup-port structure, making the decision extremely difficult. By contrast, once an influential militant leader has convinced the majority of the group to reconsider its commitment to violence, peer pressure actually encourages recalcitrant members to conform to the new worldview.

Third, the international context is important, especially the impact of demonstration effects and the growing level of counterterrorism cooperation among states. Demonstration effects operate in two ways. An *intergroup demonstration effect* occurs when one group is deradicalized. This enables other groups, which may want to emulate the deradicalized organization, to follow suit. Because these groups share the same ideology, when one group questions that worldview, it has the potential to delegitimize it for others. Alternatively, *interstate demonstration effects* occur when successful government-run deradicalization programs by one state encourage other states to adopt similar methods. At the same time, as more and more nations cooperate in global counterterrorism efforts, the possibility that a radical group can find sanctuary abroad steadily decreases. Because state repression is a critical push factor that contributes to deradicalization at the individual level, the inability to retreat to a safe haven may increase the likelihood that extremist leaders will reexamine their commitment to armed struggle.

Fourth, individual-level and group deradicalization are complementary processes that can reinforce each other; therefore, programs are most successful when they include individuals and groups. Moreover, it appears that collective deradicalization may be a more effective way of countering Islamist extremism.[6] This is not only because collective deradicalization moderates a larger number of extremist Islamists at one time but also because it appears more likely than individual disengagement to result in a change in beliefs as well as behavior.

---

[6] Della Porta (2008, p. 85) makes the same point with regard to leftist Italian terrorism.

Similarities Between Collective and Individual Deradicalization

The processes of disengagement and deradicalization for individual Islamist extremist and violent Islamist organizations share a number of significant characteristics. Most importantly, the first three stages of individual disengagement outlined in Chapter One—a trigger that weakens the commitment to violence, a debate over the costs and benefits of leaving the group, and a turning point that occurs when a member decides whether to remain or leave—closely mirror the stages of collective disengagement and deradicalization.

Thus, although this type of organizational transformation is a collective process, it often begins when the leaders of a radical group have serious misgivings about the efficacy of their actions and start to question the viability of the group's strategy.[7] Both the specific type of trigger and the circumstances that lead radicals to begin doubting their beliefs are very similar in cases of individual and collective deradicalization. As described earlier, a *strategic crisis*—that is, a reexamination of a group's methods due to state repression—is one possible trigger that can precipitate individual disengagement. Not surprisingly, then, a number of authors have established that extremists often leave violent Islamic organizations because of doubts that the group's goals can be achieved.[8]

This factor also plays a major role in the decision by militant Islamist organizations to abandon violence and recant their prior beliefs. In fact, a strategic crisis appears to be the most important and, perhaps, the only trigger in these cases. For instance, the leaders of each of the armed Islamic groups that have deradicalized—IG, EIJ, and LIFG—did so only after the vast majority of the group's key members (i.e., activists and the hard core) were imprisoned and it became clear

---

[7]   Ashour also emphasizes the importance of leadership (see Ashour, 2009, p. 15).

[8]   Demant et al., 2008, p. 155. This is also true of other terrorist organizations (see Della Porta, 2008, pp. 69–72).

that they were going to remain incarcerated for the foreseeable future.[9] Former LIFG leader Noman Benotman concluded, "It is very unlikely that any armed group would voluntarily change their ideology without their activities first being reduced physically through force."[10]

Under these conditions, the failure of the group to realize its goals becomes readily apparent, the prospects for reversing that failure in the near future appear minimal, and, as a result, militant leaders may begin to question the effectiveness of their ideological commitments. Similarly, IG leader Nagih Ibrahim's comments reflect that his group's moderation was, in part, a response to its inability to realize its objectives: "Jihad is not an end by itself. It is just a means to attain other ends. If you cannot attain these ends through jihad you should change the means."[11]

In these cases, once a trigger emerged, the leaders of the radical organization began a period of internal deliberation. When presented by credible interlocutors—usually accomplished Islamic scholars, or ex-militants—mainstream Islamic theology served to push the militant leaders to disengage and deradicalize by raising questions about their ideology. Mainstream Islamic teachings pulled the leaders toward moderation by offering them a chance to redeem themselves in the eyes of God, as well as a way to justify the strategic and ideological shift to their followers. Because Islamic jurisprudence prohibits many types of jihad, the militant leaders could present the organization's moderation as a correction of past beliefs that were the result of a misreading of Islamic theology.

Like many of the individuals who have defected from radical Islamist organizations, in many cases, the leaders of these groups had little formal religious training; if they were educated, they usually

---

[9] Omar Ashour, "De-Radicalizing Jihadists the Libyan Way," *Arab Reform Bulletin*, April 7, 2010; Diaa Rashwan, "Egypt's Contrite Commander," *Foreign Policy*, March–April 2008a; Ashour, 2007, p. 621.

[10] Quilliam Foundation, "Quilliam Roundtable—Refuting Al Qaeda Former Jihadists and the Battle of Ideologies," January 11, 2010.

[11] Quoted in Ashour, 2007, p. 621.

had attended secular schools.[12] Consequently, their imprisonment afforded them the first real opportunity to study Islamic doctrine and to deeply contemplate its meaning. Former EIJ commander Kamal Habib explained that when a jihadi is "in battle, he doesn't wonder if he's wrong or he's right. When he's arrested, he has time to wonder."[13] In the case of IG, Sheikh Ali Gomaa, the Grand Mufti of Egypt, began visiting prisons in the 1990s to "hold debates and dialogues with the prisoners," which continued for years and "became the nucleus for the group's revisionist thinking."[14] Around the same time, IG founder Karam Zuhdi explained, the leadership "began to read books and reconsider" its positions on core concepts, such as jihad and *takfir*.[15]

Similarly, the Libyan government brought moderate interlocutors into the Abu Salim prison to meet with the LIGF leaders. Sheikh Ali al-Salabi was selected for this task not only because of his stature as a theologian, but also because of his reputation for independence, which made him more credible in the eyes of the Islamists.[16] In addition to Sheikh al-Salabi, the Libyan regime also employed former commander Noman Benotman as an interlocutor to discuss Islamic theology with his former comrades. Benotman attributes much of the success of the Libyan government's efforts to moderate LIFG to the shared belief in Islam and the use of Islamic teachings to persuade the militants that they had been misguided. Benotman explains that one cannot assert that "there is no jihad in Islam whatsoever"; rather, one must recognize that "jihad, it's part of Islam because it is something that's in the Koran."[17] Once this was established, the participants in the discussions could consider the specific Quaranic rulings on the practice of jihad, ultimately concluding that the jihadist teachings were incorrect.

---

[12] Rashwan, 2008b, p. 120.

[13] Quoted in L. Wright, 2008.

[14] Quoted in L. Wright, 2008.

[15] Quoted in L. Wright, 2008.

[16] Dunne, 2010; Camille Tawil, "What Next for the Libyan Islamic Fighting Group After Rebuff from the Libyan Regime," *Terrorism Monitor*, Vol. 7, No. 24, August 6, 2009.

[17] Quoted in Erin Stackelbeck, "Ex-Terrorist Takes CBN Inside Al Qaeda," CBN News, March 9, 2010.

At other times, a group's radical Islamic ideology was called into question because it demanded actions that injured Muslims or innocents. For example, both EIJ ideologue Sayyid Imam al-Sharif and LIFG member Tarek Mufteh Ghunnay cited the attacks on 9/11 as examples of jihadist actions that hurt both Muslims and undeserving victims.[18] For these radicals, a key push factor was a militant Islamic organization's indiscriminate violent attacks, which, in turn, precipitated an ideological crisis.

As a consequence of these strategic and ideological crises, there were few benefits for the leaders in remaining steadfast; they would be maintaining their position in a defeated organization guided by a theologically untenable interpretation of Islam. In short, once the leaders concluded that they could not succeed or that their ideology was incorrect, the expected utility of abandoning violence and recanting the group's ideology seemed greater than the utility of remaining committed to violent action and an unsound worldview. IG's 1997 ceasefire initiative, for instance, was in response to the historic leadership's determination that the group's armed struggle was futile and causing needless death and destruction. In these circumstances, the leadership feared that the group would splinter and its fragments would descend into a spiral of unrestrained violence, as had occurred in Algeria.[19]

Radical Islamic organizations are especially likely to disengage and deradicalize if the government offers incentives that make this course of action attractive.[20] When this is the case, it increases the probability that militant leaders will be able to obtain enough support from their followers to enact these transformations. In other words, a key component of the utility calculation that impels a militant Islamist organization to disengage and deradicalize is inducements proffered by the state. Although the Egyptian government initially did not provide such benefits to the IG leaders, it eventually did give them preferential

---

[18] Rashwan, 2008a; Borzou Daragahi, "Libya's Coup: Turning Militants Against Al Qaeda," *Los Angeles Times*, December 15, 2009.

[19] Ashour, 2009, pp. 97, 100.

[20] Ashour, 2009, p. 15.

treatment, allow them to travel to meet with the rank and file, and promise to free those who repented and renounced the ideology.[21]

Inducements seemed to play an even larger role in the case of LIFG. It was not until Muammar al-Qhadafi's son, Saif al-Islam al-Qhadafi, offered LIFG members commuted sentences in return for the renunciation of their past actions and the disbandment of their organization that they responded favorably to his overtures to negotiate with the Libyan regime.[22] Even the exiled LIFG members in Britain cited the promise to free the prisoners as the main reason that they supported the dialogue with Tripoli.[23]

If the onset of an ideological crisis helps explain cases of collective disengagement and deradicalization among radical Islamist groups, it also helps explain why these phenomena have been relatively rare and why these processes take so long when they do occur. In general, the belief that jihad is a religious obligation and that Allah will reward jihadists for their devotion in the afterlife is perhaps the most significant exit barrier that prevents individuals and organizations from abandoning violence. (It could also be a positive inducement to stay.) According to former LIFG commander Benotman, it was difficult to question the actions of armed Islamic organizations because "their political agenda is equated with Islam and therefore questioning their agenda is seen as questioning Islam."[24] Moreover, to the extent that repression is one key factor that triggers a strategic crisis among radical groups, religiously motivated organizations are extremely reluctant to acknowledge their defeat. As a result, it often takes decades for both leaders and followers to begin questioning their ideology. For instance, although IG's historic leaders had been imprisoned since 1981, they did

---

[21] Blaydes and Rubin, 2008.

[22] Frank J. Cilluffo and F. Jordan Evert, *Reflections on Jihad: A Former Leader's Perspective—An In Depth Conversation with Noman Benotman*, Washington, D.C.: George Washington University Homeland Security Policy Institute, October 16, 2009, p. 3.

[23] NEFA Foundation, trans., "An Open Speech Regarding the Details of the Dialogue Between the LIFG and the Libyan Regime," July 3, 2009, p. 2.

[24] Quilliam Foundation, 2010.

not begin to modify their position toward violence until 1997 and did not announce their ideological revisions until 2002.[25]

To summarize, effective repressive measures triggered a strategic crisis among the leadership of militant Islamic organizations, which was often followed by an ideological crisis. However, it was not until the commanders of the radical Islamic organization decided that the expected utility of disengagement and deradicalization exceeded the expected utility of militancy that they reached a turning point and embarked on a process of convincing the rest of their organization that it needed to change its beliefs as well as its behavior. This calculation may have been entirely a result of an instrumental calculation, or, for some leaders, it may have been due to a true change in their beliefs, which, in turn, altered their decision calculus.

Figure 6.1 illustrates the initial stages of the collective deradicalization process: the trigger for an ideological crisis among a group's leadership, the leadership's decision calculus, and the decision to deradicalize.

Figure 6.1
Initial Stages of Collective Deradicalization

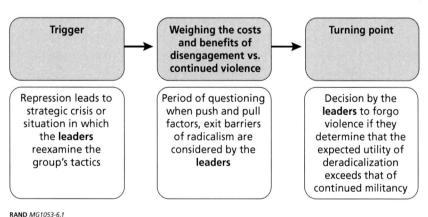

RAND *MG1053-6.1*

---

[25] Ashour 2007, p. 596, n. 1.

Differences Between Collective and Individual Deradicalization

Although there are similarities between collective and individual deradicalization, there are also important differences that should be noted. First, and most obvious, collective deradicalization is a group process that involves intragroup bargaining between the reform-minded leaders and the rest of the organization. This has a number of implications for the process of moderation, the types of change that are likely to occur, and the possibility that the group will again take up arms. Second, the international context seems to play a particularly important role in the deradicalization of militant Islamic organizations.

After the turning point—the moment at which the leaders of a militant organization agree to renounce violence—the trajectory for collective deradicalization departs from the path that is followed by individuals. It does so because the leaders cannot make such a decision alone but instead have to gain enough support within the organization to implement the desired change. The likelihood that the entire organization will moderate its behavior and its beliefs largely depends on the strength of the militant leaders, their control over the organization, and the tactics they use to build support for deradicalization.[26]

When there are capable and respected leaders who reach out to the organization's grassroots and discuss the merits of this course of action, the leadership is likely to be able to persuade significant numbers among the rank and file to support the decision. This, in turn, makes it more difficult for defiant activists to oppose deradicalization, because doing so would involve opposing their social network. At times, the leadership of a militant Islamic group may publicly declare its decision to disengage and then seek to foster support within the ranks.[27] More frequently, the leadership pursues internal deliberations before making any sort of public declaration about changes to the group's strategies or philosophy.

---

[26] Ashour (2009, pp. 137–140) argues that the leadership must be charismatic to effect such a change and that there must be social interaction within the group.

[27] This was the tactic employed by the historic leadership of IG in 1997.

During the stage of group negotiations, it is imperative that the reformers be strong and respected leaders; in the absence of this type of leadership, it is unlikely that the majority of the organization's members will accept new strategies or a revised ideology.[28] For instance, when the historic leadership of IG first announced its cease-fire in 1997, most of the organization's middle-ranking commanders opposed the initiative; nevertheless, they abided by the wishes of these venerated leaders and eventually came to accept their rationale for change.[29] By contrast, although a number of high-ranking EIJ members supported the IG cease-fire in 1997, they did not have the clout to speak for the entire group or to persuade opponents that nonviolence was the appropriate course of action.[30] It was not until 2007, when it was suddenly revealed that al-Sharif had returned to Egypt, that there was a figure within the group with enough influence to successfully lead the process of change. However, even a legendary personality like al-Sharif had to consult with rank-and-file EIJ members and incorporate their concerns into his publication revising Islamic jurisprudence on jihad.[31]

Even when capable and respected leaders spearhead the effort to moderate a radical organization's behavior and beliefs, the process is often long and difficult and usually requires the leadership to arrange numerous meeting to discuss the proposed changes with the group's followers in person. IG leader Karam Zudhi noted that many of his organization's rank-and-file members at first felt betrayed when they were informed about their leader's intentions and wondered why their commanders had not shared their reservations about the group's ideology earlier. Others accused the group's historic leadership of acting out of self-interest; these doubters suspected that their commanders were compromising their beliefs to secure their freedom. However, after the IG activists were consulted in a series of forums, many of their

---

[28] Ashour, 2009, p. 138; Rashwan, 2008b, p. 125.

[29] Ashour, 2009, p. 98.

[30] Ashour, 2009, p. 103.

[31] Ashour, 2009, p. 56.

doubts were assuaged.[32] Nevertheless, the process of gaining support for the revisions was prolonged because the leaders needed to work out numerous moral issues—ranging from core principles to minor points of interpretation—with other high-ranking commanders and with the rank and file.[33]

Although internal negotiations are often lengthy, in instances of collective deradicalization, group solidarity and emotional ties to other members encourage behavioral and ideological moderation. If respected militant leaders are able to persuade the majority of their followers to support the reforms, peer pressure and the fear of alienating one's colleagues may push doubting militants to disengage and deradicalize. By contrast, a lone individual seeking to disengage or deradicalize must defy the group and leave behind his or her social network. When radical Islamist groups deradicalize, they usually publish lengthy treatises justifying their transformation. This is notable because it has been argued that most militants who disengage from radical organizations do not alter their beliefs.[34] By contrast, most of the militant organizations that were inspired by a jihadist ideology have typically abandoned that ideology in addition to abandoning nearly all forms of violence.[35]

Deradicalization appears to be more likely in the context of a broader collective process than when a lone individual leaves a radical Islamist group that continues to exist. This seems to be at least in part a result of the fact that it is necessary for the militant Islamic leaders to convince their ideologically committed followers to approve of the reforms. Since the jihadist creed plays such an integral role in militant Islamist organizations, if the leaders want to fundamentally change the group's strategies, they must rationalize their desire to forgo violence on the basis of religion. For instance, a member of IG explained his hostility toward the 1997 cease-fire (which had not been theologically

---

[32] L. Wright, 2008.

[33] Rashwan, 2008b, p. 125.

[34] Horgan, 2009a, p. 27.

[35] An exception is the Algerian Islamic Salvation Army, which collectively disengaged but did not deradicalize. See Ashour, 2009, pp. 110–127.

justified) on the grounds that "we carried arms based on God's orders . . . we should not lay them down based on orders of humans unless they prove it to us [theologically]."[36] Moreover, by providing a religious justification, a group's leaders are better able to avoid the appearance that personal reasons motivated their recantation.

As a result of these factors, the leaders of IG, EIJ, and LIFG have claimed that they misinterpreted Islam's dictates, especially regarding the practices of jihad and *takfir*, which accounts for their organizations' past errors. This suggests that collective deradicalization may be more effective in discrediting Islamist extremism than individually focused programs that usually only result in disengagement.

Concomitantly, collective deradicalization programs may also be better able to reduce the likelihood that the rehabilitated militants reengage in violence. Collective deradicalization appears to be accompanied by low rates of recidivism because it normally results in attitudinal and behavioral moderation, and the group acts as a built-in support network for its reformed members. Although it remains difficult to establish whether the members of these militant Islamist organizations are truly deradicalized or just disengaged, when a group publishes theological justifications for its transformation, the members who accept these justifications are less likely to recidivate. According to Benotman, LIFG's *Corrective Studies* "will deny anyone in the future the opportunity or the possibility to try to re-group and re-organise for another round of struggle based on violence."[37]

In the event that a recalcitrant member does attempt to reengage in violence, rehabilitated peers may undermine this effort by reporting him or her to the authorities. For example, in Egypt, there are only two reported instances in which ex-militants became involved in violence, and, both times, they were turned in by members of their own group.[38]

Another factor that seems to play an especially important role in leading militant Islamist organizations to deradicalize is the international context, particularly the influence of demonstration effects on

---

[36] Ashour, 2009, p. 98.

[37] Cilluffo and Evert, 2009, p. 4.

[38] L. Wright, 2008.

both the radical Islamist organization and the governments fighting these groups; a related component is the increasing level of coordination among nations' counterterrorism efforts. When a militant Islamic organization is deradicalized, it creates *intergroup demonstration effects* that encourage other jihadist organizations to moderate. This is due to the fact that these groups share the same ideology, and when one radical group refutes jihadist doctrine, it poses a credible challenge to this worldview, which, in turn, can stimulate doubts in other violent Islamist groups.

After IG issued its recantation, its arguments resonated with some EIJ leaders, who then tried to follow a similar course but were unable to do so in the absence of a respected authority figure who could lead the deradicalization process.[39] In other words, IG's criticism of the radical Islamist ideology helped precipitate an ideological crisis in EIJ. In addition, by presenting evidence that the jihadist ideology was in contravention to Islamic jurisprudence, IG reduced the barriers for other groups to deradicalize. Finally, because the Egyptian government freed a significant number of the IG militants who had recanted their radical beliefs beginning in 2002, it led other groups to expect similar rewards.

EIJ's recantation clearly alarmed Ayman al-Zawahiri, al-Qaeda's second-in-command, who leveled a number of criticisms at EIJ's revised understanding of jihad, including the accusation that it took an unscientific approach and did not explain why al-Sharif had previously advocated actions that were supposedly prohibited by Islamic doctrine.[40] To avoid these criticisms, LIFG made sure that its *Corrective Studies* were rigorous and explained that previous transgressions had been due to "a lack of religious guidance and inexperience." In addition, LIFG argued that it was "imperative upon the individual who discovers these errors to fix and reform what he can, seeking the pleasure of Allah, and fearing his questioning on the Day of Judgment, and out of concern for the people of the community who might not

---

[39] Rashwan, 2008b, p. 125.

[40] Abdul Hameed Bakier, "Al-Qaeda's al-Zawahiri Repudiates Dr. Fadl's 'Rationalization of Jihad,'" *Terrorism Monitor*, Vol. 5, No. 17, April 2008.

have realized what he has."[41] In sum, as more militant Islamist groups reject the jihadist creed, they delegitimize this ideology and make it more likely that similar organizations will also deradicalize.

Second, when a government successfully uses soft-line policies to deradicalize a militant organization, it increases the likelihood that other governments will adopt similar measures, because the success of these policies has already been demonstrated. The most prominent example of this type of *interstate demonstration effect* was Libya's successful engagement of LIFG. Previously, governments were hesitant to engage violent extremists or offer them incentives in return for improved behavior for fear that the extremists would take advantage of their clemency and that they would be criticized for being soft on terrorism.

Initially, the Egyptian government was reluctant to support the IG's disengagement initiative; nevertheless, it eventually became convinced that IG's historic leaders were sincere and, as a result, the Mubarak regime took actions to facilitate this process.[42] Moreover, after the 9/11 attacks, the Egyptian regime publicized its soft-line strategy in an effort to demonstrate to international audiences that it was actively working to counter militant Islamism. Because this approach toward IG was considered a resounding success, the Egyptian authorities were willing to try these methods with EIJ as well.

Similarly, Saif al-Islam al-Qhadafi opened a dialogue with the imprisoned leaders of LIFG because he believed that engagement could lead the organization to deradicalization, which would undermine the militant Islamist threat to the Libyan government. Saif feared that the many Libyan jihadis fighting in Iraq would return home and take up arms against the regime, as the Afghan Arab mujahidin had done. He believed that if the original militants renounced their previous actions and ideology, this would stop younger radicals from turning against the regime.[43] In other words, the Qhadafi regime was willing to risk using a soft-line policy toward LIFG in part because Egypt's

[41] Ali-Musawi, 2009, p. 8.

[42] Ashour, 2009, pp. 101–102.

[43] Robertson and Cruickshank, 2010.

experiences with its militant Islamists demonstrated that this tactic was effective. In short, the interstate demonstration effect made governments more willing to take actions that would facilitate collective deradicalization.

Finally, because governments increasingly work together to combat the global jihadist movement, the international environment became increasingly hostile to the radical Islamist organizations discussed here. Domestic repression is a critical factor in bringing about a strategic crisis; although many existing extremist organizations had been contained at home, they had been able to survive in exile, often in camps with other militant Islamists. Therefore, global counterterrorism measures that deny many radical organizations safe havens may lead to the capture of influential leaders, which, in turn, seems to increase the probability that these leaders will reevaluate their commitment to jihad.

In short, as more states cooperate in global counterterrorism efforts, it is more difficult for groups like LIFG to continue their struggle from abroad; as a consequence, they are more likely to recognize that their strategy has failed—the first step toward deradicalization. Al-Sharif played a significant role in leading EIJ to deradicalize, but he only did so because the Yemeni government detained and extradited him to Egypt. Although al-Sharif reportedly had reservations about al-Qaeda's tactics before his detainment, he did not publicly put forward his critiques until he was imprisoned in Egypt. Moreover, it is not clear that he would have been able to convince most EIJ members to support his initiative if he had not been physically present in Egypt and able to discuss his ideas with them.[44]

The impact of enhanced international cooperation against terrorism is even more apparent in the case of LIFG. Because the group had been defeated in Libya by the late 1990s, most remaining members fled the country and sought to continue their struggle from exile. After the Taliban consolidated its hold over Kabul, many high-ranking LIFG members returned to Afghanistan, the group's birthplace.[45] Operation

[44] L. Wright, 2008.

[45] Alison Pargeter, 2009, p. 7.

Enduring Freedom, the U.S. invasion of Afghanistan, again displaced LIFG, forcing its members to search for a new refuge; however, many of the group's leaders were eventually apprehended and returned to Libya, where they were imprisoned. These detainees included prominent LIFG members, such as the group's emir Sheikh Abu Abdullah Sadiq, deputy emir Sheikh Abu Hazim, and the spiritual leader Abu al-Mundhir al-Sa'idi.[46] These individuals formed the core of the group that undertook a revision of LIFG's ideology.[47]

Figure 6.2 illustrates the stages of collective deradicalization after a group's leadership has chosen to deradicalize.

Figure 6.2
Latter Stages of Collective Deradicalization

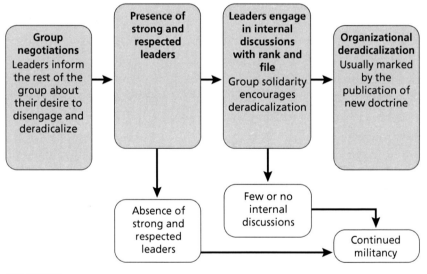

RAND *MG1053-6.2*

---

[46] Pargeter, 2009, p. 5.

[47] Other authors include Muftah al-Dudi (Sheki Abdul-Ghaffar), Mustafa Qanfid (Abu al-Zubayr), and Sheikh Abdul-Wahhab Qayid. See "Libya's Islamic Fighting Group Revises Doctrine," *Al-Awsat*, August 10, 2009.

Interaction Between Individual and Collective Deradicalization

The preceding analysis of the similarities and differences between collective and individual-level disengagement and deradicalization suggests that there are four primary ways in which the two levels interact and that these two processes are interdependent and complementary.

First, when large numbers of individual extremists leave radical organizations and, perhaps, even moderate their beliefs, it can weaken the group by denying it the manpower it needs to survive.[48] In other words, the attrition of individual members who have left the group can create a strategic crisis for a radical organization. For instance, as a growing number of the imprisoned members of the Red Brigades rejected violence and the group's ideology, it led the group's leaders to recognize that they were not going to be able to achieve their goals. This, in turn, led them to undertake a process of group deradicalization.[49]

Second, successful collective deradicalization is contingent on the presence of strong and credible leaders who can persuade grassroots members to support the process. The impact of individual disengagement and deradicalization on the group depends not only on the number of radicals who moderate but on *which* radicals moderate. If certain individuals, such as well-respected commanders, spiritual leaders, or a group's founders, renounce violence and violent Islamism, their actions increase the likelihood that the entire group will deradicalize.

Benotman resigned from LIFG after the 9/11 attacks and in 2007 openly denounced al-Qaeda's actions in a letter to Ayman al-Zawahiri that was published in a Libyan newspaper.[50] Around the same time, Benotman was also secretly escorted to Tripoli's Abu Salim prison to hold discussions with his former comrades about the merits of jihadist ideology. This former LIFG leader's intervention has been described

---

[48] Tore Bjørgo and John Horgan, "Conclusion," in Tore Bjørgo and John Horgan, eds., *Leaving Terrorism Behind: Individual and Collective Disengagement*, New York: Routledge, 2008a, p. 248.

[49] Della Porta, 2008, pp. 66–72.

[50] Bergen and Cruickshank, 2008.

as a crucial turning point that swayed LIFG's leaders to repudiate the jihadist ideology.[51]

As mentioned previously, al-Sharif's moderation had a similarly decisive impact on EIJ's decision to disavow violence and radical Islamism. Others, such as the extremely influential Saudi cleric Sheikh Salman al-Oudah, who personally reproached bin Laden for the wanton destruction caused by al-Qaeda, could potentially encourage militant Islamist organizations (as well as individuals) to forgo violence.

Third, while demonstration effects can occur between a militant Islamist group and others, the demonstration effects of a group's decision to moderate can be felt more broadly and also may lead individual jihadists to abandon violence. In other words, when an extremist Islamic group deradicalizes, it may serve as the trigger that leads individual militants to question their violent actions and ideology, ultimately resulting in their recantation. Quilliam Foundation codirector Maajid Nawaz explained that when he was in prison in Egypt, he had his "first exposure to critics of Islamist supremacy via writings by Egypt's largest terrorist organization—al-Gama'a al-Islamiyya," which "made me rethink my own affiliations with Hizb ut-Tahrir."[52] When an organization deradicalizes, it produces particularly strong demonstration effects that may affect other groups and individuals, because a group's decision to abandon jihad is a powerful symbol that inevitably garners a significant amount of publicity and attention—more so than most individual defections. Its impact is also enhanced by the fact that, often, the militant Islamist group publishes tracts that challenge the premises of jihadist ideology.

Fourth, when most members of a militant organization support the decision to deradicalize, the group may be able to persuade individual members who would not otherwise moderate to do so. This may be the product of the persuasiveness of the group's leaders or of group solidarity and the desire not to estrange one's social network. Although collective disengagement and deradicalization will not prevent truly

---

[51] Ashour, 2010.

[52] Quilliam Foundation, 2010.

irreconcilable individuals from engaging in continued militancy, it may be able to persuade most of a group's members to accept the moderate transformation. This was seen in the case of IG: The historic leadership was eventually able to persuade most of the group's initially very unconvinced commanders that they should abandon violence.

Individual and collective deradicalization are interdependent processes that are more likely to succeed in tandem. This suggests that states combating Islamic radicals should implement measures to encourage both individuals and entire Islamic groups to deradicalize. Moreover, these efforts can have a larger impact if they successfully target the group's leadership. Although it will be difficult to convince committed radicals to change, it is possible. Although a state may want to focus on encouraging collective deradicalization, it may also want to simultaneously run individually focused programs in an effort to bolster the group process by convincing skeptics and helping to prevent recidivism, thereby mitigating the chances that a radical splinter group will emerge from the collective process of deradicalization.

Conclusions

Collective and individual deradicalization are interdependent processes that have a number of similarities but also some critical differences. Because collective deradicalization begins when an individual leader begins to question the utility of jihad, its trajectory closely follows that of an individual disengaging from a radical organization: There is a trigger, which is nearly always a strategic crisis, that leads to a period of questioning and an ideological crisis. If the expected utility of disengaging and deradicalizing exceeds the expected utility of continued radicalism, the leaders reach a turning point and decide to moderate. Then, the collective aspect of collective deradicalization truly becomes significant; the reform-oriented commanders work to convince the rest of the organization to change its behavior and ideology. Figure 6.3 illustrates the stages of this process, plus subsequent demonstration effects.

Figure 6.3
Interaction Between Individual and Group Deradicalization

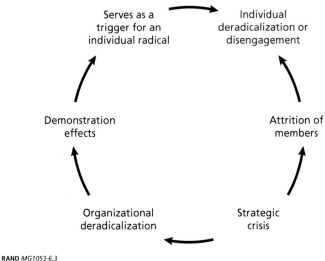

To succeed, this process must be led by influential leaders who garner support from rank-and-file militants through a series of discussions. If the militant leaders are able to convince a majority of the organization's members to moderate, social bonds and peer pressure encourage the defiant holdouts to accept the decision. Due to the high-profile nature of collective deradicalization, it produces particularly salient intergroup and interstate demonstration effects that increase the likelihood that other militant organizations will undergo their own transformative process. Furthermore, enhanced cooperative efforts by states have made it increasingly difficult for radical Islamist groups to safely operate abroad, helping to precipitate strategic crises within these groups. Finally, collective deradicalization can also encourage individual deradicalization by provoking an ideological crisis through the processes described earlier.

Demonstration effects appear to be one of the less appreciated but more important aspects of collective deradicalization, which raises the question: What is the likely impact of LIFG's *Corrective Studies* on the broader global jihadist movement? Undoubtedly, the IG and EIJ's denunciations of radical Islamist ideology had little impact on the core members of al-Qaeda in Afghanistan and Pakistan; the same is likely true for LIFG. Nevertheless, LIFG was a credible militant Islamic organization due to its origins as a part of the jihad against the Soviets in Afghanistan, as well as its less successful efforts to overthrow the Qhadafi regime. Moreover, the most respected members of LIFG—Sheikh Abu Abdullah Sadiq and Abu al-Mundhir al-Sa'idi—led the deradicalization initiative, which increases the probability that their actions and writings will influence other radical Islamists.

In the end, LIFG is a strong additional voice in the rising chorus of groups and individuals who have become critical of al-Qaeda and jihadist ideology more broadly. It alone is not likely to defeat the movement, but its input into the debate over the legitimacy of violence will have a demonstration effect at the individual and collective levels. This growing criticism is increasingly likely to raise doubts in the minds of radical Islamists about whether they are truly going to be rewarded in heaven for their actions or whether most violence is proscribed and will elicit punishment in the afterlife. Since they are motivated by religion, this is a critical concern that may give more and more Islamists pause. Moreover, it may discourage Muslims toying with the idea of radicalizing from doing so. In short, the deradicalization of LIFG is not going to strike a fatal blow against al-Qaeda or the jihadist movement, but it is likely to reduce its appeal and further weaken it.

CHAPTER SEVEN

Implications and Recommendations

There is emerging consensus among analysts and practitioners that to defeat the threat posed by Islamist extremism and terrorism, there is a need to go beyond security and intelligence approaches; it is necessary to take proactive measures to prevent vulnerable individuals from radicalizing and to rehabilitate those who have already embraced extremism. This broader conception of counter-radicalization is manifested in the counter- and deradicalization programs of a number of Middle Eastern, Southeast Asian, and European countries.

A key question is whether the objective of these programs is the disengagement or the deradicalization of militants. Disengagement entails a change in behavior—refraining from violence and withdrawing from a radical organization. Deradicalization is the process of changing an individual's belief system. There can be disengagement without radicalization but not deradicalization without disengagement. A person could exit a radical organization and refrain from violence but nevertheless retain a radical worldview.

Deradicalization, in fact, may be particularly difficult for Islamist extremists because they are motivated by an ideology that is rooted in a major world religion. The requirements of the ideology are regarded as religious obligations. Nevertheless, deradicalization may be necessary to permanently defuse the threat posed by these individuals. If a militant disengages solely for instrumental reasons, when the circumstances change, the militant may once again take up arms. Conversely, when deradicalization accompanies disengagement, it creates further barriers to recidivism.

Besides their primary objective of rehabilitating imprisoned extremists, deradicalization programs have two other important goals. One is obtaining intelligence on extremist organizations. One measure of the success of these programs is the willingness of reformed militants to provide information about their former associates. Indonesian National Counterterrorism Agency head Ansyaad Mbai attributes the success of Indonesian counterterrorism efforts in disrupting the terrorist network in that country to the broad and deep knowledge of the network that the police acquired through their interactions with detainees.

Another goal is discrediting the extremist ideology. Challenging the extremist ideology with an alternative interpretation of Islam is likely, if accepted, to effect a more permanent change in the militant's worldview and to reduce the risk of recidivism; it also helps weaken the appeal of radical Islamism. An important indicator of success is convincing rehabilitated militants to speak out against extremist groups and ideology.

Because counter-radicalization and deradicalization programs are embedded in a war of ideas, the counterideological component of these programs is extremely important. Most Middle Eastern and Southeast Asian programs employ a form of theological dialogue in which mainstream scholars and sometimes even former radicals engage extremists in discussions of Islamic theology in an effort to convince the militants that their interpretation of Islam is wrong.

As discussed earlier, this counterideological component is an essential part of any effective counter-radicalization or deradicalization program. However, the content of the theological dialogue in some of these programs should be treated with caution. Because the priority of these governments is combating the domestic terrorist threat, their programs may stress the unacceptability of terrorism domestically (on the basis that the government is an Islamic government, for instance, or that the country is not under occupation) but condone it outside the country in zones of conflict, such as Iraq and Afghanistan. This approach might address the immediate security needs of the country in question, but it does not truly deradicalize militants; it just deflects them to other theaters.

With that caveat, we can turn to an assessment of these programs and whether they are successful on their own terms—that is to say, with regard to disengaging militants from violent groups.

There are not enough reliable data to reach definitive conclusions about the short-term, let alone the long-term, effectiveness of most existing deradicalization programs. Many of the state-sponsored programs closely guard information about the content of their initiatives and about the militants who have been rehabilitated. Moreover, the ostensibly good track record of some programs, such as Saudi Arabia's, can be misleading because these efforts focus on reforming terrorist sympathizers and supporters, not hard-core militants. This has become increasingly apparent in light of the number of Saudi Guantanamo detainees who have returned to terrorism.

By contrast, there is more information available on the content of European efforts to counter radicalization, but the need to maintain participant confidentiality often precludes the dissemination of data about the effectiveness of interventions to help at-risk youth. It is also difficult to measure the success of counter-radicalization policies because these effects are more diffuse. In some cases (for instance, the Slotervaart Action Plan in Amsterdam), measurable indicators to assess the success of programs have not been used, and it is very difficult, if not impossible, to estimate the effects of the programs on the exposure group.

It follows that knowledge about deradicalization programs remains limited and there are reasons to remain skeptical about the programs' claims of success. Nonetheless, our analysis of the processes of disengagement and deradicalization has a number of important policy implications. In Chapter One, we presented a disengagement trajectory that indicates that individuals often leave a radical organization and choose to forgo violence for instrumental reasons. Taken alone, this finding would suggest that programs that aim to rehabilitate radical Islamists should focus on influencing the participants' decision calculus by offering material incentives, practical assistance, and alternative support networks.

However, Islamists differ from other extremists or antisocial elements, such as gang members, in that they are motivated by an ideology based on religion, which makes them particularly resistant to material rewards and punishments. As a consequence, a counter-ideological component designed to induce the militant to question the radical ideology is a crucial element for a deradicalization program that addresses this type of extremism. There are, in fact, numerous examples of radical Islamists who determined for various reasons that their ideology was incorrect, and this, in turn, contributed to their decision to renounce extremism.

In addition to reducing the probability of recidivism, deradicalization is necessary because ideology plays a significant role in maintaining the cohesion of these organizations and motivating militants to engage in violence. Therefore, it must be countered to weaken the appeal of Islamist extremism.

Furthermore, an individual who joins an extremist organization comes to rely on the group for comraderie and practical support. To convince radical Islamists to disengage or deradicalize, a program should work to break their affective, practical, and ideological commitment to the group. Individuals may vary in terms of the level of each type of commitment, but because it is prohibitively costly to tailor a deradicalization program to each person, rehabilitation efforts should include components to address each type of attachment. None of these components on its own is sufficient; programs appear more likely to succeed when these processes are implemented in tandem. Since there is no single path to disengagement or deradicalization, it is best if the programs provide individuals with multiple reasons to abandon violence and their radical ideology.

In sum, because many deradicalization initiatives challenge radical Islamist principles, in addition to offering emotional and practical support, it is difficult to disentangle each component's effects and to determine which part of these efforts produces moderation. The most effective deradicalization programs have been comprehensive efforts that dissolve the three types of commitment. Therefore, in contrast to Horgan and Braddock, who argue that trying to deradicalize militants is both "premature and naïve," we believe that deradicalization programs should be broad efforts that not only encourage militants to instrumentally give up violence but also work to change their worldview.[1]

Although programs aiming to deradicalize radical Islamists should have affective, pragmatic, and ideological components, these efforts often vary considerably and should be fitted to the particular circumstances. One can make the broad distinction among Middle Eastern and Southeast Asian programs to rehabilitate imprisoned individual Islamists, prison-based collective deradicalization programs, and European efforts that focus on increasing the resiliency of Muslim communities and, in particular, youths at risk of radicalization.

Middle Eastern and Southeast Asian Individual Rehabilitation Programs

Middle Eastern and Southeast Asian governments have established prison-based individual rehabilitation programs that usually promote a particular state-sanctioned brand of Islam. These efforts are often modeled after Yemen's theological dialogue and based on the assumption that most of the militant Islamists do not have a proper understanding of Islam and therefore can be reeducated and reformed.[2] Since these nations (with the exception of Singapore) have explicitly Islamic governments or are Muslim-majority countries, the government is willing to become involved in matters of religious interpretation to promote an official version of Islam. Our examination of these programs has four key policy implications.

First, these efforts seem to hinge on the ability of the state to find credible interlocutors who can develop relationships with imprisoned militants and use their legitimacy and personal ties to convince the radicals of the error of their ways. Credibility may stem from the interlocutor's standing as a theologian, history as a former militant, or personal piety. Using interlocutors whom the militants respect and

---

[1] Horgan and Braddock, 2010, p. 280.

[2] As discussed earlier, the exception to the theological dialogue model is Indonesia, which has no organized religious component.

who are able to connect with the prisoners appears to be essential to establishing rapport with the detainees.

Second, deradicalization programs need to be balanced, with affective, pragmatic, and ideological components that continue after the prisoners have been released. It is clear that prison-based rehabilitation programs cannot rely solely on religious debates to reform detainees. Dialogue alone does not break militants' affective and practical ties to a radical movement or equip them with the skills they need to become self-reliant, productive members of their community. Moreover, it is difficult to assess whether a radical has truly changed his or her beliefs. Since prisoners have an incentive to cooperate with the authorities to earn their freedom, it is best to create a situation that provides incentives for disengagement and disincentives to recidivism.

Third, to ensure that militants remain disengaged, deradicalization programs need to continue to monitor former detainees and offer extensive support after their release. In particular, aftercare should include locating the ex-radical in a supportive environment and facilitating reintegration into society. The best-designed rehabilitation programs (for instance, the one in Singapore) continue to offer (and sometimes require) theological and psychological counseling for those who have been released. Continued interaction with a credible interlocutor provides ongoing emotional support, helps to dispel doubts, and ensures that behavioral and ideational changes endure.

Fourth, programs that include the militant's family appear to increase the probability that the individual will remain disengaged. Deradicalization programs may incorporate militants' families by offering practical support or counseling or by making them guarantors of the former radical's behavior. All of these are effective ways of investing the radical's family in his or her rehabilitation and making it likely that family members will urge the former radical to remain disengaged from extremism.

As noted earlier, the state-sanctioned interpretation of Islam being promoted in some rehabilitation programs often contains radical elements; in particular, some programs propagate the idea that violence at home is illegitimate but that violence in zones of conflict, such as Afghanistan and Iraq, is legitimate and necessary. This suggests that the United States should learn more about these programs before it agrees to repatriate militants currently held in U.S. detention facilities. The United States should also carefully consider all aspects of a deradicalization program before offering support. Finally, it should encourage states with deradicalization programs to provide more information about their efforts so that they can be better evaluated and improved.

Prison-Based Collective Deradicalization

Collective deradicalization has occurred infrequently—only when a state has defeated an extremist organization by killing or imprisoning most of the group's leaders. Collective deradicalization differs from the programs established to rehabilitate individual extremists in that states in which collective deradicalization has occurred have not established extensive, organized programs to rehabilitate imprisoned militants. Instead, governments have responded to overtures from a radical group's leaders who have already begun to reconsider their positions and then engaged these leaders to facilitate their process of disengagement.

Our analysis of collective deradicalization has a number of implications for policymakers.

First, policymakers should encourage group deradicalization where it seems feasible and facilitate the public disclosure of the writings and arguments of militants who renounce extremism. When an influential ideologue or operational leader renounces an extremist ideology—and, more importantly, explains the reasons for doing so—it raises doubts in the minds of radicals who subscribe to a similar worldview. Because of the stature and credibility of some of the authors, these treatises pose the greatest and most serious challenge to extremist ideology, which must be delegitimized to permanently remove the threat posed by radical Islamism. Extremists who are still at large will predictably argue that these recantations have been made under duress, so governments should avoid embracing the recanting extremists too closely in order to avoid compromising their credibility.

Second, governments must maintain a high level of international cooperation in suppressing terrorist groups. This is particularly important because Islamist extremist organizations are part of a global network that allows them to survive even if they have been defeated at home. Repression or, more accurately, effective containment of extremist groups is an essential antecedent condition to deradicalization. When a critical mass of a group's key leaders and members are imprisoned with little chance of being released, this hopeless situation precipitates a strategic crisis that is often followed by an ideological crisis. Experience has shown that a mixed strategy—one that relies on hard-line counterterrorism measures as well as soft-line measures—is the most effective way to encourage militants to disengage and deradicalize.

Third, most programs focus on reforming less committed radicals. Although it is extremely difficult to induce committed militants to renounce extremism, governments may want to target the more devoted militants—the activists and the hard core—because these individuals have more influence on the rank and file. Collective deradicalization is the most efficient way to change the behavior and beliefs of a large number of militants at once and ultimately discredit the extremist ideology. Of course, some committed militants may be impervious to efforts to induce them to change. These recalcitrant individuals, or irreconcilables, may have to be segregated from other group members to prevent them from impeding the rehabilitation of other inmates. However, if some leaders or influential militants show some indications of openness to alternative ideas, it would be advisable to include them in deradicalization programs.

European Counter-Radicalization and Voluntary Deradicalization Efforts

European governments have taken a very different approach to combating Islamist extremism from governments in the Muslim world. In particular, most European states have been very reluctant to become involved in religious matters and therefore do not directly challenge the extremist ideology. Moreover, rather than attempting to rehabilitate imprisoned militants, European governments have emphasized policies aimed at countering radicalization by enhancing social cohesion and the integration of their Muslim populations, as well as small, voluntary deradicalization programs for young people who are at risk of radicalization but have not yet broken the law. Based on our examination of these efforts, we have identified three policy recommendations.

First, European nations must carefully select their partners in the Muslim community to ensure that they are working with authentic voices with grassroots support and not those who promote values contrary to liberal democracy. This is a difficult task, and many European governments have been reluctant to pick and choose partners within their Muslim populations. However, it is not clear that simply promoting democratic and national values, which is the approach that some European governments have taken, is sufficient to ward off radicalization. These governments may need to identify moderate Muslim intermediaries and strengthen these groups to enable them to compete with extremists in the war of ideas. Of course, there is a risk that extremists will attempt to discredit moderates as government tools. As we discussed in an earlier RAND publication, the key question is not whether but *how* governments should channel their assistance and engage prospective partners effectively. Assistance must be channeled in ways that are appropriate to local circumstances and, to the extent possible, involve NGOs with existing relationships in the community.[3]

Second, although the voluntary deradicalization programs that some European states have created need to protect the privacy of their participants, these efforts must be critically evaluated. Therefore, baselines and benchmarks need to be established and data collected to permit independent assessments of the programs' effectiveness. If it is found that locally directed interventions are successful, the programs should be expanded. But their effectiveness needs to be verified first.

Third, given the increasing severity of the problem of Islamist radicalization and recruitment in prisons, European governments may want to consider establishing prison deradicalization programs. The secular character and legal systems of European states make it difficult to emulate some of the practices of prison-based rehabilitation programs in the Middle East and Southeast Asia, but there may be experi-

---

[3]   See Rabasa, Benard, et al., 2007, pp. 78–79.

ences in the case of Singapore, a secular, non–Muslim-majority state facing challenges similar to those confronted by European countries, that are relevant to the European context.

Implications for the United States

The United States does not have a domestic counter-radicalization strategy, much less deradicalization programs. Nevertheless, the results of the programs analyzed here can have important implications for the United States. First, Islamist extremism and terrorism constitute a global threat. Would-be airliner underwear bomber Umar Abdulmutallab is a Nigerian citizen who was apparently radicalized in London. He prepared for a suicide mission in Yemen under the guidance of a U.S.-born Yemeni cleric before he boarded a flight to the United States in Amsterdam with the intention of detonating a bomb aboard the plane. Since the United States is a prime target of attacks by extremists abroad, how successful these programs are in mitigating global terrorism can have a direct impact on the security of the United States.

Second, the United States could derive lessons from the experiences of some of these programs for the purposes of preventing domestic radicalization or to put in place similar programs in areas where U.S. forces are engaged in counterinsurgency operations (for instance, in Afghanistan).

The question is, can or should the United States adopt a domestic counter-radicalization or deradicalization approach at the national or local level? One part of the answer relates to the characteristics of the Muslim population in the United States and the nature of the domestic Islamist terrorist threat. It has been noted that American Muslims are well integrated into American society, are well educated (a majority are college graduates), and have per capita incomes that are higher than those of the U.S. population at large.[4] The United States also does not

---

[4] Zogby International, *Muslims in the American Public Square: Shifting Political Winds and Fallout from 9/11, Afghanistan, and Iraq*, October 2004.

have a large Muslim prison population, as is the case in some European countries, although there is certainly a risk of prison radicalization.

Nevertheless, some of the same features that facilitate the spread of Islamist extremism in Europe are also present in the United States. Most disturbingly, there has been an uptick in the number of Islamist terrorist plots and attacks over the past two years, which suggests that the United States is not immune to the same risks of radicalization and recruitment into terrorist groups that have been observed in Europe.

There are legal, political, and cultural reasons for the lack of an official U.S. interest in domestic counter-radicalization. For constitutional reasons, it is difficult for any level of government in the United States to address the religious component of radicalization, or even radicalization itself. U.S. governmental bodies lack the tools and legal authority to reach out to individuals at risk of radicalization if these individuals have not yet committed crimes. Once the radicalized individual crosses the line into violence, the matter is treated strictly as a law enforcement responsibility. What this means is that replicating a program like the British Channel initiative in the United States would inevitably raise concerns about civil liberties. The British have attempted to finesse this problem by ensuring that individuals nominated for inclusion in Prevent programs were not the subject of surveillance by law enforcement because they were suspected of engaging in potentially illegal activities.[5]

Moreover, U.S. authorities have been reluctant to address the ideological challenge of radical Islamism because of an unwillingness to acknowledge an association, however indirect, between Islam (actually, its radical ideological variant) and terrorism, although the terrorists themselves justify their actions on religious grounds. Even when the actual or attempted acts of terrorism have an obvious connection to radical Islamism—as in the case of the Fort Hood shootings—U.S. authorities have gone out of their way to downplay the relationship between the violence and the religious or ideological driver.

---

[5] Charles Farr, testimony in UK House of Commons, Communities and Local Government Committee, *Preventing Violent Extremism: Sixth Report of Session 2009–10*, London: Stationery Office, March 30, 2010, p. 16

All these factors make a counterideological approach to Islamist radicalization in the United States very challenging. Nevertheless, there are lessons in the experiences of some Western European countries that share with the United States secular political institutions, liberal values, and a reluctance to become directly involved in what are ostensibly religious matters. The British practice of working with Muslim NGOs that are combating radicalization could be replicated in the United States. There are numerous Muslim organizations in the country that oppose Salafism and other forms of Islamist extremism and could be a critical vector for democratic ideas in U.S. Muslim communities and beyond. Such partnerships should be indirect and carefully constructed to avoid compromising the credibility of these partners.

The Dutch model of empowering local communities to assist at-risk individuals and combat the spread of radical ideas could also be more suitable to the U.S. political culture, would track with U.S. federalism, and would accommodate the heterogeneity of the U.S. population better than a more centralized approach. In any event, local governments, social service agencies, and community organizations may be in a better position to detect the early stages of radicalization and undertake interventions as needed.

Final Observations

Culture matters. As this monograph shows, the deradicalization programs that we studied all reflect the social and cultural characteristics of the countries in which they have been implemented. The best-designed plans leverage local cultural patterns to achieve their objectives. One implication of this observation is that deradicalization programs cannot simply be transplanted from one country to another, even within the same region. They have to develop organically in a specific country and culture.

That is not to say that best practices cannot be identified. When they appear to be successful, deradicalization programs have been comprehensive efforts that break extremists' affective, pragmatic, and ideological commitment to a radical organization and worldview. This is a very difficult and expensive undertaking that does not guarantee success. Some states—Yemen, for instance—may not have the means to implement a comprehensive program. In other cases, there may be legal or political obstacles that prevent a government from developing programs that intrude on the religious sphere.

Disengagement and deradicalization programs will likely remain a necessary part of larger counter-radicalization and counterterrorism strategies. However, governments cannot afford to be naïve or careless when seeking to rehabilitate extremists. To succeed, deradicalization programs must be extensive efforts that include affective, pragmatic, and ideological components and considerable aftercare. Prison-based deradicalization programs, in particular, need to exercise caution, carefully evaluating each individual before release and implementing safeguards, such as monitoring, to protect against the eventuality that former militants could once again take up arms.

Bibliography

Abedin, Mahan, "Al-Qaeda: In Decline or Preparing for the Next Attack? An Interview with Saad al-Faqih," *Spotlight on Terror*, Vol. 3, No. 5, June 15, 2005.

Abu-Ali, Nidaa, "Saudi Arabia: Between Radicalisation and Terrorism," *RSIS Commentaries*, Singapore: S. Rajaratnam School of International Studies, Nanyang Technological University, April 24, 2008.

Abuza, Zachary, *Uncivil Islam: Muslims, Politics, and Violence in Indonesia*, New York: Routledge, 2006.

———, "The Rehabilitation of Jemaah Islamiyah Detainees in South East Asia: A Preliminary Assessment," in Tore Bjørgo and John Horgan, eds., *Leaving Terrorism Behind: Individual and Collective Disengagement*, New York: Routledge, 2008, pp. 193–211.

Active Change Foundation, homepage, undated. As of September 23, 2010: http://www.activechangefoundation.org/

Ahmad, Zaleha, presentation at the International Conference on Terrorist Rehabilitation, International Centre for Political Violence and Terrorism Research, S. Rajaratnam School of International Studies, Nanyang Technological University, Singapore, February 24–26, 2009.

Al-Ariqi, Amel, "Gitmo Returnees Need Rehabilitation Program, Lawyers Speculate," *Yemen Times*, December 5, 2007.

Al-Hathloul, Alaa, and Johan Bodin, "Aprés Guantanamo" ["After Guantanamo"], France 24, December 7, 2007. As of September 23, 2010: http://www.france24.com/fr/20071207-apres-guantanamo-

Al-Hitar, Hamoud Abdulhameed, *Dialogue and Its Effects on Countering Terrorism: The Yemeni Experience*, undated.

Al-Jabri, Abd al-Mun'im, "Yemeni Interior Minister Discusses Terrorism Issues, Cooperation with US," *26 September News* (Sana'a, Yemen), October 17, 2003.

Al-Khalifah, Abdullah, *Suspects' Families and the Relationship with Terrorism and Extremism in Saudi Society*, Riyadh: Imam Mohammed University, 2008.

Al-Naja, Badea Abu, "Challenging Task of Integrating Ex-Convicts into Society," *Arab News*, October 28, 2007.

Al-Obathani, Sultan, "Saudi Arabia: Over 400 Extremists Released in the Last Six Months," *Asharq Alawsat*, November 22, 2005.

Al-Saheil, Turki, "Al-Ubaykan: Al-Qa'ida and Books of Abu Qatadah Al-Maqdisi Have the Most Prominent Influence on the Minds of the Deceived Youths," *Asharq Alawsat*, September 9, 2005a.

———, "Saudi Arabia: Decisive Turnaround for Takfiris Through Counseling and Release of Detainees for Security Reasons; al-Washm Blast Has Caused Imbalance Within al-Qa'ida Organization's Ranks," *Ashraq Alawsat*, November 30, 2005b.

———, "Rehabilitating Reformed Jihadists," *Asharq Alawsat*, September 6, 2007a.

———, "Former Saudi Guantanamo Inmates Get a New Start," *Asharq Alawsat*, October 3, 2007b.

Al-Ziyadi, Abdallah, "Interior Ministry: Seminars and Lectures in Schools and Universities to Combat Terrorist Ideology," *Asharq Alawsat*, November 29, 2006.

Ali-Alkaff, Sharifah Sakinah, and Yayasan Mendaki, presentation at the International Conference on Terrorist Rehabilitation, International Centre for Political Violence and Terrorism Research, S. Rajaratnam School of International Studies, Nanyang Technological University, Singapore, February 24–26, 2009.

Ali-Musawi, Mohmmed, trans., *A Selected Translation of the LIFG Recantation Document*, London: Quilliam Foundation, 2009.

Allen, Charles E., Assistant Secretary for Intelligence and Analysis and Chief Intelligence Officer, U.S. Department of Homeland Security, *Threat of Islamic Radicalization to the Homeland*, written testimony to the U.S. Senate Committee on Homeland Security and Governmental Affairs, Washington, D.C., March 14, 2007.

Almond, Gabriel A., R. Scott Appleby, and Emmanuel Sivan, *Strong Religion: The Rise of Fundamentalisms Around the World*, Chicago, Ill.: University of Chicago Press, 2003.

Anne Frank House, *Racism and Extremism Monitor: Eighth Report*, Leiden, the Netherlands, 2008. As of September 23, 2010:
http://www.monitorracisme.nl/content.asp?PID=320&LID=1

"Arab Veterans of Afghanistan War Lead New Islamic Holy War," *Compass*, October 28, 1994.

Arianti, V., "Legacy of the Bali Trio: A Changing Threat Pattern from Jemaah Islamiyah," Singapore: S. Rajaratnam School of International Studies, Nanyang Technological University, November 14, 2008.

Arnaz, Farouk, "Embassy Bomb Planner Remorseless in New Book," *Jakarta Globe*, March 15, 2009.

Ashour, Omar, "Lions Tamed? An Inquiry into the Causes of De-Radicalization of Armed Islamist Movements: The Case of the Egyptian Islamic Group," *Middle East Journal*, Vol. 61, No. 4, Autumn 2007, pp. 596–625.

―――, "Islamist De-Radicalization in Algeria: Successes and Failures," *Middle East Institute Policy Brief*, No. 21, November 2008.

―――, *The De-Radicalization of Jihadists: Transforming Armed Islamist Movements*, New York: Routledge, 2009.

―――, "De-Radicalizing Jihadists the Libyan Way," *Arab Reform Bulletin*, April 7, 2010. As of June 15, 2010:
http://www.carnegieendowment.org/arb/?fa=show&article=40531

Audit Commission, *Preventing Violent Extremism: Learning and Developing Exercise*, London, October 2008. As of September 23, 2010:
http://www.audit-commission.gov.uk/communitysafety/goodpractice/Pages/preventingviolentextremism.aspx

Azarva, Jeffrey, "Is U.S. Detention Policy in Iraq Working?" *Middle East Quarterly*, Vol. 16, No. 1, Winter 2009, pp. 5–14.

Bakier, Abdul Hameed, "Al-Qaeda's al-Zawahiri Repudiates Dr. Fadl's 'Rationalization of Jihad,'" *Terrorism Monitor*, Vol. 5, No. 17, April 2008.

Barker, Eileen, "Defection from the Unification Church: Some Statistics and Distinctions," in David G. Bromley, ed., *Falling from the Faith: Causes and Consequences of Religious Apostasy*, Newbury Park, Calif.: Sage Publications, 1988.

Barrett, Richard, and Laila Bokhari, "Deradicalization and Rehabilitation Programmes Targeting Religious Terrorists and Extremists in the Muslim World: An Overview," in Tore Bjørgo and John Horgan, eds., *Leaving Terrorism Behind: Individual and Collective Disengagement*, New York: Routledge, 2008, pp. 170–180.

Bartels, Edien, and Inge De Jong, "Civil Society on the Move in Amsterdam: Mosque Organizations in the Slotervaart District," *Journal of Muslim Minority Affairs*, Vol. 27, No. 3, December 2007, pp. 455–471.

Bartlett, Jamie, and Jonathan Birdwell, *From Suspects to Citizens: Preventing Violent Extremism in a Big Society*, London: Demos, July 2010.

Benard, Cheryl, Edward O'Connell, Cathryn Quantic Thurston, Andres Villamizar, Elvira N. Loredo, Thomas Sullivan, and Jeremiah Goulka, *The Battle Inside the Wire: U.S. Prisoner and Detainee Operations from World War II to Iraq*, Santa Monica, Calif.: RAND Corporation, forthcoming.

Bennett, Drake, "How to Defuse a Human Bomb," *Boston Globe*, April 13, 2008.

Bergen, Peter, and Paul Cruickshank, "The Unraveling: Al Qaeda's Revolt Against Bin Laden," *New Republic,* June 11, 2008.

Birk, Ane Skov, *Incredible Dialogues: Religious Dialogue as a Means of Counter-Terrorism in Yemen,* London: King's College International Centre for the Study of Radicalisation and Political Violence, April 2009.

Bjørgo, Tore, "How Gangs Fall Apart: Process of Transformation and Disintegration of Gangs," paper presented at the annual meeting of the American Society of Criminology, November 17–20, 1999.

———, "Processes of Disengagement from Violent Groups of the Extreme Right," in Tore Bjørgo and John Horgan, eds., *Leaving Terrorism Behind: Individual and Collective Disengagement,* New York: Routledge, 2008, pp. 30–48.

Bjørgo, Tore, and Yngve Carlsson, "Early Intervention with Violent and Racist Youth Groups," Norwegian Institute of International Affairs, Working Paper No. 677, 2005.

Bjørgo, Tore, and John Horgan, "Conclusions," in Tore Bjørgo and John Horgan, eds., *Leaving Terrorism Behind: Individual and Collective Disengagement,* New York: Routledge, 2008a, pp. 245–255.

———, "Introduction," in Tore Bjørgo and John Horgan, eds., *Leaving Terrorism Behind: Individual and Collective Disengagement,* New York: Routledge, 2008b, pp. 1–13.

Blanford, Nicholas, "Saudis Mount Intense Drive Against Terror," *Christian Science Monitor,* May 29, 2003.

Blaydes, Lisa, and Lawrence Rubin, "Ideological Reorientation and Counterterrorism: Confronting Militant Islam in Egypt," *Terrorism and Political Violence,* Vol. 20, No. 4, 2008, pp. 468–470.

Boucek, Christopher, "The Saudi Process of Repatriating and Reintegrating Guantanamo Returnees," *CTC Sentinel,* Vol. 1, No. 1, December 2007, pp. 10–12.

———, "Jailing Jihadis: Saudi Arabia's Special Terrorist Prisons," *Terrorism Monitor,* Vol. 6, No. 2, January 25, 2008a.

———, "The Sakinah Campaign and Internet Counter-Radicalization in Saudi Arabia," *CTC Sentinel,* Vol. 1, No. 9, August 2008b, pp. 1–4.

———, "Courts Open New Chapter in Counter-Terrorism," *Arab Reform Bulletin,* September 2008c.

———, *Saudi Arabia's "Soft" Counterterrorism Strategy: Prevention, Rehabilitation, and Aftercare,* Carnegie Papers, No. 97, September 2008d.

———, "Examining Saudi Arabia's 85 Most Wanted List," *CTC Sentinel,* Vol. 2, No. 5, May 2009.

Boucek, Christopher, Shazadi Beg, and John Horgan, "Opening Up the Jihadi Debate: Yemen's Committee for Dialogue," in Tore Bjørgo and John Horgan, eds., *Leaving Terrorism Behind: Individual and Collective Disengagement*, New York: Routledge, 2008, pp. 181–192.

Brandon, James, "Koranic Duels Ease Terror," *Christian Science Monitor*, February 4, 2005.

———, "The UK's Experience in Counter-Radicalization," *CTC Sentinel*, Vol. 1, No. 5, April 2008, pp. 10–12.

Briggs, Rachel, "Community Engagement for Counterterrorism: Lessons from the United Kingdom," *International Affairs*, Vol. 86, No. 4, July 2010, pp. 971–981.

British Muslim Forum, homepage, undated. As of October 6, 2010:
http://www.britishmuslimforum.org.uk/

"British Muslim Forum: Sufis Rise," MPACUK Muslim Discussion Forum, April 28, 2005. As of September 23, 2010:
http://forum.mpacuk.org/showthread.php?t=1060

Bromley, David G., "Deprogramming as a Mode of Exit from New Religious Movements: The Case of the Unification Movement," in David G. Bromley, ed., *Falling from the Faith: Causes and Consequences of Religious Apostasy*, Newbury Park, Calif.: Sage Publications, 1988.

Bures, Oldrich, "EU Counterterrorism Policy: A Paper Tiger?" *Terrorism and Political Violence*, Vol. 18, No. 1, 2006, pp. 57–78.

Carey, Liz, "Anderson Teens Share Gang Experiences, Difficulty of Getting Out," *Independent Mail* (Anderson, S.C.), October 26, 2009.

Casciani, Dominic, "Minister Backs New Muslim Group," BBC News, July 19, 2006. As of September 23, 2010:
http://news.bbc.co.uk/2/hi/uk_news/5193402.stm

Castle, Stephen, and Steven Erlanger, "Dutch Voters Split, and Right Surges," *New York Times*, June 10, 2010.

Cavendish, Camilla, "From Drug Dealer to Bomber in Weeks," *Times* (London), July 12, 2007. As of September 23, 2010:
http://www.timesonline.co.uk/tol/comment/columnists/camilla_cavendish/article2062060.ece

Chaiyanukit, Charnchao, "Vision for Establishing a Rehabilitation Programme in Thailand," presentation at the International Conference on Terrorist Rehabilitation, International Centre for Political Violence and Terrorism Research, S. Rajaratnam School of International Studies, Nanyang Technological University, Singapore, February 24–26, 2009.

Chalk, Peter, *The Malay-Muslim Insurgency in Southern Thailand—Understanding the Conflict's Evolving Dynamic: RAND Counterinsurgency Study—Paper 5*, Santa Monica, Calif.: RAND Corporation, OP-198-OSD, 2008. As of September 23, 2010:
http://www.rand.org/pubs/occasional_papers/OP198/

Checkel, Jeffrey T., "International Institutions and Socialization in Europe: Introduction and Framework," *International Organization*, Vol. 59, No. 4, Fall 2005, pp. 801–826.

Choudhury, Tufyal, *The Role of Muslim Identity Politics in Radicalisation (A Study in Progress)*, London: UK Department for Communities and Local Government, 2007.

Christanto, Dicky, "Dulmatin Confirmed Dead in Raids," *Jakarta Post*, March 11, 2010. As of September 23, 2010:
http://www.thejakartapost.com/news/2010/03/11/dulmatin-confirmed-dead-raids.html

Cilluffo, Frank J., and F. Jordan Evert, *Reflections on Jihad: A Former Leader's Perspective—An In-Depth Conversation with Noman Benotman*, Washington, D.C.: George Washington University Homeland Security Policy Institute, October 16, 2009.

Clubb, Gordon, "Re-Evaluating the Disengagement Process: The Case of Fatah," *Perspectives on Terrorism*, Vol. 3, No. 3, September 2009.

Conciliation Resources and Quaker Peace and Social Witness, *Coming Home: Understanding Why Commanders of the Lord's Resistance Army Choose to Return to a Civilian Life*, May 2006.

Council of the European Union, *The European Union Counter-Terrorism Strategy*, Brussels, November 30, 2005. As of September 23, 2010:
http://register.consilium.europa.eu/pdf/en/05/st14/st14469-re04.en05.pdf

Crenshaw, Martha, "Why Violence Is Rejected or Renounced: A Case Study of Oppositional Terrorism," in Thomas Gregor, ed., *A Natural History of Peace*, Nashville, Tenn.: Vanderbilt University Press, 1996, pp. 249–272.

Cronin, Audrey Kurth, "How Al-Qaida Ends: The Decline and Demise of Terrorist Groups," *International Security*, Vol. 31, No. 1, Summer 2006, pp. 7–48.

———, "Historical Patterns in Ending Terrorism," in *Ending Terrorism: Lessons for Defeating al-Qaeda*, Adelphi Papers, No. 394, 2008.

Curcio, Sharon, "The Dark Side of Jihad: How Young Men Detained at Guantanamo Assess Their Experience," in Cheryl Benard, ed., *A Future for the Young*, Santa Monica, Calif.: RAND Corporation, WR-354, 2005, pp. 50–64. As of September 23, 2010:
http://www.rand.org/pubs/working_papers/WR354/

Danish Ministry of Refugee, Immigration and Integration Affairs, "Denmark's Deradicalisation Efforts," fact sheet, May 2010. As of June 10, 2010: http://www.nyidanmark.dk/NR/rdonlyres/AAF35358-232A-4189-9375-1AF5C9 EBC623/0/Faktaarkafradikaliseringengelskudgave.pdf

Daragahi, Borzou, "Libya's Coup: Turning Militants Against Al Qaeda," *Los Angeles Times*, December 15, 2009.

Decker, Scott H., and Janet L. Lauritsen, "Leaving the Gang," in C. Ronald Huff, ed., *Gangs in America III*, Thousand Oaks, Calif.: Sage Publications, 2001, pp. 51–67.

Decker, Scott H., and Barrik van Winkle, *Life in the Gang: Family, Friends, and Violence*, Cambridge, UK: Cambridge University Press, 1996.

Della Porta, Donatella, "Leaving Underground Organizations: A Sociological Analysis of the Italian Case," in Tore Bjørgo and John Horgan, eds., *Leaving Terrorism Behind: Individual and Collective Disengagement*, New York: Routledge, 2008, pp. 66–87.

Demant, Froukje, and Beatrice De Graaf, "How to Counter Radical Narratives: Dutch Deradicalization Policy in the Case of Moluccan and Islamic Radicals," *Studies in Conflict and Terrorism*, Vol. 33, No. 5, May 2010, pp. 408–428.

Demant, Froukje, Marcel Maussen, and Jan Rath, *Muslims in the EU: Cities Report—the Netherlands*, New York: Open Society Institute, EU Monitoring and Advocacy Program, 2007.

Demant, Froukje, Marieke Slootman, Frank Buijs, and Jean Tillie, *Decline and Disengagement: An Analysis of Processes of Deradicalization*, Amsterdam: IMES Report Series, 2008.

"Denmark and the Far Right: Fear of Foreigners," *Economist*, November 14, 2007.

Dobson, William J., "The Best Guide for Gitmo? Look to Singapore," *Washington Post*, May 17, 2009.

Dodd, Vikram, "Government Anti-Terrorism Strategy 'Spies' on Innocent," *Guardian*, October 16, 2009.

Dunne, Charles W., "Terrorist Rehabilitation and Succession Politics in Libya: Opportunities for the United States?" Middle East Institute, March 31, 2010.

Dutch Ministry of the Interior and Kingdom Relations, *Polarisation and Radicalisation Action Plan: 2007–2011*, 2007. As of September 23, 2010: http://english.minbzk.nl//subjects/public-safety/publications/@108447/polarisation-and

———, *Operational Action Plan: Polarisation and Radicalisation*, 2008.

Ebaugh, Helen Rose Fuchs, "Leaving Catholic Convents: Toward a Theory of Disengagement," in David G. Bromley, ed., *Falling from the Faith: Causes and Consequences of Religious Apostasy*, Newbury Park, Calif.: Sage Publications, 1988.

Elster, Jon, "Introduction," in John Elster, ed., *Rational Choice*, New York: New York University Press, 1986, pp. 1–33.

"Ex–Guantanamo Inmates 'Fail Rehab,'" Aljazeera, June 20, 2010. As of June 23, 2010:
http://english.aljazeera.net/news/middleeast/2010/06/201062013047249951.html

"Extremists Have No Firm Religious Beliefs," *Khaleej Times* (Dubai), November 27, 2005.

Faith Matters, "Board of Directors," web page, undated. As of September 23, 2010:
http://faith-matters.org/about-us/who-we-are

Fandy, Mamoun, *Saudi Arabia and the Politics of Dissent*, New York: Palgrave, 2001.

Fink, Naureen Chowdhury, and Ellie B. Hearne, *Beyond Terrorism: Deradicalization and Disengagement from Violent Extremism*, New York: International Peace Institute, October 2008.

Firdaus, Irwan, "Noordin M Top Reportedly Killed in a Bathroom After 16 Hour Siege," Associated Press (*Jakarta Post*), August 8, 2009. As of September 23, 2010:
http://www.thejakartapost.com/news/2009/08/08/noordin-m-top-reportedly-killed-a-bathroom-after-16-hour-seige.html

Florez-Morris, Mauricio, "Why Some Colombian Guerrilla Members Stayed in the Movement Until Demobilization: A Micro-Sociological Case Study of Factors that Influenced Members' Commitment to Three Former Rebel Organizations: M-19, EPL, and CRS," *Terrorism and Political Violence*, Vol. 22, No. 2, March 2010, p. 216–241.

Ford, Richard, "Jail Imams Vetted by Security Services and Muslim Books Screened for Code," *Times* (London), February 26, 2007. As of September 23, 2010:
http://www.timesonline.co.uk/tol/news/uk/article1437916.ece

Frieden, Jeffry A., "Actors and Preferences in International Relations," in David A. Lake and Robert Powell, eds., *Strategic Choice and International Relations*, Princeton, N.J.: Princeton University Press, 1999, pp. 39–76.

Galanter, Marc, *Cults: Faith, Healing, and Coercion*, New York: Oxford University Press, 1989.

Gallis, Paul, Kristin Archick, Francis Miko, and Steven Woehrel, *Muslims in Europe: Integration Policies in Selected Countries*, Washington, D.C.: Congressional Research Service, RL33166, November 18, 2005.

Gambetta, Diego, and Steffen Hertog, *Engineers of Jihad*, Oxford, UK: University of Oxford, Sociology Working Paper 2007-10, 2007.

Garfinkle, Renee, *Personal Transformations: Moving from Violence to Peace*, Washington, D.C.: United States Institute of Peace, Special Report 186, April 2007.

General Intelligence and Security Service, Communications Department, *Annual Report 2003*, The Hague: Dutch Ministry of the Interior and Kingdom Relations, July 2004.

Gerges, Fawaz A., *The Far Enemy: Why Jihad Went Global*, New York: Cambridge University Press, 2005.

———, "Al Qaeda Has Bounced Back in Yemen," CNN, January 7, 2010. As of June 6, 2010:
http://www.cnn.com/2010/OPINION/01/07/gerges.yemen.us.terrorism/

Giordano, Peggy C., Stephen A. Cernkovich, and Donna D. Holland, "Changes in Friendship Relations over the Life Course: Implications for Desistance from Crime," *Criminology*, Vol. 41, No. 2, May 2003, pp. 293–328.

Goodstein, Laurie, "Defectors Say Church of Scientology Hides Abuse," *New York Times*, March 6, 2010.

Government of Denmark, *A Common and Safe Future: Proposal for an Action Plan to Prevent Extremist Views and Radicalisation Among Young People*, June 2008.

———, *A Common and Safe Future: An Action Plan to Prevent Extremist Views and Radicalisation Among Young People*, January 2009.

Government of Singapore, Ministry of Home Affairs, "Singapore Government Press Statement on ISA Arrests," January 11, 2002. As of September 23, 2010:
http://www.mha.gov.sg/news_details.aspx?nid=Mjgz-HVbv3ryewWc%3D

———, *The Jemaah Islamiyah Arrests and the Threat of Terrorism*, white paper, January 2003.

Gregg, Heather S., "Fighting the Jihad of the Pen: Countering Revolutionary Islam's Ideology," *Terrorism and Political Violence*, Vol. 22, No. 2, April 2010, pp. 292–314.

Halafoff, Anna, and David Wright-Neville, "A Missing Peace? The Role of Religious Actors in Countering Terrorism," *Studies in Conflict and Terrorism*, Vol. 32, No. 11, November 2009, pp. 921–932.

Hannah, Greg, Lindsay Clutterbuck, and Jennifer Rubin, *Radicalization or Rehabilitation: Understanding the Challenge of Extremist and Radicalized Prisoners*, Santa Monica, Calif.: RAND Corporation, TR-571-RC, 2008. As of September 23, 2010:
http://www.rand.org/pubs/technical_reports/TR571

Harrison, Roger, and Javid Hassan, "Al-Qaeda Chief in Kingdom Killed," *Arab News*, August 19, 2005.

Hassan, Ustaz Mohamed Feisal Mohamed, Secretary of the Religious Rehabilitation Group, presentation at the International Conference on Terrorist Rehabilitation, International Centre for Political Violence and Terrorism Research, S. Rajaratnam School of International Studies, Nanyang Technological University, Singapore, February 24–26, 2009.

"Head of Yemeni Dialogue Committee Interviewed on Work with Afghanistan Returnees," *Al-Quds al-Arabi* (London), March 4, 2004.

Hegghammer, Thomas, "Terrorist Recruitment and Radicalization in Saudi Arabia," *Middle East Policy*, Vol. 13, No. 4, December 2006, pp. 39–60.

———, *Violent Islamism in Saudi Arabia, 1979–2006: The Power and Perils of Pan-Islamic Nationalism*, dissertation, Paris: Sciences-Po, 2007.

———, "Islamist Violence and Regime Stability in Saudi Arabia," *International Affairs*, Vol. 84, No. 4, July 2008, pp. 701–715.

———, *Jihad in Saudi Arabia: Violence and Pan-Islamism Since 1979*, Cambridge, UK: Cambridge University Press, 2010.

Helqvist, Iben, and Elizabeth Sebian, "Islam in Denmark," Euro-Islam.info, undated. As of September 23, 2010:
http://www.euro-islam.info/country-profiles/denmark/

HM Government, *Countering International Terrorism: The United Kingdom's Strategy*, London, July 2006.

———, *The Prevent Strategy: A Guide for Local Partners in England*, London, June 2008. As of September 23, 2010:
http://publications.education.gov.uk/default.aspx?PageFunction=productdetails&PageMode=publications&ProductId=288324&

———, *Pursue Prevent Protect Prepare: The United Kingdom's Strategy for Countering International Terrorism*, London, March 2009.

———, *Channel: Supporting Individuals Vulnerable to Recruitment by Violent Extremists*, London, March 2010a.

———, *Pursue Prevent Protect Prepare: The United Kingdom's Strategy for Countering International Terrorism, Annual Report*, London, March 2010b. As of September 23, 2010:
http://www.official-documents.gov.uk/document/cm78/7833/7833.pdf

HM Government, Research, Information and Communications Unit, *British Muslim Media Consumption Report*, London, March 2010a.

———, *Counter-Terror Message Testing: Qualitative Research Report*, London, March 2010b.

———, *Credible Voices: Exploring Perceptions of Trust and Credibility in Muslim Communities*, London, March 2010c.

————, *Understanding Perceptions of the Terms "Britishness" and "Terrorism,"* London, March 2010d.

————, *Young British Muslims Online*, London, March 2010e.

Hoffman, Bruce, *Inside Terrorism*, New York: Columbia University Press, 2006.

"Home Office Statement on Muslim First, British Second," BBC News, February 16, 2009. As of June 10, 2010:
http://news.bbc.co.uk/panorama/hi/front_page/newsid_7888000/7888793.stm

Horgan, John, "Individual Disengagement: A Psychological Analysis," in Tore Bjørgo and John Horgan, eds., *Leaving Terrorism Behind: Individual and Collective Disengagement*, New York: Routledge, 2008, pp. 17–29.

————, *Walking Away from Terrorism: Accounts of Disengagement from Radical and Extremist Movements*, New York: Routledge, 2009.

Horgan, John, and Kurt Braddock, "Rehabilitating the Terrorists? Challenges in Assessing the Effectiveness of De-Radicalization Programs," *Terrorism and Political Violence*, Vol. 22, No. 2, April 2010, pp. 267–291.

Human Rights Watch, *No Direction Home: Returns from Guantanamo to Yemen*, New York, March 2009. As of September 23, 2010:
http://www.hrw.org/en/reports/2009/03/28/no-direction-home

Hurst, Steven R., "Mentally Retarded Women Used in Bombings," Associated Press, February 1, 2008.

International Crisis Group, *Understanding Islamism*, Cairo and Brussels, Middle East/North Africa Report No. 37, March 2, 2005.

————, *Terrorism in Indonesia: Noordin's Network*, Jakarta and Brussels, Asia Report No. 114, May 5, 2006.

————, *Deradicalisation and Indonesian Prisons*, Jakarta and Brussels, Asia Report No. 142, November 19, 2007.

————, *Recruiting Militants in Southern Thailand*, Bangkok and Brussels, Asia Report No. 170, June 2009a.

————, *Southern Thailand: Moving Towards Political Solutions?* Bangkok and Brussels, Asia Report No. 181, December 8, 2009b.

Jacobson, Michael, *Terrorist Dropouts: Learning from Those Who Have Left*, Washington, D.C.: Washington Institute for Near East Policy, Policy Focus No. 101, January 2010.

Jamieson, Alison, "Identity and Morality in the Italian Red Brigades," *Terrorism and Political Violence*, Vol. 2, No. 4, Winter 1990, pp. 508–520.

Jenkins, Russell, "Killers May Have Been Recruited at Youth Centre," *Sunday Times*, July 16, 2005.

Jervis, Robert, *Perception and Misperception in International Politics*, Princeton, N.J.: Princeton University Press, 1976.

Johnsen, Gregory D., "In Yemen, a Benevolent Alternative to Osama Bin Laden," *Pacific News Service*, January 20, 2004.

―――, "Yemen's Passive Role in the War on Terrorism," *Terrorism Monitor*, Vol. 4, No. 4, February 23, 2006.

―――, "Yemen Faces Second Generation of Islamist Militants," *Terrorism Focus*, Vol. 4, No. 27, August 14, 2007a.

―――, "Al-Qaeda's Generational Split," *Boston Globe*, November 9, 2007b.

Jones, Seth G., and Martin C. Libicki, *How Terrorist Groups End: Lessons for Countering al Qa'ida*, Santa Monica, Calif.: RAND Corporation, MG-741-1-RC, 2008. As of September 23, 2010:
http://www.rand.org/pubs/monographs/MG741-1/

Jones, Sidney, International Crisis Group, presentation to the Center for Strategic and International Studies, Washington, D.C., May 24, 2010.

Juergensmeyer, Mark, *Terror in the Mind of God: The Global Rise of Religious Violence*, Berkeley, Calif.: University of California Press, 2003.

Kader, Halim, President, Taman Bacaan, presentation at the International Conference on Terrorist Rehabilitation, International Centre for Political Violence and Terrorism Research, S. Rajaratnam School of International Studies, Nanyang Technological University, Singapore, February 24–26, 2009.

Karnavian, Brigadier General Tito, Indonesian National Police, presentation at the International Conference on Terrorist Rehabilitation, International Centre for Political Violence and Terrorism Research, S. Rajaratnam School of International Studies, Nanyang Technological University, Singapore, February 24–26, 2009.

Klein, Malcolm W., *The American Street Gang: Its Nature, Prevalence, and Control*, Oxford, UK: Oxford University Press, 1995.

Knights, Michael, "Internal Politics Complicate Counterterrorism in Yemen," *Jane's Intelligence Review*, February 2006.

Kohlmann, Evan F., with Josh Lefkowitz, *Dossier: Libyan Islamic Fighting Group (LIFG)*, NEFA Foundation, October 2007. As of June 22, 2010:
http://www.nefafoundation.org/miscellaneous/nefalifg1007.pdf

Kühle, Lene, and Lasse Lindekilde, *Radicalization Among Young Muslims in Aarhus*, Aarhus, Denmark: Center for Studies in Islamism and Radicalisation, January 2010.

Kundnani, Arun, *Spooked! How Not to Prevent Violent Extremism*, London: Institute of Race Relations, 2009.

Lambert, Robert, "Empowering Salafis and Islamists Against al-Qaeda: A London Counterterrorism Case Study," *PS: Political Science and Politics*, Vol. 41, No. 1, January 2008, pp. 31–35.

————, "Salafi and Islamist Londoners: Stigmatised Minority Faith Communities Countering al-Qaida," *Crime, Law and Social Change*, Vol. 50, Nos. 1–2, September 2008, pp. 73–89.

Lawson, Guy, "Osama's Prodigal Son," *Rolling Stone*, January 20, 2010.

Lee, Sue-Ann, "Managing the Challenges of Radical Islam: Strategies to Win the Hearts and Minds of the Muslim World," paper presented at the John F. Kennedy School of Government, Harvard University, April 1, 2003.

Leiken, Robert S., "Europe's Angry Muslims," *Foreign Affairs*, Vol. 84, No. 4, July–August 2005.

"Libya's Islamic Fighting Group Revises Doctrine," *Al-Awsat*, August 10, 2009.

Lynch, Marc, "Islam Divided Between *Salafi-Jihad* and the *Ikhwan*," *Studies in Conflict and Terrorism*, Vol. 33, No. 6, June 2010, pp. 467–487.

Magnus, Richard, senior fellow at the S. Rajaratnam School of International Studies and former Chief Judge in Singapore, presentation at the International Conference on Terrorist Rehabilitation, International Centre for Political Violence and Terrorism Research, S. Rajaratnam School of International Studies, Nanyang Technological University, Singapore, February 24–26, 2009.

Maher, Shiraz, "Saudi Care for Jihadis," *Wall Street Journal*, January 11, 2010.

Martin, Di, "Bali Bomber Now Campaigns to Stop Terrorism," Australian Broadcasting Corporation News, September 20, 2007.

Martinez, Luis, *The Libyan Paradox*, New York: Columbia University Press, 2007.

Ma'ruf, Mahmud, "Chairman of the Committee for Religious Dialogue with al-Qa'ida Supporters in Yemen Humud al-Hattar Tells Al Quds al-Arabi: Violence Is Due to Restricting Freedom of Islamists and the Positions Toward Arab Issues, Especially Palestine," *al-Quds al-Arabi* (London), December 18, 2004.

McAuley, James W., Jonathan Tonge, and Peter Shirlow, "Conflict, Transformation, and Former Loyalist Paramilitary Prisoners in Northern Ireland," *Terrorism and Political Violence*, Vol. 22, No. 1, January 2010, pp. 22–40.

Mellis, Colin, "Amsterdam and Radicalisation: The Municipal Approach," in *Radicalisation in Broader Perspective*, The Hague: National Coordinator for Counterterrorism, October 2007.

Mitchell, Claire, "The Limits of Legitimacy: Former Loyalist Combatants and Peace-Building in Northern Ireland," *Irish Political Studies*, Vol. 23, No. 1, February 2008, pp. 1–19.

Morris, Norval, *The Future of Imprisonment*, Chicago, Ill.: University of Chicago Press, 1977.

Mount, Mike, "Report: 20 Percent of Released Detainees Returning to Terrorism," CNN, January 11, 2010. As of March 9, 2010:
http://www.cnn.com/2010/POLITICS/01/11/detainees.terror.return/

Murshed, S. Mansoob, and Sarah Pavan, *Identity and Islamic Radicalization in Western Europe*, Brighton, UK: MICROCON, Research Working Paper 16, August 2009. As of September 23, 2010:
http://www.microconflict.eu/publications/RWP16_MM_SP.pdf

NEFA Foundation, trans., "An Open Speech Regarding the Details of the Dialogue Between the LIFG and the Libyan Regime," July 3, 2009. As of June 22, 2010:
http://www.nefafoundation.org/miscellaneous/FeaturedDocs/nefa_lifgaq0709.pdf

"Netherlands-Labour Icon Aims for 'Blooming Muslim Community' in Amsterdam West," NIS Dutch News, January 13, 2009. As of October 6, 2010:
http://www.newenglishreview.org/blog_days.cfm/d/13/m/1/y/2009

Network of Comparative Research on Islam and Muslims in Europe, "A Convergence Crisis? A Study of Muslim Immigration, Security Strategy, and the Rise of Xenophobia in the European Union," 2003. As of September 23, 2010:
http://homepage.mac.com/kmcspadden/ConvergenceCrisis_Full.htm

Ottaway, David, "Saud Effort Draws on Radical Clerics to Combat Lure of al-Qaeda," *Washington Post*, May 7, 2006.

Padil, Ustaz Iszam, "Terrorist Rehabilitation: Malaysia's Experience," presentation at the International Conference on Terrorist Rehabilitation, International Centre for Political Violence and Terrorism Research, S. Rajaratnam School of International Studies, Nanyang Technological University, Singapore, February 24–26, 2009.

Paley, Amit R., "In Iraq, 'A Prison Full of Innocent Men,'" *Washington Post*, December 6, 2008.

Pargeter, Alison, "LIFG Revisions Unlikely to Reduce Jihadist Violence," *CTC Sentinel*, Vol. 2, No. 10, October 2009, pp. 7–9.

Peraino, Kevin, "The Reeducation of Abu Jandal," *Newsweek*, May 29, 2009.

Piazza, James, "Is Islamist Terrorism More Dangerous? An Empirical Study of Group Ideology, Organization, and Goal Structure," *Terrorism and Political Violence*, Vol. 21, No. 1, January 2009, pp. 62–88.

Pluchinsky, Dennis A., "Global Jihadist Recidivism: A Red Flag," *Studies in Conflict and Terrorism*, Vol. 31, No. 3, March 2008, pp. 182–200.

"Preventing Extremism Together" *Working Groups, August–October 2005*, London: UK Home Office, October 2005. As of June 7, 2010: http://www.communities.gov.uk/documents/communities/pdf/152164.pdf

Porges, Marissa L., "Can We Retrain Terrorists?" *Philadelphia Inquirer*, November 18, 2009.

———, "The Saudi Deradicalization Experiment," Council on Foreign Relations, Expert Brief, January 22, 2010a.

———, "Deradicalisation, the Yemeni Way," *Survival*, Vol. 52, No. 2, April 2010b, pp. 27–33.

———, "Getting Deradicalization Right," letter to the editor, *Foreign Affairs*, May–June 2010c.

"Prisons," *Terrorism Monitor*, Vol. 6, No. 2, January 24, 2008.

Progressive British Muslims, homepage, undated. As of October 6, 2010: http://www.pbm.org.uk/

Quilliam Foundation, "About Us," web page, undated(a). As of September 23, 2010: http://www.quilliamfoundation.org/about-us.html

———, *Preventing Terrorism: Where Next for Britain?* London, undated(b).

———, "Quilliam Roundtable—Refuting Al Qaeda Former Jihadists and the Battle of Ideologies," January 11, 2010. As of September 23, 2010: http://www.quilliamfoundation.org/index.php/component/content/article/613

Quita, Carlos, "The Philippines' Counter-Terrorism Approach," *Asian Conflicts Reports*, No. 5, May 2009, pp. 8–9.

Qusti, Raid, "Coupons Instead of Cash for Needy," *Arab News*, September 21, 2007.

Rabasa, Angel, Cheryl Benard, Lowell H. Schwartz, and Peter Sickle, *Building Moderate Muslim Networks*, Santa Monica, Calif.: RAND Corporation, MG-574-SRF, 2007. As of September 23, 2010: http://www.rand.org/pubs/monographs/MG574/

Rabasa, Angel, Peter Chalk, Kim Cragin, Sara A. Daly, Heather S. Gregg, Theodore W. Karasik, Kevin A. O'Brien, and William Rosenau, *Beyond al-Qaeda: Part 1, The Global Jihadist Movement*, Santa Monica, Calif.: RAND Corporation, 2006. As of September 23, 2010: http://www.rand.org/pubs/monographs/MG429/

Raghavan, Sudarsan, "Former Militants Now Wage Battle Within Libya to Discredit al-Qaeda," *Washington Post*, May 29, 2010.

Ramakrishna, Kumar, "A Holistic Critique of Singapore's Counter-Ideological Program," *CTC Sentinel*, Vol. 2, No. 2, January 2009, pp. 8–11.

Rashwan, Diaa, "Egypt's Contrite Commander," *Foreign Policy*, March–April 2008a.

———, "The Renunciation of Violence by Egyptian Jihadi Organizations," in Tore Bjørgo and John Horgan, eds., *Leaving Terrorism Behind: Individual and Collective Disengagement*, New York: Routledge, 2008b, pp. 113–131.

RICU—*see* HM Government, Research, Information and Communications Unit.

Risse, Thomas, "International Norms and Domestic Change: Arguing and Communicative Behavior in the Human Rights Area," *Politics and Society*, Vol. 27, No. 4, December 1999, pp. 529–559.

———, "Let's Argue! Communicative Action in World Politics," *International Organization*, Vol. 54, No. 1, Winter 2000, pp. 1–39.

Robertson, Nic, "Failed Suicide Bomber Turns on al-Qaeda," CNN, September 14, 2007.

Robertson, Nic, and Paul Cruickshank, "New Jihadi Code Threatens al Qaeda," CNN, November 10, 2009.

———, "In Bid to Thwart al Qaeda, Libya Frees Three Leaders of Jihadi Group," CNN, March 23, 2010. As of April 8, 2010:
http://edition.cnn.com/2010/WORLD/africa/03/23/libya.jihadist.group/

Rondonuwu, Olivia, "Changing the Militant Mindset: Few Signs of Success," Reuters, September 24, 2009.

Ross, Jeffrey Ian, and Ted Robert Gurr, "Why Terrorism Subsides: A Comparative Study of Canada and the United States," *Comparative Politics*, Vol. 21, No. 4, July 1989, pp. 405–426.

Rothbaum, Susan, "Between Two Worlds: Issues of Separation and Identity After Leaving a Religious Community," in David G. Bromley, ed., *Falling from the Faith: Causes and Consequences of Religious Apostasy*, Newbury Park, Calif.: Sage Publications, 1988.

Roy, Olivier, *Al-Qaeda in the West as a Youth Movement: The Power of a Narrative*, Brussels: Centre for European Policy Studies, Policy Brief No. 168, August 2008.

Sageman, Marc, *Leaderless Jihad: Terror Networks in the Twenty-First Century*, Philadelphia, Pa.: University of Pennsylvania Press, 2008.

Sampson, Robert J., and John H. Laub, "Crime and Deviance Over the Life Course: The Salience of Adult Social Bonds," *American Sociological Review*, Vol. 55, No. 5, October 1990, pp. 609–627.

"Saudi Arabia: Official Prison Visit Leads to the Pardoning of 1,000 Detainees," *Asharq Alawsat*, May 4, 2006.

"Saudis Helping Freed Terror Suspects; Trying to Pull Militants Away from Terrorism," *Vancouver Province*, April 26, 2007.

Scheuer, Michael, "Bin Laden Identifies Saudi Arabia as the Enemy of Mujahideen Unity," *Terrorism Focus*, Vol. 5, No. 1, January 8, 2008.

Schimmelfennig, Frank, "Strategic Calculation and International Socialization: Membership Incentives, Party Constellations, and Sustained Compliance in Central and Eastern Europe," *International Organization*, Vol. 59, No. 4, Fall 2005, pp. 827–860.

Schonhardt, Sara, "Terrorists Go Back to School in Indonesia," *Asia Times*, July 22, 2010. As of September 23, 2010:
http://www.atimes.com/atimes/Southeast_Asia/LG22Ae01.html

Schulze, Kristen E., "Indonesia's Approach to Jihadist Deradicalization," *CTC Sentinel*, Vol. 1, No. 8, July 2008, pp. 8–10.

Schweighöfer, Kerstin, "Ahmed Marcouch—A Man of Action," *Qantara.de: Dialogue with the Muslim World*, 2007. As of September 23, 2010:
http://www.qantara.de/webcom/show_article.php/_c-478/_nr-662/i.html

Shaikh, Habib, "Makkah Committee Gives 40 Ex-Convicts a Fresh Start in Life," *Khaleej Times* (Dubai), May 8, 2007.

Shuaib, Ali, and Salah Sarrar, "Libya Frees Jailed Leaders of Islamist Group," Reuters, March 23, 2010.

Shuja, Sharif, "Gauging Jemaah Islamiyah's Threat in Southeast Asia," *Terrorism Monitor*, Vol. 3, No. 8, May 5, 2005.

Slack, Megan K., "Saudis Confront Extremists with Convert's Passion," *Los Angeles Times*, November 17, 2003.

Slotervaart Council, *Progress Report: Slotervaart Action Plan—Countering Radicalisaton*, Amsterdam, February 2008. As of September 23, 2010:
http://www.slotervaart.amsterdam.nl/aspx/download.aspx?file=/contents/pages/97375/slotervaartprogressreport.pdf

Stackelbeck, Erin, "Ex-Terrorist Takes CBN Inside Al Qaeda," CBN News, March 9, 2010. As of September 23, 2010:
http://www.cbn.com/cbnnews/world/2010/March/Ex-Terrorist-Gives-CBN-Glimpse-Inside-Al-Qaeda/

Stern, Jessica, "Mind Over Martyr," *Foreign Affairs*, Vol. 89, No. 1, January–February 2010.

Stockman, Sarah, "Nationality Plays Role in Detainee Release," *Boston Globe*, November 22, 2007.

Stone, Major General Douglas M., Commander, Detainee Operations, Multi-National Force–Iraq, transcript of press conference, June 1, 2008, As of September 23, 2010:
http://www.usf-iraq.com/?option=com_content&task=view&id=20028&Itemid=128

Stracke, Nicole, "Arab Prisons: A Place for Dialogue and Reform," *Perspectives on Terrorism*, Vol. 1, No. 4, 2007.

Sufi Muslim Council, "Sufi Muslim Council's Core Principles," web page, undated. As of September 23, 2010:
http://sufimuslim.homestead.com/about/principles.html

Taarnby, Michael, "Yemen's Committee for Dialogue: The Relativity of a Counter Terrorism Success," in Cheryl Benard, ed., *A Future for the Young: Options for Helping Middle Eastern Youth Escape the Trap of Radicalization*, Santa Monica, Calif.: RAND Corporation, WR-354, September 2005, pp. 129–139. As of September 23, 2010:
http://www.rand.org/pubs/working_papers/WR354/

Tajjudin, Razia, "Islam in Amsterdam," Euro-Islam.info, undated. As of September 23, 2010:
http://www.euro-islam.info/country-profiles/city-profiles/amsterdam

Task Force on Confronting the Ideology of Radical Extremism, *Rewriting the Narrative: An Integrated Strategy for Counterradicalization*, Washington, D.C.: Washington Institute for Near East Policy, March 2009.

Tawil, Camille, "What Next for the Libyan Islamic Fighting Group After Rebuff from the Libyan Regime," *Terrorism Monitor*, Vol. 7, No. 24, August 6, 2009.

Teitelbaum, Joshua, *Holier Than Thou: Saudi Arabia's Islamic Opposition*, Washington, D.C.: Washington Institute for Near East Policy, 2000.

"Terrorist 'Rehab' a Failure: Minister," *Jakarta Globe*, June 26, 2010. As of September 23, 2010:
http://www.thejakartaglobe.com/home/terrorist-rehab-a-failure-minister/382698

TNS Media Intelligence, *The Language of Terrorism: Analysing the Public Discourse and Evaluating RICU's Impact*, January 2007–March 2008.

Travis, Alan, "Time to Tackle the Non-Violent Extremists, Says Smith," *Guardian*, December 11, 2008.

UK Department for Communities and Local Government, *Building Community Resilience: Prevent Case Studies*, London, December 2009. As of September 23, 2010:
http://www.communities.gov.uk/publications/communities/preventcasestudies

UK House of Commons, Communities and Local Government Committee, *Preventing Violent Extremism: Sixth Report of Session 2009–10*, London: Stationery Office, March 30, 2010.

United Nations Counter-Terrorism Implementation Task Force, *First Report of the Working Group on Radicalisation and Extremism That Lead to Terrorism*, September 2008. As of March 6, 2010:
www.un.org/terrorism/pdfs/Report%20of%20the%20Working%20Group%20-%20Workgroup%202.pdf

United States Institute of Peace, *How Terrorism Ends*, Washington, D.C., Policy Brief, May 25, 1999.

U.S. Department of State, Bureau of Intelligence and Research, "The Wandering Mujahidin: Armed and Dangerous," *Weekend Edition*, August 21–22, 1993.

U.S. Military Academy, Combating Terrorism Center, *Militant Ideology Atlas*, West Point, N.Y., November 2006.

Vasil, Raj, *Governing Singapore: A History of National Development and Democracy*, St. Leonards, Australia: Allen and Unwin, 2000.

Vidino, Lorenzo, "A Preliminary Assessment of Counter-Radicalization in the Netherlands," *CTC Sentinel*, Vol. 1, No. 9, August 2008, pp. 12–14.

———, "Europe's New Security Dilemma," *Washington Quarterly*, Vol. 32, No. 4, October 2009, pp. 61–75.

———, "Toward a Radical Solution," *Foreign Policy*, January 5, 2010.

Warr, Mark, "Life-Course Transitions and Desistance from Crime," *Criminology*, Vol. 36, No. 2, May 1998, pp. 183–216.

Wasmund, Karl, "The Political Socialization of West German Terrorists," in Peter H. Merkl, ed., *Political Violence and Terror: Motifs and Motivations*, Berkeley, Calif.: University of California Press, 1986, pp. 191–228.

Watkins, Eric, "Landscape of Shifting Alliances," *Terrorism Monitor*, Vol. 2, No. 7, April 8, 2004.

"Wawancara Fauzi Hasbi: 'Saya Dijebak ICG'" ["Fauzi Hasbi Interview: 'I Was Framed by ICG'"], *Tempo* (Indonesia), January 1, 2003. As of September 23, 2010: http://www.tempo.co.id/hg/nasional/2003/01/01/brk,20030101-09,id.html

Westervelt, Eric, "Growing Repression in Yemen May Feed al-Qaeda," *All Things Considered*, National Public Radio, November 10, 2005. As of September 23, 2010: http://www.npr.org/templates/story/story.php?storyId=5007776

Whewell, Tim, "Yemeni Anti-Terror Scheme in Doubt," BBC News, October 11, 2005. As of June 4, 2010: http://news.bbc.co.uk/2/hi/programmes/crossing_continents/4328894.stm

Whine, Michael, "The Radicalization of Diasporas and Terrorism: United Kingdom," in Doron Zimmermann and William Rosenau, eds., *The Radicalization of Diasporas and Terrorism*, Zurich: Center for Security Studies, ETH Zurich, 2009, pp. 17–39.

Whitaker, Brian, "Yemen Overview 2003–4," British-Yemeni Society, August 2005. As of September 23, 2010: http://www.al-bab.com/bys/articles/whitaker04.htm

Wiedemann, Erich, "Moroccan-Born Mayor Dispenses Tough Love to Immigrants," *Spiegel Online*, July 30, 2007. As of September 23, 2010: http://www.spiegel.de/international/europe/0,1518,497404,00.html

Willems, Peter, "Unusual Tactics," *Middle East*, October 2004.

Woods, Andrew K., "The Business End," *Financial Times*, June 27, 2008.

Wright, Lawrence, "The Rebellion Within: An Al Qaeda Mastermind Questions Terrorism," *New Yorker*, June 2, 2008.

Wright, Stuart A., "Leaving New Religious Movements: Issues Theory, and Research," in David G. Bromley, ed., *Falling from the Faith: Causes and Consequences of Religious Apostasy*, London: Sage Publications, 1988.

———, "Reconceptualizing Cult Coercion and Withdrawal: A Comparative Analysis of Divorce and Apostasy," *Social Forces*, Vol. 70, No. 1, September 1991, pp. 125–145.

Zimmermann, Doron, "The European Union and Post-9/11 Counterterrorism: A Reappraisal," *Studies in Conflict and Terrorism*, Vol. 29, No. 2, March 2006, pp. 123–145.

Zogby International, *Muslims in the American Public Square: Shifting Political Winds and Fallout from 9/11, Afghanistan, and Iraq*, October 2004. As of October 6, 2010: http://www.zogby.com/AmericanMuslims2004.pdf